PRAISE FOR THE NORWEGIAN EDITION

"There is no alternative to facing up to Hege Storhaug and her book.
Read it – and experience vexation, surprise, insight, and involvement."
– Unni Wikan, MORGENBLADET

"A necessary and brave book."
– Henrik Gade Jensen, JYLLANDS-POSTEN

"A sharp and necessary book, one of the most important of the
season."
– Lars Saabye Christensen

 "A painful but necessary book to read. It is the most important
contribution ever to the Norwegian immigration and integration
debate….It should be obligatory reading for everyone who works with
foreigners in Norway."
– Tore Andreas Larsen, FREMSKRITT

"If Hege Storhaug's revelations…are not taken seriously by the
powerful politicians, we will, within a few years, see a different, illiberal
European in which a mentality out of the Middle Ages will wield
absolute power…..One of the most important books of opinion that
have come along in recent years."
– Oddbjørn Solstad, DRAMMENS TIDENDE

"Read as a book of opinion, or as a political book, this is perhaps one of
the most interesting books written in Norwegian."
– AGDERPOSTEN

"Has the power and substance to be the year's book of opinion in
Norway."
– Aud Farstad, SUNNMØRSPOSTEN

"Hege Storhaug is brave…. Read this book and become uneasy."
– Berit Kobro, VG

"A feminist work that wages the battle for democracy and women's
rights and against the naïve tolerance that tolerates intolerance in Islam.
This is a struggle of values, and it must be fought now – otherwise it
will be too late."
– WEEKENDAVISEN

ABOUT THE AUTHOR

Hege Storhaug is one of Europe's leading experts and commentators on immigration, integration, and Islam, and is the author of several highly regarded books on these subjects. Since 2002, she has served as information director of Human Rights Service, Norway's first think tank, which performs research and formulates policy proposals relating to integration and the human rights of women and girls, especially those living in European immigrant neighborhoods. The work done by Storhaug and HRS on issues such as female genital mutilation, forced marriage, and honor killing has resulted in major legislative reforms in Norway and elsewhere. The original edition of this book was a bestseller and award-winner in Norway in 2006; for this first English-language edition, Storhaug has written a substantial new afterword that includes extensive and highly illuminating updates.

ABOUT THE TRANSLATOR

Bruce Bawer, the author of *A Place at the Table, Stealing Jesus, While Europe Slept, Surrender,* as well as several volumes of literary and film criticism, has translated a dozen books from Norwegian to English.

But the Greatest of These Is Freedom

ALSO BY HEGE STORHAUG

Rundlurt: Om innvandring og islam i Norge
(Duped: On Immigration and Islam in Norway)
Kagge Forlag

Tilslørt. Avslørt. Et oppgjør med norsk naivitet
(Covered, Uncovered: A Critique of Norwegian Naïveté)
Kagge Forlag

Feminin integrering – utfordringer i et fleretnisk samfunn
(Human Visas: A Report from the Front Lines of Europe's
Integration Crisis)
(with Human Rights Service)
Kolofon

Hellig tvang – unge norske muslimer om kjærlighet og ekteskap
(Holy Force: Young Norwegian Muslims on Love and Marriage)
Aschehoug Publishing House

Mashallah - en reise blant kvinner i Pakistan
(Mashallah: A Journey among Women in Pakistan)
Aschehoug Publishing House

But the Greatest
of These Is Freedom

The Consequences of Immigration
in Europe

Hege Storhaug

Translated from the Norwegian and with an
introduction by Bruce Bawer

With a new afterword by the author

"There are moments in history when confrontation is a necessary precondition for honest dialogue."

> – *Harald Stanghelle,* "Expression under Pressure" (an opinion piece on the Danish cartoon crisis), *Aftenposten,* 14 February 2006

To Reidar Storhaug (1924-2001)

Resistance fighter and father

Contents

Introduction

By Bruce Bawer

In recent decades, as Hege Storhaug notes in these pages, those of us fortunate enough to live in the Western world have enjoyed a degree of freedom unparalleled in human history. This freedom did not come easily. It is the product of centuries of struggle – a product of the Renaissance, of the Protestant Reformation, of the seventeenth-century Enlightenment, and of a long series of hard-won reforms in various countries, of which the most notable and influential were probably the American Revolution and American Declaration of Independence, which in 1776 affirmed the then remarkable notion that human beings – every last one of them – had a right to the pursuit of happiness.

Among the things that freedom frees up are human creativity and innovation. Thus freedom has brought with it a remarkable array of technological developments and cultural achievements as well as unprecedented levels of prosperity.

But freedom, alas, also leads to complacency. People who are born into a free society, and who never know anything else, can all too easily come to think of freedom as the natural order of things, the default situation of humankind. Many of them can even be taught to mock the idea that they are free, and to look up to totalitarian heroes such as Mao Tse Tung or Che Guevara. It can be terribly difficult for free people to imagine what it is like *not* to be free; terribly difficult for them to conceive of the ordeal undergone by millions who, in living memory, have inhabited Communist Gulags and "re-education camps"; terribly difficult for them to recognize the heroism of such men and women as Vaclav Havel and Aung San Suu Kyi, who at extraordinary personal risk stood up to tyranny; terribly difficult for them to recognize that the freedom they fail even to appreciate is, in fact, an extremely rare and precious exception to the state of affairs throughout virtually the entire history of human civilization. This ignorance and indifference result in an alarming shortage of the very vigilance that is necessary to keep freedom alive and well. So it is that freedom, in the freest of times and places, rests upon exceedingly fragile pillars.

In the last century, Western freedom faced threats in the form of German, Italian, and Japanese fascism and Soviet Communism. Today it is once again threatened – this time not only by ideological enemies beyond our borders but by the steady accumulation and empowering of ideological enemies in our very midst.

Let there be no confusion about one thing: immigration, in and of itself, is not an enemy of freedom. On the contrary, immigration played a crucial role in renewing, generation after generation, the promise and reality of American freedom. Over the last two centuries, millions of people from every corner of the globe have been drawn to America by its freedom and opportunity and have contributed to it their energy and imagination, their hard work, and a diversity of skills and talents. They made American science and technology, and the American economy, the marvels of the world – all the while helping American liberty to flower ever more abundantly.

But the immigrant wave that is sweeping over Europe today, and that is poised to do the same, in time, to America, differs drastically from the immigrant waves of the past. The existence of Muslim enclaves in Europe – enclaves governed not according to democratic principles but according to illiberal Islamic law – testify to the fact that all too many of those who have come to the West in recent decades have come here not to enjoy Western freedoms but to exempt themselves from them, to exploit them, and ultimately to undo them. The burgeoning welfare rolls that seem destined to bankrupt one European country after another, moreover, reflect the fact that all too many of the Muslims who have established residences in Europe have done so not with the intention of working hard but with the intention of coolly and systematically draining dry social-services systems that were designed to be used by native populations only in cases of catastrophe or desperate need.

Rather than being built up by these new immigrants, then (many of whom are, properly speaking, not immigrants, since they still spend much if not most of their time in their homelands), Europe is being torn down by them. The true nature of this situation is still insufficiently understood by many in the United States, and the seriousness of the problem appreciated by only a few. Even highly placed individuals in the American government and the media – people whose job descriptions, one might think, would require that they have a clear sense of what is going on in Europe – don't get it, or don't want to. For many of them, to speak the unvarnished truth about the present crisis (and a crisis is assuredly what it is) is to express prejudice. On the contrary, to face up to the unpleasant reality now afflicting Europe is a matter of social responsibility, pure and simple – and to turn away from it in discomfort or confusion, or out of a sense of hopelessness or helplessness or fear of being called a bigot, is a grave abdication of that responsibility.

The simple fact is that no one in the U.S. understands the reality of today's Europe as well as a few well-placed observers in Europe do – if only for the simple reason that the latter have experienced that reality firsthand and on a daily basis for a number of years. And in all of Europe, Norway – which is Hege Storhaug's turf, and the main focus of this book – occupies a special position. In terms of population, this mountainous northern kingdom is tiny, with only four and a half million residents. While in the larger countries of Western Europe there are significant Muslim communities in a number of cities, in Norway the Muslim community as such is largely confined to a single city, Oslo. Norway and its capital thus represent a very handy microcosm of the European crisis.

17

In the larger Western European nations, such as Britain and France and Germany, the sheer scale of the immigrant communities makes it impossible for any one person to have a detailed familiarity with those communities and their problems. In little Norway, however, it *is* still possible for a single tireless individual to have a handle on everything having to do with Islam, immigration, and integration, and to be personally acquainted with all the major players – the politicians, the imams, the community spokespeople, and so forth.

In Norway, that single tireless individual is Hege Storhaug.

Hege is, let it be understood from the outset, no defender of white against black, no standard bearer for ethnic or cultural purity. On the contrary, she was led to her concern for immigration and integration policy and the challenge of Islam by the noblest of motives: a passion for secular democracy, an unwavering insistence upon the equal rights of women, and a fervent dedication to the respectful treatment and responsible upbringing of children. She came to this issue, in short, not as a basher of immigrants or Muslims but as a critic of policies and ideologies that oppress individuals who, she fervently believes, should enjoy the same rights she does – no matter what community, religion, or ethnic group they may happen to have been born into. Hege wears many hats: she is a writer and journalist, a researcher and formulator of policies, and a lobbyist and activist on behalf of those policies' implementation; she is also a brilliant debater who has passionately championed the causes of freedom and human rights on countless Scandinavian television and radio debates, in talks and lectures and colloquia. She has made enemies among sundry imams and Islamist community leaders and their variously naïve and spineless defenders in the media, government, and academic and literary intelligentsia, and won devoted admirers among ordinary Norwegians of every religious and ethnic background who recognize her as a stalwart advocate for the freedoms of all. For like Jefferson and Adams and Franklin, Hege believes, quite simply, that liberty belongs to everyone, and that no country that calls itself democratic can afford to allow tyranny in the name of any ideology to exist within its borders. No one in Europe can surpass Hege as a sheer witness to the consequences of Europe's disastrous immigration policies both on the largest and the most intimate of scales; no one has given more thought to, or understands better than she does, the reasons for those policies' colossal failure; and no one has addressed the situation with deeper insight, fuller humanity, or greater eloquence and courage. For those of us who wish to grasp what is going on – and it is important, for the sake of our civilization and our children's futures, for *all* of us to grasp what is going on – she is an indispensable resource, and this book an essential starting point.

Preface

By Hege Storhaug

The freedom we enjoy today as citizens of Western democracies is unique. Nowhere else in the world, and at no other time in history, have human beings been blessed with such a high degree of personal liberty. I am thinking in particular of the free and open relationship that exists between men and women, their equality before the law, and the respect of members of each sex for the rights and personhood of members of the other. In the West, individuals of both sexes have the same rights and the same opportunities to shape their lives and pursue their dreams. Men and women can establish lifelong friendships. We are free to follow our hearts and to marry whom we wish. And if a marriage doesn't live up to our expectations, we are free to dissolve it. Women's bodies, moreover, are their own: it is up to them to decide whether they wish to be mothers and how many children they will have. Women can go where they want, when they want. And they are free to speak their minds. Freedom of speech permits all of us to challenge ourselves and those around us and thereby influence and improve the society in which we live.

This freedom did not float down from the skies. Nor does it come with a guarantee that it will last forever.

Immigration is changing key aspects of life in the West in ways that individual citizens have little opportunity to influence – except at election time. A few years from now, most of the people living in my own city, Oslo, will be immigrants, and by the end of this century the majority of Norway's inhabitants will be persons with non-European roots. The more individuals who come to Norway or who are born here to parents who live outside of mainstream society, the more difficult it will become to achieve real integration. As the number of people who need to be integrated grows, so will the need for clear, comprehensive efforts at integration.

In recent decades, immigration has brought to Norway larger and larger groups of people who live by values that are at odds with Western liberty. Is integration going smoothly? Far from it. Indeed, the challenges are greater than many believed just a few years ago.

For what is it that's actually happening? Let's start with immigrant children, a large percentage of whom fall through the cracks in school and many of whom end up in gangs rather than in the labour market. In a typical classroom, a grand total of five Norwegian pupils may be expected to do the job of integrating no fewer than fifteen immigrant children – a virtually impossible task. Many *grandchildren* of immigrants start their first day of school without the slightest knowledge of the Norwegian language or Norwegian culture. An unknown number of Norwegian-born children don't even get to grow up in Norway; instead their families send them to their homelands (and, often, enroll them in Koran schools) and store them there for years in order to keep them as far as possible from Norway and its secular values.

Young women who want to live like their Norwegian neighbours, who desire an education and an active social life, and who wish to share their lives with the people they love, can end up spending their lives on the run. Some women are under such serious threat that the authorities don't see any alternative other than to give them new identities and find them a place to live outside of Norway's borders. Mothers who seek to escape violent or unhappy marriages are kept on tight leashes; and those who break those leashes run the risk of being killed by their own families. Violent crime has also risen dramatically in recent years. Gangs terrorize and rob children and young people, selecting their victims at random. A few decades ago, the rape of a young woman would be a big news story; today it is rare for even a gang rape to make the front page.

At the same time, more and more immigrant boys label girls as whores, and as honourless, because they dare to exercise the personal freedom to which everyone in Norway is supposed to be entitled. In parts of Oslo, gays don't dare to hold hands, for they know that their love might provoke some of "our new countrymen" to commit acts of violence. Freedom of expression is also in danger. In 2006, Norwegian embassies were attacked because a small Christian newspaper published Danish cartoons of a religious leader who lived in the seventh century. Since that episode, hardly anyone in Norway has dared to say anything critical or negative in public about Muhammed and Islam; such comments are reserved for safe, private conversations. (Given this state of affairs, it is interesting to note that Muhammed is now one of the most common names for baby boys in Oslo.) Today almost every fifth resident of Oslo has a non-Western background – a background, that is, in a part of the world which lacks the freedoms we treasure so highly. Many of these new citizens live in separate societies within mainstream society. These parallel societies are not sustainable and are dependent on steadily increasing financial support by Norwegian taxpayers. Thus immigration also costs Norway dearly in money.

Unfortunately, many of the perpetrators of assaults on individuals have their roots in the Muslim world. The integration of Muslims in the West faces a number of challenges. Islam's view of women is an especially significant obstacle to the integration of Muslims in democratic Europe. Islam's problematic relationship to both human rights and critical reflection also plays a role in the development in Europe of parallel Muslim subcultures and a Muslim underclass. For these reasons, Islam is a major topic in this book. To be sure, to write about Islam and Muslims is to step into a linguistic minefield. I myself am often furious when I hear Muslims discussed as if they were a single uniform group of people all of whom share the same needs, the same opinions, and the same visions. It is not only non-Muslims who talk about Muslims this way; Muslim spokespersons and politicians do it, too. I could not care less whether a certain person was born Muslim or not. What interests me is whether the person seeks to lift his or her religion out of the private sphere and into the public arena, and to use it as a basis for political activity and the drafting of legislation.

The general term for Muslims who have such aspirations is *Islamists* – they are, in other words, politicized Muslims. Islamism can in turn be divided into many categories. What all Islamists share is the desire to create a state run according to Islamic laws and principles. The main division within the Islamist camp is between those who only wish to employ words and missionary activity to achieve their goal and those who also consider politically motivated violence a legitimate tool. It is, of course, no secret that some members of other faith traditions blur the line between religion and politics – as evidenced, for example, by the opposition of many Christians to abortion and gay rights. But no Christian in Norway seeks to establish gender-discriminatory Christian marriage, divorce, and inheritance laws based on ancient Christian texts. By contrast, a family law based on religion – and at odds with human rights in a multiplicity of ways – is a sacred goal for Islamists.

I should mention that there is widespread disagreement about the proper interpretation and understanding of the concept of human rights. The United Nations' 1948 Declaration of Human Rights was a reaction to the massive assaults by certain governments on groups and individuals during World War II. Some argue, therefore, that human rights are meant, first and foremost, to protect individuals and groups from abuse by the state. I believe, however, that in a democratic and humanistic country such as Norway – where the state does not represent a major threat to human rights – those rights should be recognized as protecting the individual, in addition, from abuse committed within families and groups.

I have spent fourteen years dealing professionally with a range of immigration-related issues. Today I work as information director of the independent political think tank Human Rights Service (HRS), which was founded in 2001 and focuses especially on the integration of women and children with immigrant backgrounds. At HRS we have the freedom of not representing anybody; we work in the cause of a well-functioning democracy that is worthy of the name. In this book, however, I am speaking only for myself.

During the nine years prior to my employment by HRS, I was a journalist and author. I spent more than two of these years in Pakistan, the non-Western country that has sent the largest number of immigrants to Norway. These years brought me much joy, not least because of the Pakistanis' generosity and helpfulness. Norwegians encounter great hospitality in Pakistan, and it is also easy to form close, long-term friendships with the people of that country. Pakistani humour – including the black humour of which so many Pakistanis are masters – is one of the things I most valued during my time there.

But it was also in Pakistan that I lost my political and cultural innocence. I saw close-up how inhuman ideologies can systematically destroy individuals' lives. And on returning to Norway I encountered at close quarters the same collectivist and reactionary social systems I had observed there. In the years since, I have seen those social systems grow ever more deeply rooted.

I have always reacted to acts of injustice directed at individuals and groups by people in power – no matter who those people in power were. In recent years, there has been a new reason to resist such abuses: a concern for the future of secular democracy. Democracy, we must never forget, has lasted for only a very brief period of humanity's very long history, and it is profoundly vulnerable. The new immigration to the West, and the consequent growth in influence of religio-political ideologies, threatens to drastically weaken democracy's ideological foundations.

Norwegian asylum policies are not a subject of this book. To me, it is obvious that a free, prosperous country such as Norway should provide protection to political dissidents in flight from despotic regimes. At the same time, I also believe that we

25

should do more to help people in need in the places where they live. To tear them away from familiar and beloved settings, and move them to entirely alien societies where they may spend years in government-run asylum centres, is not always the best solution.

Immigration itself, in my view, will be the most crucial determinant of Norway's future. Today, the country's asylum policy is far more regulated than its immigration policy. Most of our new countrymen come here as immigrants, not asylum seekers. It is immigration, in particular, that leads to the infringement of individuals' basic human rights, and thus it is immigration policy that requires a radical change of course. The immigration debate is also crippled by myths and a lack of factual knowledge – a failing that has led to prejudice on the part of top politicians, social commentators, members of the media, and ordinary citizens. One goal of this book, then, is to help fight those prejudices that have made it more difficult for people to reflect openly and critically upon the consequences of immigration.

This book is intended to be a contribution to the debate about Norway's – and the West's – future. Immigration from the non-Western world is today's and tomorrow's greatest policy challenge. Immigration concerns *you;* it concerns me; it especially concerns the non-Western immigrants in the West today. And it concerns, not least, our children and our children's children.

Oslo, 1 August 2006

1

Anooshe: A Woman in Norway

It is early morning in the Norwegian coastal town of Kristiansund. Two cabs stop outside the courthouse. Out of one of them step a lawyer and her client, a young woman. A man steps out of the other while his lawyer, still inside, pays the driver. The man shoves his hand in a plastic bag. A second later, six shots are fired. The young, unguarded woman falls to the ground. The killer throws down the revolver and walks into the police station, where he confesses to the crime. The long-planned job has been done. Anooshe Sediq Gholam, only twenty-two and the mother of two, has been executed by her estranged husband because she availed herself of the right to divorce.

Anooshe, who was from Afghanistan, found it almost incredible that a woman in Norway has the same right as her husband to dissolve their marriage. Anooshe had been only thirteen years old when she was forced into a marriage bed. In Afghanistan she could hardly have dreamed of escaping the union that had been thrust upon her. But in Norway, as she had been told by workers at the refugee centre, you can legally divorce. Legally divorce! For an Afghani child bride, it was almost too good to be true. And, as it turned out, it *was* too good to be true. As her murder demonstrated, Afghani law and traditional Afghani punishments apply on Norwegian soil, too.

No honour killing has made a deeper impression on me. This was because of Anooshi's background – who she was as a person – and because she had contacted me the year before.

On that red-letter day in recent Norwegian history, Friday, 26 April 2002, I was still working part-time as a freelance journalist. The newspaper *Dagbladet* informed me that an Afghani woman had been killed, and asked me to cover the story. The year before, staffers at the Svanviken refugee centre had phoned me on Anooshe's behalf, and I'd written an op-ed about gender-based persecution and asylum policies. Anooshe and the head of the centre wanted advice. She had received death threats from her ex-husband – threats so venomous that she was sure it was only a matter of time before he would succeed in taking her life. The head of the centre was thus considering various residency alternatives for her. One alternative was an island without a connecting bridge, but with a local ferry. The idea was that any stranger who tried to cross to the island would immediately be identified by the locals and stopped.

Anooshe wasn't worried mainly about her own life, she said on that occasion. She was worried how life would be for her two small sons when she was gone. That's how certain she was that all the threats weren't empty. Anooshe also feared for her parents and her six underage siblings. Her husband's family had played a major role in the civil war under the Taliban, she said. The family had been represented in the leadership of the warlike Northern Alliance. They were powerful, and after Anooshe had taken her life into her own hands and divorced, they had threatened the lives of her closest relatives in Afghanistan, who as a result had been forced to flee to Pakistan. With intense anxiety and sincere love in her voice, Anooshe told about her parents' sorrow and powerlessness when her husband's warrior family forced them to give their child in marriage to "an evil and bestial" man. Anooshe saw no solution for her father, mother, and siblings other than that to bring them to safety in Norway.

Who was Anooshe? Born in northern Afghanistan, she was ethnically Uzbeki. Her father was well educated, and Anooshe received good schooling. She grew up in a gentle and loving family, but it had no power in the clan- and tribe-based Afghani society. Thus, when a powerful and violent warrior family demanded the thirteen-year-old's hand in marriage, her family had pretty much no choice in the matter. Protests would likely have been met with a brutality that could have cost human lives.

Anooshe, then, was a child who had been forced to marry a man ten years her senior. She was a child who had children after having been raped by her husband. She had her first child when she was only fifteen years old. The next year came the second, who was born very prematurely because of the physical violence to which Anooshe was subjected every day of her life. Anooshe was still a child when she saw her own small children, too, being kicked and smacked around. And when the children were only a few years old, it was their turn to be forced – forced, that is, to abuse their own mother.

Anooshe moved to Norway in May 1999 with her then husband, who had decided to seek asylum there. She would then have been nineteen and a half years old. Her husband, however, told the authorities that she was twenty-two. He wanted, Anooshe explained to me on the phone, to avoid uncomfortable questions about her having had children while still a minor. Her husband had two wives, but it was Anooshe, the younger, whom he chose to take with him to Norway. It made sense: she was "book-smart" and spoke English, while he was illiterate. Her knowledge and wisdom, he decided, would be of value in a new society.

As a private person and journalist, I couldn't do anything on that occasion other than to refer Anooshe to a lawyer, Elisabeth Tørresby, who could present her case to Norwegian authorities. I never even considered interviewing her for a news article, not even anonymously: she was so obviously in a life-threatening situation that could be made even worse by public attention.

The first phone call I placed on that 26 April was therefore to the Svanviken refugee centre in the West Norway county of Møre and Romsdal. I wanted to talk to Anooshe. Perhaps, I thought, she had known the woman who was killed, or perhaps she had other important information she could share with me. I was shocked when the director of the centre, Trygve Siira, told me that the murdered woman had in fact been Anooshe – a victim of an honour killing in the Kingdom of Norway in the year 2002.

A letter that Anooshe had sent me just before the telephone conversation in 2001 was published in *Dagbladet* in its entirety on 14 May 2002. Anooshe had lived in Norway for only one year and ten months, but had managed to write the letter in Norwegian. Two days later she was granted asylum on account of the harassment she was enduring at the hands of her ex-husband.

Here are some excerpts from her letter:[1]

Hi,

> *I am a woman from Afghanistan. I am married to an Afghani man and have two children (…) I am very scared, and consider myself to be in danger and have many problems. I was thirteen years old when I was forced to marry my ex-husband. My family and I were forced to marry me off to him. Because my husband and his family and his seven uncles were powerful and rich people in the town that we lived in there (…) All of them were generals and worked in the government in Afghanistan. (…) When they said that I had to marry him, my father was against it. (…) My father had reason to be against it. The first reason was that I was a girl of thirteen, and didn't know anything about marriage or such things, and the second reason was that he and his family were illiterate, and almost the whole town knew that they had no humanity and were like animals.*

> *My husband's uncle has six wives, and all of them, like me, were forced into marriage. (…) They pressured and threatened the girls' families, and said that if the families didn't agree, they'd kill them. My husband's uncle had killed one girl's father, who didn't want his daughter to marry him.*

> *It is terrible in Afghanistan. In particular they're so strict with women. Those with power and money make decisions about other*

people's lives. Therefore my family feared that perhaps my father, too, would be killed if he said no to the marriage, after I was raped. (…) I grew up in an intelligent, kind family. If my father had not been threatened by my husband and his family, he would never have married me to him, my husband.

(…) He slept with me against my will. I was only thirteen, and was unaware of all these things. I can't find the words to describe hard and difficult things, and what has happened to me.

I have only prayed to God that I would die, but God didn't listen to me.

(…) He began to hit me after two months of marriage. He has threatened me with weapons, and he has said that he would shoot me (…) every single day I had wounds on my body (…) My life was an endless round of abuse, beating, shoving (…) I couldn't sleep at night and live out the day in peace. When he wasn't home it was his family that threatened me and his brothers who hit me. I have lost all the good things and joys and the fun times that a girl of thirteen experiences.

(…) When I was fifteen, I had my first son. It was so difficult to raise a child and look after him all by myself, but I looked after him anyway, while I was abused by my husband. I think my in-laws had hearts of stone. They didn't have love or any feelings for one another, or for others. They were inhuman …

I had never thought that I might be able to divorce him one day, and live a new and safe life in peace. If I were in my country I wouldn't have been able to leave him, because in Afghanistan people have the worst culture (…) Women have no opportunities in my country (…) no opportunity to divorce. If they do it they're killed by their husband or his family.

I believe that I am lucky to live in a country that has humanity, and a country where people can tell right from wrong.

When we came to Norway I had not decided to leave him (…) When we lived at the refugee centre in Oslo, he began to hit me even more. And said to me that I mustn't think that I'm in Norway and that I'm free or that I can make my own decisions (…) therefore he hit me every single day, and the children, and said that we mustn't tell anybody about it (…) or he would cut me up into small pieces and throw me in the trash.

Eventually I started taking a Norwegian course (…) When I was in the course I met many other women, and we talked together. He was scared, because I might meet other people in the course and learn more about Norwegian law and leave him. Then he abused me very roughly, and I had to tell him whom I talked with in the course and what we talked about every day. He burned me by throwing boiling water on me, and hit me with a hard, heavy bicycle lock (…) then I couldn't take it any more (…) I would have been glad if he had killed me at once, it would have been better than dying every day.

It wasn't easy to leave such a man, but I did it anyway for my children's sake. I didn't know then that I was placing my family in great danger (…) He threatens to kill my father or my brothers. He told me that I had to think of my future. He would get his revenge at some time and place, because I had made a huge mistake. And he said that if I loved my family, I had to come back to him. But I would not go back to that hell, and I know that he will kill when he gets his hands on me.

I don't see any solution to this.

I am very scared of losing my family. I've talked with the police and with the Norwegian Directorate of Immigration, and those who work in this centre where I live, and I asked them to help me. But they say that they can't do anything.

I heard about you, and decided to write to you and ask for help. I hope you can read my letter and understand what I mean and how hard I have it. I would like very much to get in touch with you in order to get good advice (…) Please help me.

Anooshe Sediq Gholam, 19 March 2001

No document in our time, I would submit, has provided more consequential testimony about the inhuman brutality that can follow women to the West – and none has brought home more clearly the fact that this brutality persists in homes not far from our own.

What a loss Anooshe's death was for Norway! She could have made a real difference.

"Do we dare to take her in?"

In the wake of the honour killing, I was contacted by several of Anooshe's neighbours in Rabben, a residential neighbourhood in the tiny township of Eide with a population of 3200. They told me about the meeting to which they'd been summoned by local officials before Anooshe moved in. At the meeting they had been told that a woman with two children was to be their new neighbour, and that she had received such serious death threats that she needed the local community's protection.

Were they willing to step forward? Would they take her into their homes, into their hearts? Would they risk the possibility that they might one day grieve her death?

Several were hesitant. But they stepped up to the plate anyway. On Friday, 26 April 2002, there were many who regretted it. They regretted it because they'd fallen in love with the unusually good and wise Anooshe, and also with her boys. Anooshe's sons had become their children's best friends. Their pain over the loss gnawed at them every day.

Anooshe was a remarkable woman in many ways. She integrated herself in record time. She wanted to live in modern democratic Norway with both her head and heart. She began attending secondary school. Her plan was to become a doctor, and according to her teacher this was not an unrealistic dream. The neighbours incorporated Anooshe quickly into their private and social lives. They celebrated holidays together. They shared Anooshe's dreams, and they shared her sorrows and hard times.

Anooshe also told some of her neighbours about her marriage. Not just about the violence she'd suffered, but about the violence directed against her children, and about how the children had been pressured to discipline her, their own mother. The neighbours also knew that her husband had been fined after being reported to the police for violent behavior, and that he had been imprisoned for violating a restraining order.

More than a few times while Anooshe had lived in secret (supposedly) at the refugee centre in Svanviken, she had had to be taken into hiding because her husband had been observed in the area. Most likely, he had tracked her down with the help of others like himself. Anooshe feared that he would try to kidnap her children and take them to Iran or Afghanistan, thus putting pressure on her to follow. In those countries, no judgment is passed on a man who kills a disobedient wife – especially not a woman who has taken her life entirely into her own hands by divorcing him against his will. Apprised of all this, Anooshe's neighbours did what they had promised the police during the meeting with local officials: they kept a close eye on strangers who turned up in the area.

For security reasons, Anooshe was transported by car to her Norwegian class. One day, driving through Eide in the car, she saw her husband. Yes, there was a very good reason why Anooshe didn't take part in public celebrations. It wasn't a question of not wanting to; it was because she feared that her husband or one or more of his co-conspirators might be in the crowd.

How was it that a man who represented such a threat to Anooshe and her children could be permitted to take legal action to ensure his parental rights? Anooshe didn't understand how the Norwegian democracy she had come to know would afford her husband such an opportunity.

As it turned out, it was precisely this that led to her death. When she stepped out of the car with her lawyer, Elisabeth Tørresby, at about 8:30 that morning, she was about to attend a child-custody hearing. Not a single police officer was there to protect her. The pistol her ex-husband pointed at her was loaded with ammunition that is intended for hunting and that isn't even allowed to be used in war. It is manufactured in such a way as to cause the greatest possible damage. When the shots were fired, Anooshe was halfway turned away from her husband.

Apparently she didn't see the pistol pointed at her. She died on the spot.

"Impossible not to love Anooshe"

A few hours after the murder, armed police officers turned up in peaceful Eide.

They feared that Anooshe's ex-husband had co-collaborators who would kidnap Anooshe's boys, aged six and seven. The police took up positions outside the township's government building, the grade school, and the day nursery. On 28 April 2003, the mayor of Eide, Oddbjørn Silteth, described the police action as follows: "They tried to be anonymous, but it's not so easy in a place like this. It was a bit special. In fact it reminded me of the war."

Anooshe's boys were taken underground. During the first days after the murder, they were protected by the police twenty-four hours a day.

None of the neighbours were told where they were; they were only assured that the boys were safe. Through local officials, they were able to send the boys letters and gifts.

The boys were given new identities and a new home, which may or may not be in Norway.

Anooshe's memorial service took place at the church in Eide on 7 May 2002. It was there that her neighbours got a last glimpse of her children. There was an extensive police presence at the service, both because of the danger of kidnapping and because a Muslim group had called for a demonstration to protest Anooshe's burial in Christian ground.

Despite the danger of kidnapping, Anooshe's sons sat in the front pew, guarded by police. Each of the two little boys placed a red rose on his mother's casket. With a heart-shaped wreath of white roses, the boys said a last thank-you to her.

The church was virtually packed. "It was impossible not to love Anooshe," one woman told me. The woman had worked with refugees in Kristiansund, Anooshe's first home in Norway, and had made the long trip to Eide along with colleagues to say a final farewell.

During the brief time she had been permitted to live in Norway, Anooshe had left a clear mark on the people she met. In his remarks at the memorial service, the pastor also mentioned how easy it had been to love Anooshe: "Anooshe had become one of us here in Eide, our fellow human being, whom many had come to love." Neighbours, friends, classmates, and teachers who spoke at the service agreed.

The verdict

Shortly after the murder, I contacted one of Norway's leading experts on Muslim cultures, Walid al-Kubaisi, an author and refugee from Baghdad. He was in no doubt about the killer's motive. On 28 April 2003, he explained to *Dagbladet:* "Anooshe was a Muslim woman with children. By getting a divorce in Norway, she challenged Islam's sharia law about obedience to one's husband. She protested against her husband, and she sought to join the Norwegians' – the infidels' – society, which has a different honour code. Therefore her husband probably thought that she might sleep with men outside of marriage, since this isn't considered immoral in Norwegian culture. This, in turn, would make his sons the children of a whore; and this is enough to provoke a conservative Muslim man to commit murder."

Another man in Norway with roots in the same cultural region as Anooshe only dared to speak out anonymously, and he explained the murder as follows: "As the children's father, Shamsi [the ex-husband] can never accept that the boys have been taken from him and that they are growing up with people who aren't Muslims. Norwegians live, as he sees it, without morals." That Anooshe had left her husband in the summer of 2000, he further explained, could be considered an act of treachery: "An Afghani Muslim woman has no right to divorce and to have her own life. If she does, she is considered a whore. By leaving her husband against his will, moreover, she violates her obligation to obey her husband. He loses face." The fact that Anooshe lived among Norwegians was viewed as apostasy, this source believed; and under sharia law, apostasy is punished by death. This man also maintained that the ex-husband's family in Afghanistan knew that Anooshe was dead before the shots were fired – meaning that the murder had been ordered at the highest levels of the family in Afghanistan, and that the ex-husband had carried out his obligation to his family by firing those shots in Kristiansund. The murder, in other words, was the result of a collective sentencing.

In his way, then, Anooshe's ex-husband, too, was a victim – even though his fate can't be compared at all, of course, with Anooshe's suffering and death. He was the product of a culture in which individuals are brought up within rigid boundaries, and in which there is virtually no room for empathy with those who cross those boundaries. All he knew was that as a Muslim husband, his job was to enforce his authority. Hence he had two alternatives to choose from: either set Anooshe free and participate fully in Norwegian society – thereby losing respect and status among his own people – or kill Anooshe and then continue to live in the conservative Afghani Muslim subculture in Norway.

The year after the honour killing, an appeals court sentenced Anooshe's ex-husband to eighteen years in prison for premeditated murder. The court's written verdict described him as a vulnerable and unstable person. But his level of awareness before and during the murder was high. During the murder itself, aggression was more conspicuous than despair. The verdict stated that he could not accept being abandoned – something he himself had explained during the criminal proceedings.

Then there was the report from the refugee centre at Eide that had been entered into evidence. It said that he had reacted to the fact that Anooshe had shown her wounded body to a male doctor and a male police officer. He had called her a whore, and said that she had probably slept with everybody in

Eide. It turned out, in short, that Walid al-Kubaisi's assessment of the motive for the murder had been right on the money.

The verdict further stated that when Anooshe had left her husband, he had felt not only despair, but also shame and humiliation. His oppressive Afghani view of women, the court believed, made it impossible for him to accept Anooshe's liberation; her conduct made him feel that he had been "brought down to a lower social level by his young wife." The appeals court called the murder a planned execution.

The sentence was appealed to the Supreme Court. It refused to hear the case. It noted that Anooshe had managed to adapt to Norwegian society: she had wanted an education, wanted freedom of movement, wanted an escape from the strict regimen for women prescribed by her homeland's traditions. Anooshe's liberation, wrote the Supreme Court, had "exposed her to the danger of being killed in accordance with longstanding local traditions from Afghanistan." The Court further noted that immigrants who choose to conduct themselves in accordance with Norwegian society's norms have the right to the protection of the law.

Anooshe's ex-husband was ordered to pay damages of 300,000 kroner to each of his children, Baborsha and Sharokh, for having deprived them of the woman they themselves called "the world's best mother."[2]

2

Marriage Immigration

Anooshe and her children came to Norway as refugees and applied for residency here. Most non-Westerners who settle in Norway, however, come here through marriage. Let's take a look at who the immigrants in Norway are.

The immigrant population in numbers

Today there are immigrants living in every township in Norway. In recent years, about twenty thousand new immigrants have settled in Norway every year. Given that Norway's population is about four and a half million, this corresponds roughly to an annual influx into the U.S. of 1.3 million people. Annual immigration through so-called family reunification – which usually means importing spouses, sometimes with children – has in recent years amounted to approximately thirteen to fifteen thousand persons. About three-quarters of the immigrants to Norway come through family reunification, while one fourth come as refugees.

Norway accepts about one thousand quota refugees per year through the U.N.; the other refugees come on their own, and are either accorded asylum status or granted residency on humanitarian grounds (or are placed under the category "other protection").

The total number of immigrants in Norway is now 386,000. This represents 8.3 percent of the nation's total population, according to Statistics Norway's figures for 2006. The non-

Western population is 285,000, which represents 6.1 percent of the population. The number of Western immigrants is 101,400, or 2.2 percent of the population. The immigrant population is rising steadily as a proportion of the total. In 2002, immigrants made up only 6.9 percent of the population.

For Statistics Norway, the "immigrant population" consists of immigrants themselves and their Norwegian-born children. The so-called "third generation" – which consists of individuals one or both of whose parents were born in Norway – is defined in the statistics in Norwegian. Although Norwegians have traditionally referred to all descendants of immigrants as immigrants, Statistics Norway does not do so, because it assumes that integration will take place naturally over time, and that people whom many Norwegians would call "third-generation immigrants" can thus not be characterized as immigrants. As Statistics Norway demographer Lars Østby said in *Klassekampen* on September 6, 2003, "If a person in 2033 has a bunch of Pakistani great-grandfathers, I won't be able to have a basis for saying that this person will be particularly different from my great-grandchildren." A total of 180,000 current Norwegian residents were born in Norway and have one foreign-born parent, which means that they fall outside of the statistics cited above. Statistics on the number of "second-generation" couples that have had children are not released to the public.

The country that has given Norway the largest number of non-Western immigrants is Pakistan; today the number of individuals in this group is 27,700. No non-Western group has lived in Norway longer than Pakistanis, and therefore, naturally enough, the "second generation" is largest among Pakistanis. Owing to high immigration levels from Iraq in recent years, however, the number of "first-generation" Iraqis now exceeds the number of "first-generation" Pakistanis. Iraqis are now the second largest non-Western group in Norway (20,100), followed by Vietnamese (18,300), Somalis (18,000), Bosnians (14,800), Iranians (14,400), Turks (14,100), and people from Serbia and Montenegro (12,900). Without question, it is the Somali community that has experienced the largest growth during the last five years, from 10,100 to 18,000.

While the numbers of Swedes, Danes, and Britishers living in Norway have held stable during the past few years, the non-Western population has increased steadily, and the number of non-Western children and young people is high.[3] Statistics Norway explains these differences largely by pointing not only to the group's length of residency in Norway but also to various nationalities' marriage patterns.

Almost every fourth person in the township of Oslo, or 123,900 people in all (23 percent of the township's population), is now a first- or second-generation immigrant. Western immigrants constitute four percent of Oslo's population, while non-Westerners make up nineteen percent. In the neighbourhood of Søndre Nordstrand, 41 percent of the residents are immigrants, the great majority of them non-Western. Statistics from 2006 that were published in *Aften* on 15 June 2006, show that non-Western immigrants account for 86 percent of the capital's growth during the last ten years: of the almost 50,000 new residents, only 4,000 are ethnic Norwegians. After Oslo, Drammen is the township with the highest percentage of immigrants, almost 18 percent.

The marital route to Norway

Marriage is at the heart of the immigration policy challenge, because marriage is the main route to Norway. It's by far the simplest way to immigrate, and also the fastest way to attain Norwegian citizenship. After three years of cohabitation, one can be independently granted permanent residency, and after four more years of cohabitation, one can apply for Norwegian citizenship. Labour immigrants can apply for citizenship after seven years' residency.

About 75 percent of all those who immigrate to Norway come through so-called reunification with persons in Norway. An adult can be reunified with someone to whom he or she was married before emigrating, and with whom he or she may have children. Most of those who come, however, are newly married to a person living in Norway. An important question is: Whom do immigrants in Norway marry and bring to Norway? The statistics tell an unambiguous story of the one-way shipping of spouses.[4] In other words: one person leaves; two come back.

The most important statistics concern the nine-year period 1996-2004. Let us first examine the marriages in the largest immigrant group in Norway, the Pakistanis.Of those Pakistani-Norwegians who married during this period, 75 percent of the first-generation men and 74 percent of the first-generation women married in Pakistan.[5] Eighteen percent of the men and 23 percent of the women married an ethnic Norwegian. Three percent of the men and one percent of the women married a person of another national origin living in Norway.

Second-generation Norwegian-Pakistani girls and boys married people of the same national origin at an even higher rate than did members of their parents' generation. Seventy-six percent of the boys who married during the period were married in Pakistan; for the girls, the figure is 77 percent. Twenty percent of the boys and 21 percent of the girls married a Norwegian-Pakistani in Norway. Three percent of the boys and one percent of the girls married a Norwegian. The same percentages married individuals with other backgrounds. The year 2004 was a record year for both boys and girls: fully 80 percent of the marriages were with individuals in Pakistan. Of the exactly 100 boys who married that year, only one married a Norwegian girl. Of the 91 girls who married, only one married a Norwegian boy.

Over the years, it has often been claimed that the marriage pattern would change between the first and second generation. The hypothesis is that the children of immigrants will, in much higher numbers than their parents, get married in Norway to people with national backgrounds different from their own. The underlying assumption is that the longer a population group has lived in Norway, the better integrated it will be: in both the social and professional spheres, the children of immigrants will meet ethnic Norwegians and find partners, and the marriage pattern will change. Immigrant groups will increasingly melt together with both the majority population and one another, and marriage across cultural and religious lines will become common. Among non-Western groups, Pakistanis have lived in Norway the longest, and thus, according to this hypothesis, should thus have gone the furthest of any group toward being absorbed into mainstream society. One can safely maintain that this hypothesis has so far proven wrong.[6]

The hypothesis is also wrong as regards another large group that has been in Norway nearly as long as the Pakistanis – namely, the Turks. Among Norwegian-Turks as among Norwegian-Pakistanis, members of the second generation marry members of their own ethnic group to an even greater extent than do members of the first generation, their spouses being resident either in Norway or in Turkey. They also marry Norwegians less often than do members of the first generation. Between 1996 and 2004, 77 percent of first-generation Turkish women married in Turkey, 13 percent married a Turk in Norway, three percent married a man in Norway with a different national origin, and eight percent married an ethnic Norwegian. In the second generation, the respective figures are 74 percent, 20 percent, three percent, and three percent. Among men, too, there are many more in the first than in the second generation who have married a Norwegian. Second-generation Turks are more likely to marry within their own group than are first-generation Turks, and most of them marry spouses whom they bring to Norway from Turkey.

Almost identical patterns are found among Norwegian Moroccans and Indians, both of which groups also have long histories of residence in Norway. For most of the countries of origin represented in Norwegian statistics, the percentage of spouses brought over from abroad has been high and stable during the entire nine-year period. The rates of fetching marriages have in fact *risen* in the largest immigrant groups, which first began to emigrate to Norway nearly forty years ago.

43

The same applies to new groups, such as men from Bosnia, Gambia, India, Eritrea, Ethiopia, Somalia, Serbia and Montenegro, Sri Lanka, and Vietnam. Similar increases are found among women from Bosnia, Chile, Iraq, Iran, Serbia and Montenegro, Somalia, Sri Lanka, and Vietnam.

Fetching marriage is about several things. One major factor in its popularity is the desire of non-Westerners in Norway to help both relatives and non-relatives in their ancestral homelands to achieve prosperity in the West. The pressure to emigrate in those homelands is strong. Another factor is immigrants' opposition to marrying outside their respective groups. A third factor is immigrants' desire to ensure the preservation and perpetuation in Norway of the culture and the social and religious values of their homelands. A fourth factor is immigrants' close ties to their countries of origin, where many of them own significant amounts of property. Many of them, in fact, live mentally, as it were, in their country of origin, with Norway serving only as an economic base. Modern transportation enables a number of them to commute, in effect, between continents – a way of life that was impossible, of course, for Norwegians who emigrated to the U.S. a hundred or more years ago.

There is a widespread myth that needs to be dispelled. Statistics Norway, leading politicians, and others maintain that it is not immigrants but ethnic Norwegian men who enter into the most fetching marriages.[7] The reason why they make this claim is that they seek to make the problems involving non-Western marriage patterns seem less serious than they are. But what enables them to make this claim is that they include in their statistics Norwegians' marriages to Swedes, Danes, and other Europeans. Such marriages, of course, are not pro forma or arranged by families, and the expectations for the spouses' integration are very good. To be sure, many marriages between Norwegian men and women from poor countries such as Thailand, the Philippines, and Russia, as well as the Baltic countries, may be suspect, but the number of marriages with these groups is far lower than the number of fetching marriages among non-Western immigrants.[8]

Marrying relatives – a ticket to Norway

The public discussion of several subjects associated with immigration and integration has been plagued by a lack of empirical evidence. I am thinking especially of matters relating to children and women, as well as social and family structures. But thanks to an initiative conceived of by personnel at the Norwegian embassy in Pakistan, we now know far more about the brand-new spouses who come to Norway from countries like Pakistan.[9]

During the year and a half from the beginning of 2004 to mid 2005, 436 Pakistanis applied to immigrate to Norway after marrying Norwegian-Pakistanis. Almost 60 percent of the applicants told the Norwegian embassy that they were related to their new spouses. Thirty-four percent were first cousins, 11 percent were second cousins, and 12 percent were more distantly related.

Sixty percent percent said that their marriages had been arranged by their families. Six percent said it had been their own idea, and three percent said they had used a so-called matchmaker, such as a marriage agency. Seventeen percent said they didn't know who was behind their marriage. But how many said that they had married out of love? Three percent.

Many were young when they married. Almost 50 percent of the spouses in Norway were under twenty-three years old at the time of their marriages. Eleven of them were under eighteen. In 2004, one Norwegian-Pakistani partner was fourteen years old when that individual's prospective spouse in Pakistan applied for an engagement visa. In eight out of twenty engagements, either the Norwegian or the Pakistani party was underage.[10] The age difference between the spouses ranged up to 40 years.

The educational level of the spouses in Pakistan tended to be low. Seventeen percent had less than five years of schooling

45

or none at all. Thirty-one percent had finished lower secondary school, and 39 percent had completed upper secondary school. Only ten percent had any higher education.

It is among this ten percent with higher education that the fewest marriages to relatives take place. And it is among those with the least schooling that the most marriages to close relatives take place. Seventy percent of those with less than five years of schooling, or none at all, married a relative. Sixty-five percent of those who had completed lower secondary school married a relative; for those who had completed upper secondary school, the figure dropped to 52 percent. Among those with higher education, the percentage is 38. The embassy's figures also showed that the less schooling the partner in Pakistan had had, the more likely it was that his or her spouse would be a first cousin.

Honour killing awakens Scandinavia

The year 2002 marked a turning point in the Scandinavian integration debate. The reason: two honour killings.

First Fadime Sahindal was killed in Uppsala on 21 January. Fadime's father shot her because he believed she had dishonoured him by marrying a Swedish-Iraqi man named Patrik. (Her father had wanted her to marry a cousin in Turkey.) On TV, in newspaper interviews, and even in a speech to the Swedish Parliament, Fadime had spoken straightforwardly about her life and death struggle to live with the man she loved. She talked about death threats and about the oppressive values that left their mark not only on her life but also on the lives of so many other immigrant girls and women in Sweden. These public appearances only intensified her father's feeling that he had lost his honour and respectability among his own people. Fadime was banished from her immediate family and the Kurdish community. Before she was to leave Sweden to begin studies abroad, her mother and siblings visited her to say goodbye. With this visit, she entered the "territory" to which the men of her family had forbidden her access. It was this that motivated her father to take up arms.

Fadime's murder shook all of Scandinavia, perhaps especially because public warning had been given that she would be killed. Indeed, the victim herself had warned that it would happen. Thanks to all the TV pictures and newspaper interviews of Fadime, who had been a vivid presence among us, she didn't become – like so many others – a faceless name and an unheard voice.

It was three months after Fadime's murder that Anooshe was shot in Krustiansund. For the public in general, and especially for some segments of the media and the political establishment, these events served as a wake-up call. As a result, assaults on girls and women with non-Western backgrounds were given a higher priority on the government agenda. Debates on the subject filled the opinion pages. Young women with non-Western backgrounds went to the barricades in both Norway and Sweden and bravely recounted their experiences. They demanded to be taken seriously; they demanded political action.[11] They demanded the same freedoms, the same right to self-determination, as ethnic Norwegian and Swedish women. And they demanded the right to live with those they loved.

Mina makes contact

Most Scandinavians now recognized that immigrant women may be running a serious risk if they violate cultural and religious norms. One sign of this recognition was a phone call I received in the summer of 2002 from a hospital physician who wanted advice. He was desperate: he was treating a patient who'd been abused by her husband. Now she was about to be released. But to what? She couldn't return home to her abuser, and she didn't want to go to a crisis centre. She had explained to the doctor that in the eyes of her people – not just her extended family but her entire community – the crisis centres were "whorehouses." Muslim women, they believed, should be under the supervision of the men in their families. The woman had told the doctor about death threats she had received from members of her immediate family. The doctor, it was clear, grasped the seriousness of the situation.

I spoke briefly on the telephone with the woman, whom I will call Mina. By pure coincidence, it turned out that we had met each other outside her apartment in an Oslo suburb the year before. When I had noticed, on that occasion, that she was of Pakistani origin, I had been moved to strike up a conversation, and with her husband at her side Mina and I had chatted together for several minutes. She got a kick out of the fact that I was familiar with the Pakistani village of her birth. Speaking to me on the telephone in the summer of 2002, she was glad to discover that we had this slight acquaintance: for her, my familiarity with Pakistani culture was comforting. She insisted that we meet: she wanted to tell me about her situation, receive some support, and come up with solutions. The doctor had arranged a place for her at a crisis centre. There was no alternative. Mina wanted me to come there.[12]

The next day I met her outside the crisis centre. Mina had not taken a chance that her extended family might pass judgment on her decision to live at a "whorehouse." Instead she'd sought shelter at the home of her older brothers the night before, and her niece had driven with her to the crisis centre. We sat on a bench with our backs to the wall of the building for a couple of hours while Mina talked. She made it absolutely clear that she'd reached her limit. She wanted to go home to her children, and wanted her husband out of the house. The violence in the marriage had lasted for fourteen years. She'd had enough. She wanted to get a divorce and live in peace.

While we sat on the bench, Mina took out a photo of herself to prove the seriousness of the violence to which she'd been subjected. The photo, which had been taken at a hospital twelve years earlier, showed her roughed up to the point of being unrecognizable. She had lost count of how many times she had been abused in that fashion.

The death threats begin

Mina definitely needed a lawyer to initiate divorce and child custody proceedings, arrange for the division of assets, and pursue any legal action against her husband. And what about their home? She had gone to the crisis centre against her will, and had spent several days there; then, under pressure from her brothers, she had moved in under their "honour-protecting wings." Again she was pressured to give her husband another chance. No woman in the family, she was told, had ever divorced of her own volition. The implication, Mina explained, was that if she divorced against her husband's will, it would show other women in the family that they, too, could escape.

The pressure on Mina had soon escalated into threats to (for example) break her arms and legs. Then her husband, his brothers, and Mina's eldest brother had made explicit death threats. During this time, Mina had hardly ever been permitted to speak with her children on the phone. She had been able to spend some time with a couple of them, but the others had been kept completely apart from her. It was clear that they were being manipulated in the most serious way. Several of them expressed outright hostility to Mina and called her a "whore." Even the smallest child, who was five years old, talked to her like this.

During my first meeting with Mina, she rattled off the names of several male relatives – brothers-in-law, cousins, brothers – who had threatened her life. It was impossible for me to follow it all. In order to give me a handle on who was who, and also with thought to Mina's security, we decided to construct a family tree. As it turned out, it not only gave me an overview of her extended family – it painted a vivid picture of the practical consequences of Norwegian immigration policy.

How they came to Norway

Mina's family tree first took root in Norway in 1973 when her father, whom I will call Ahmed, left his Pakistani village to

49

work in Norway. Contrary to the erroneous claims that are still made by many pundits, journalists, and editors today, neither Ahmed nor any other non-Western persons were invited by the Norwegian government to work in Norway. No: they came of their own accord – and Norwegian officials were caught napping.

This became clear in the summer of 1971, when so-called Pakistani "tourists" received extensive coverage in the press. That summer, young and middle-aged Pakistani men on tourist visas were roaming the streets, almost on the verge of starvation. Many had been brought here by smugglers in Germany. They weren't alone. Many Moroccans, Turks, and men from various African countries had also come to Norway on tourist visas. Under the law as it existed at that time, they should have been sent home at once because they hadn't come here with working permits. But cabinet member Oddvar Nordli, on behalf of the Labour Party government, allowed the law to be overlooked and gave the men working permits even though they were already in the country. The idea was that these poor men should be permitted to earn the money they needed to buy plane tickets home, thus sparing Norwegian taxpayers the expense.[13] History shows that something entirely different happened. Officials closed their eyes, and the men stayed.

In 1971, 990 Pakistanis, 450 Moroccans, and 390 Turks were living legally in Norway. In 1975, when a formal stop was put to labour immigration to Norway, over 3,700 Pakistanis, 600 Moroccans, and 1100 Turks had received work and residency permits.[14] Among them was Ahmed, Mina's father.

After working in Norway for five years, Ahmed brought over his wife and children under the rules permitting reunification with one's immediate family. Ahmed had ten children in his native village. Two of the sons were over eighteen years old, and thus too old to be reunified with him under the law. But Ahmed brought ten children over anyway: he adopted two of the sons of a brother of his who was still living back in the family's home village.

During the 1980s, Ahmed's children reached marriageable age. Thereupon began the migration of new spouses from Pakistan to Norway. First out of the gate was Ahmed's oldest son, who was paired off with a female cousin of his back in their home village. Second son, same procedure. The first marriageable daughter was hooked up with a cousin in the village. Of Ahmed's ten children, nine married cousins from back home. All of the cousins immigrated to Norway. When the tenth daughter was ready to marry, there was no marriage-ready male cousin available in the village, so she was married off to another man from the home village, who then immigrated to Norway.

After a few years, one of Ahmed's sons divorced and was married again, this time to a close relative in the village. She, too, immigrated to Norway. Hence Ahmed's ten children yielded eleven marriage immigrations, nine of them with cousins.

It didn't stop there. Mina's husband had five brothers left in the village. Even though Mina's husband had been illiterate when he came to Norway, he had figured out quickly enough how best to exploit Norwegian immigration policy. He met a Norwegian woman who had, shall we say, limited social prospects. He made an arrangement with her, and one day they traveled together to Pakistan, where she wed a man twenty years her junior – Mina's husband's brother.

At this point, Ahmed's ten children had yielded twelve marriage immigrations.

After Mina's husband's brother had been married for four years to the much older Norwegian woman, he won the right to Norwegian citizenship. What did he do? He divorced, just as Mina had predicted he would, and married a cousin of his in the family's home village to whom he had been engaged since childhood. She immigrated to Norway.[15]

Ahmed's ten children had now yielded thirteen marriage immigrations.

Mina's husband repeated the successful process for another brother of his in the family's home village. This time he found a

Norwegian woman who, like his as yet unmarried brother, was in her early twenties.

She, too, had limited social prospects. A little over four years after the marriage, the man became a Norwegian citizen. What did he do then? Exactly what Mina had predicted that he, too, would do: he divorced the Norwegian woman and married the cousin to whom he had been engaged since he was a child. The cousin immigrated to Norway.

Ahmed's ten children had now yielded fourteen marriage immigrations.

Mina's husband decided to repeat the successful procedure for a third brother in the village. But this time Norwegian authorities put a stop to it. The third brother could not speak a word of English; thus the "married couple" didn't have a shared language in which they could communicate. The "marriage" was rejected as being without foundation.

But Mina's husband knew what to do. How about finding a divorced woman or widow in Norway with Pakistani origins? Then the couple would have a common language, and if they didn't meet before the wedding day it wouldn't matter to Norwegian authorities, since arranged marriages were legitimate grounds for immigration. The plan was put into effect, and the marriage was recognized as valid in Norway. At this writing, the third brother is counting the days until he gets Norwegian citizenship and can divorce his Norwegian wife.

Ahmed's ten children had now yielded fifteen marriage immigrations.

Mina's husband, from whom she was now divorced, no longer had five brothers left in his native village. He had two. He took a break from arranging marriages for others and, as Mina predicted, traveled to the village himself and married a woman seventeen years his junior. She moved to Norway in 2006.

Ahmed's ten children had now yielded sixteen marriage immigrations.

The genealogical chart and the family history behind it have been thoroughly documented by means of official records in the national register and conversations with the police, Mina, the Norwegian women, and many others.

The story told here is the reality of Norway today. And the history isn't over.

Ahmed's grandchildren: is integration improving?

Today several of Ahmed's grandchildren are of marriageable age. One might imagine that as a result of integration they would marry people born in Norway. So far, four of them have married. Three were sent to the family village in Pakistan to marry their cousins, who have immigrated to Norway.

One of Ahmed's grandchildren refused to marry a cousin from the village. I will call her Nadia. At one time, I had just under a hundred text messages from Nadia stored on my cell phone, most of them sent at night from a lonely soul shivering under her blanket.[16] The messages were about being threatened with (for example) "being stabbed all over your face," about her younger brother calling her a whore, about her mother going to bed and playing dead to pressure her into marrying. The messages told of threats from her family to kill her if her mother died, of hospital visits for the treatment of neck and head wounds sustained in beatings, of her father's statement that he "would rather die than live if she married outside the family's house in the village," of nightly nightmares about being killed. And the messages communicate her hope that she might someday be able to marry a Pakistani man in Norway with whom she was in love, that the two of them might be able to live in peace without fear of what tomorrow might bring in terms of threats and violence, and that she might not, after all, be turned out her family – a family that, in spite of everything, she was closely bound to and still loved – should she choose to follow her heart.

In the end, Nadia was compelled to break off relations with her family in order to escape marrying her cousin. Instead, she married the Norwegian-Pakistani man whom she loved, and who was about her own age. They moved into their own apartment with support from his family, with whom they are in close contact. A year later they had their first child. The threats from Nadia's family persisted after the marriage, but after the marriage passed its two-year point they stopped. Nadia and her husband have finally found peace and quiet in their daily life. They're doing well together, and are convinced that – despite the costs – the struggle to which they had committed themselves in order to be together had been the only proper course of action.

By the summer of 2006, the labour immigrant Ahmed, who had come to Norway thirty-three years earlier, had been transformed into an extended family with eighty-one members.

"A financial milk cow"

The immigration history of Ahmed's family is entirely a product of Pakistani culture and Norwegian policy – a policy that creates the optimal conditions for the use of marriage as a tool of immigration.

How Norwegian policy functions at the individual level can be shocking. I want to say a few things about Mina's life – a life that provides insight into what happens in such families when a wife and mother tries to establish a dignified life for herself and her children. Mina's life also provides insight into how an extended Norwegian-Pakistani family establishes the same social structure in Norway as in its homeland, aided in large part by the fetching of new spouses.

Mina came to Norway as a child. When she was sixteen years old, her schooling in Norway ended and she was put to work. Why? Because she was of marriageable age. At that time, Norwegian authorities required that a person wanting to import a spouse to Norway have a certain minimum income. Mina needed to go to work in order to fulfill this requirement.

The summer Mina was eighteen years old, she accompanied her father and a couple of her brothers to their home village in

Pakistan. One day Mina's father put three photos on a table in front of her. They showed three of Mina's male cousins, all of them brothers. Mina's father asked her to choose one of them as a lifemate. Some choice. I asked Mina what chances she had of escaping her father's plan. She replied: "Whom could I turn to? Whom could I cry to?"

Mina was, then, given a "choice" among three cousins. And she was pressured to choose a particular one – the one who had the weakest position on the marriage market, because he hadn't been to school and was darker than most people in a region where dark skin is equated with low status and ugliness. This young man, according to Ahmed, was the one who most desperately needed a visa to the West. In the end, therefore, he was the one who got Mina – a human being reduced to the status of a living visa.

When Mina's husband came to Norway, there was an apartment waiting for him with a table already set and a wife ready to support him. He was as good as helpless in modern Norway. He was illiterate, couldn't speak Norwegian, and knew nothing about Norwegian society. His only professional experience was with horses and the soil. Mina became the household's sole provider. She had to arrange every detail of his life. It was a major burden. It goes without saying, moreover, that the situation was also untenable for her husband, a product of a patriarchal, conservative Pakistani village. Soon enough, he resorted to the remedy of the impotent: he began to abuse Mina. One reason why he did it was that, according to his own world picture, he had no sexual control over her. Mina worked outside the home. On her way to and from work, and at her workplace, she encountered other men. It was unavoidable. For him, it was entirely unheard of for a wife to have contact with men outside her closest family.[17]

Once her husband had found employment and taken up the role of family provider, Mina was forced to give up her job. She was only allowed contact with close family members. Sometimes her husband locked the outside door behind him with an extra lock. He coded the telephone so that she couldn't place calls. If Mina wanted to go to her private female doctor, he accompanied her from the door of their home all the way in to the doctor's office, where he took part in the consultation.[18]

The economic aspects are a chapter in and of themselves. Mina's control over her own finances changed gradually as her husband grew familiar with the Norwegian system. Having put an end to Mina's career, he took full control of the family's income and child care. Mina told me that he had gained access by force to all the family accounts, emptied them from time to time, and sent the money to his parents in Pakistan.

When he had first come to Norway, his parents had lived in a small clay house with a dirt floor and were among the poorest people in their village. After he had lived in Norway for a few years, his parents and their nearest kin moved into a large two-story brick house and acquired a car, servants, and top-quality modern furniture.

At first Mina had nothing against helping her husband's family to improve their standard of living. There were two main reasons for her increasing opposition to the money transfers: her husband's financial priorities lowered her and her children's quality of life: "We'll stay home as much as possible," her husband would say, "because it doesn't cost anything." Nor was she ever shown any respect or gratitude: "I have never been anything other than a financial milk cow for them. If it hadn't been for me and the children, neither my husband nor his family would have had anything at all. Yet they have never thanked me or been nice to me."

"Just like in our homeland"

Shortly after Mina was discharged from the hospital in the summer of 2002, she went to the police and filed a long list of charges against her husband: abuse, rape, systematic imprisonment, possession of illegal firearms, participation in illegal immigration through pro forma marriage, and abuse of the welfare system (while working full time in his brother's store, he was receiving government rehabilitation support, which is for people who cannot work). She charged not only her brother but two of his brothers with threatening her with death. At her first meeting with the police, Mina produced documentation showing that charges had been filed against her husband for raping the Norwegian woman whom he had used to bring his first brother to Norway, that other charges had been filed against him for threatening to assault Norwegian-Pakistani men, and that he had earlier been subject to a restraining order that denied him the right to visit Mina.[19] The police also were given a written statement by Mina's doctor expressing concern that she might be killed by her husband.

Mina's greatest desire was for the police to remove her husband from the apartment and let her move in with her children. When she was told that the police didn't have the authority to do this, she cried out to the police officer: "This is just like in our homeland. The man does what he wants. He tosses out his wife and takes the children. She has no rights. It shouldn't be that way in Norway. Do you know what they [the men] say? They say that the police don't do anything, no matter how much we women try. So they can do whatever they want. They feel so safe."

Mina was referred to a lawyer and to Barnevernet, the Norwegian Directorate for Children, Youth and Family Affairs.

"Taking over custody" – of Mina

Barnevernet was already familiar with some aspects of the family situation, having been informed earlier about Mina's abuse. At a meeting I attended, I heard a Barnevernet representative tell Mina that her case was "exceedingly complicated" because of "cultural factors." The focus was particularly on Mina; Barnevernet was especially concerned about her decision to divorce her husband. They were scared that there was a danger of an honour killing – as with Anooshe.

Mina fought hard to obtain temporary custody of her children until a decision could be made about permanent custody. The pressure placed on her and the threats directed at her by her brothers, her female relatives, and her husband intensified by the day. Her relatives were very tired of having her living with them. "They think only of honour," Mina told me. "They're scared that I might be a role model for other women in the family – that they'll see that they don't have to live like animals."

Behind Mina's back, her husband and Mina's brothers had been laying plans for a long time to "take over custody" of Mina. One day her husband came driving to the extended family's house with a copy of the Koran beautifully wrapped in a silk headscarf. In front of both the adults and the children in the family, Mina was forced to swear on the book that she didn't have a lover, which everybody thought was the reason why she wanted a divorce. Mina also agreed to return to her husband and promised that she would take responsibility for the marriage working. She was then driven home.

Barnevernet continued to monitor the situation. Growing more and more resigned to her fate, Mina withdrew both her police report and her divorce application – chiefly because of pressure from her husband and the rest of the family, but also because she felt the authorities had failed her.

"You are a dog"

Three months later, the situation changed dramatically. Mina's youngest daughter told another child in the extended family that she had been sexually assaulted while Mina had been living away from home. The assailant: her father. The information reached the police, Barnevernet, and me before it reached Mina. When Mina heard the news, she didn't dare to report it. She was scared of being accused by her relatives of having manipulated the girl to make the accusation. But they accused her of it anyway.

How did the little girl's family and her father's acquaintances treat her when her accusation became known? They made fun of her and accused her of being a liar. They called her, among other things, a "dog" – a common term of abuse among many Muslims because Islam considers dogs unclean. They believed that the little girl and Mina had conspired. The fact that the girl had told her story to a judge, and that both the judge and the police believed her, did not alter this view.

Disobedience can pay off, and this proved to be the case with Mina. In an unguarded moment, she left her home on an errand. Her husband tracked her down and attacked her, beating her until her face bled horribly. She was still bleeding when he got her home, where all the children were. He told them that Mina had attacked him, and that he'd been forced to defend himself. For their own protection, he told the children, they would have to go to his brothers' house for the evening. He took them all there, except for the daughter whom he was suspected of having abused. The next day he couldn't get into the house. Mina had changed the locks.

A new round of interviews with the lawyer, the police, and Barneveret in the autumn of 2003 finally brought results: Mina received temporary custody of all the children and was given a body alarm; a restraining order was put out against her husband. Mina's extended family froze her and her children out while giving her husband their love and support.

Not until 2006 did Mina manage to make a decent life for herself. She received custody of all of her children, while her husband was denied all contact with them. She has been allowed to keep her home. Her relatives still reject her and she lives with a body alarm. All the crimes of which she has accused her husband are still being investigated by the police, with the exception of the purported sexual attack on the youngest daughter. Even though the authorities believe that she was indeed sexually assaulted by her father, they feel that there is insufficient evidence to convict him.

The spider web

Needless to say, I would never claim that Mina and her children's experiences of violent assault by criminal and semi-criminal men in their extended family is a widespread phenomenon in tradition-bound families in Norway. Mina's story does, however, show how such a family is likely to react when a woman wants to escape an unhappy life. In my experience, very few women manage to break out – indeed, very few even dare to try. Their dreams hardly ever come to anything. Mina was thus an exception. She stood up against everybody, including Norwegian authorities, and did so against all odds. She challenged the higher powers in the spider web – the extended family – in which the oldest men are both the prosecuting authorities and the courts of law. In that spider web, one woman standing alone is as helpless against the system as the next, and is every bit as prepared as the others to stab a "sister" in the back if she violates the old village's cultural norms and values, especially those involving sexual conduct.

In the extended-family system, virtually no one dares to trust anyone else entirely, for everyone knows that the tolerance level is virtually zero. Thus there is lying, manipulation, game-playing, and deception aplenty – the purpose being to hide the truth about oneself and to protect oneself from punishment.[20] It's inhuman, of course, to have to live up to the demands of such a system. Whether by thought or by action, large or small, you're bound to break the code in the course of daily life. And when your potential informer is sleeping in the same room, or the next room, you're obliged to be dishonest, to be suspicious. You're trapped, and you hold your head down for fear of the possible consequences. As we've seen in the case of various despotic regimes during the postwar era, such as those of Stalin and Hoxha, the informer can be at the heart of one's innermost family circle. Under those regimes, if you had thoughts and opinions that went against the ideology of the ruling leadership, you risked being turned in to the authorities by your own father, mother, sister, or brother. So it is in a traditional extended family: the oldest man in the clan can function as a small-scale Stalin or Hoxha. And it doesn't matter whether he wants to be a Stalin or not: the role is imposed upon him, and if he fails – if, that is, he neglects to exercise his power in such a way as to inspire fear and submissiveness among the other family members, especially where women's sexual conduct is concerned – he'll lose face within the family, and the family will lose face outside the family. In such a case the man will lose his "peacock throne," and his power will devolve upon the next oldest man.

How a culture based on honour and shame results in gossip, suspicion, and out-and-out lies has also been described by Ayaan Hirsi Ali, the Somali-born former member of the Dutch Parliament, in her book *The Son Factory: About Women, Islam and Integration:* "Lies and honour play an important role in this culture of honour and shame; ignoring or simply denying what has really happened is normal. The tribal culture has a strongly developed sense of mistrust, not only of outsiders, but also of the members of one's own family or clan" (*The Caged Virgin*, p. 50). Hirsi Ali maintains that lies in the innermost private sphere are routine: "lies are continually being told about the most intimate matters. It is a survival strategy, but it also becomes a way of living." In this way, children learn from their mother's daily conduct that if they don't want to be punished, they must lie. Children learn that "it pays to lie," says Hirsi Ali (*The Caged Virgin*, pp. 25-6).[21]

The hotbed of honour

Honour thinking has its origins in countries and regions where the central government is weak and where power is instead organized – in feudal fashion – according to clan, caste, or tribal membership. In such places there is no welfare system to serve as a safety net should some accident befall an individual or family. Therefore the individual is dependent upon a larger group – namely, the family, clan, caste, or tribe. This kind of situation obtains, for example, in Kurdish areas, in Somalia, in the Arabic world, in Pakistan, and in Afghanistan. These are societies marked by a lack of modernity and democracy – societies where the status of women is extremely low and entirely conditional on their sexual conduct.

In these societies, girls and women are bearers of the clan's honour, the tribe's honour, and the extended family's honour. They carry the men's honour on their shoulders – an honour upon which men are entirely dependent if they wish to obtain, and retain, the respect of other members of their community. This respect is based on fear: a fear that protects one against external enemies, that secures one from being exploited in business, and that ensures that one is treated with dignity outside one's own circles. A girl, or woman, who breaks with the strict sexual morality enshrined in unwritten rules and norms, or who is suspected of having done so, or who is thought capable of doing so, places the honour of the men in her family in jeopardy. She is showing that she doesn't fear her own men – on the contrary, she is, by her very behavior, mocking them and exposing their weakness. She is saying indirectly to outsiders: look! These men are nothing to be feared. They can't control me or other women in our family. These are men with whom one can do as one wishes. They're without honour.

Needless to say, a man's all-embracing fear of losing control over the women in his family takes a huge daily toll in both energy and attention. The exercise of control leads to a lack of innovation and creativity.

Result: conformism.

Either one has honour, or one doesn't. There's no in-between. So it's only through constant vigilance that men can recover their honour – that is, reinstate fear. The vigilance takes the form of sanctions against disobedient women – and against any men outside of the family who have touched the family's women. And the most extreme sanction of all is murder.

That was why Anoonse, an Afghani, was murdered. That was why Fadime, the Kurd, was killed.

Fadime's challenge was answered in a way that sent a clear message to the world: namely, that her family's men were not weak. And the other women in the family received a clear message, too – about what awaited them if they followed her example of disobedience. For the same reason, Mina's desire for a divorce never won any support from the men in her family: such support would have sent all the wrong signals. Nor did Mina get any sympathy from her female relatives – for a woman who stands by a disobedient woman becomes herself an object of suspicion: Is she cut from the same cloth? And since it's a mother's responsibility to bring her daughter up to follow the moral code, that mother is fully responsible if her daughter violates that code. No wonder, then, that Mina's own mother didn't back her up. On the contrary: her own mother, Mina told me, believed that the family's men had every right to kill her.

The village lives on – in Norway

There wasn't a single person in Mina's circle of intimates who was willing to take her side. When her daughter told the extended family about the sexual assault, I was there. Mina wanted someone from outside the family to communicate to them that it was important that they believe the girl and not discuss the case in her or the other children's presence (as had happened on several occasions).

I felt I'd been there before. Visiting that family in Oslo was like visiting an extended family in a village, or a lower middle-class or middle-class family in a city, in Pakistan. Several generations under the same roof. Women in traditional clothes. The age-based hierarchy among the women, with the daughters-in-law at the bottom of the ladder. The men coming and going between servings of hot casseroles. The big TV set in the middle of the house, always turned on, at high volume, with the satellite dish tuned in to the channels coming in from the "homeland." One bedroom per married couple, often including children's beds. No private life for anyone, for private life is suspect; a need to be alone, if only for a half hour, is suspect. For being alone is the same as being able to sin. And in these families, sin is virtually identical with forbidden sexuality. There is a total control over one another and a thoroughgoing mutual suspicion, which is reflected in the conversations: gossip about one another and about acquaintances; criticism of one another and of acquaintances. And during these conversations children of all ages are present, though they have no input into the choice of topics.

And anyone who might yearn for a life different from the one being lived inside this cocoon knows that that choice would essentially involve an automatic severing of all family ties. I'm referring here to young people who might wish to move out so they can study or work, and to grown men or women who might want to live alone, unmarried, or enter into non-traditional relationships. Hardly anything is more sensitive in these milieux than the idea of choosing one's own life partner on the basis of one's emotions. Love and romance are so taboo that even married couples aren't supposed to display affection for each other in the sight of others. A woman is especially discouraged from showing affection for her husband – for if she does, other people might suspect that she can't control her feelings.

This was how I experienced the mental and social circumstances of Mina's extended family. For them, Norway is only a financial base. And Mina, as she herself said, has only been a financial milk cow for her husband and his family in Pakistan. But it's a lot harder for her today to live with all the immigration cheating by which her imported husband has profited. That her marriage to her cousin also led to three new visas for his brothers, plus two visas for their cousins, makes her as furious now as it did then. I have no idea how many times in recent years Mina has phoned me in despair over Norwegian immigration policy, over politicians who allow the endless fetching of new spouses from abroad, and over the fact that no policy has been put in place to stop to this abuse. For, as she says, her young nieces and nephews will be used in exactly the same way that she and her siblings were used, as pure tools of immigration. And as a result they'll never escape the village, never be freed from the spider web, never get to live completely in Norway.

They'll live here only part of the time – and with only part of their selves.

3

Family-Arranged Marriage

The statistical information presented in the previous chapter about fetching marriage among non-Western immigrant groups in Norway is the most extensive and detailed material of its kind in all of Europe. Most European countries – among them Sweden, Germany, and France – have no official statistics at all about these matters. A few do. One of them is Denmark.

A 2000 study in Denmark showed that about 90 percent of all married male immigrants and children of immigrants from the former Yugoslavia, Pakistan, Somalia, Turkey, and Vietnam married individuals with the same national origin, who either were already living in Denmark or were "fetched." Another 2003 study awakened great interest. For the first time, it was possible to say why the majority of immigrants bring over spouses from their homelands.[22] Researchers examined the family backgrounds, educational levels, and personal attitudes of 693 children of immigrants from Turkey, Pakistan, and the former Yugoslavia. All the children had come to Denmark at age seven, had lived in Denmark for at least twenty years, and were between twenty-eight and thirty-six years old when the study was carried out.

Of those who had had no education, about 90 percent were married off in their country of origin. Meanwhile, fewer than half of those with more education brought spouses over from their homelands. The researchers concluded as follows: in most such cases, it's the family that decides whom one marries. The less conflict young people have with their parents, the greater the chance that they'll marry in their homeland. From childhood on, young people in these communities have adapted themselves to the authoritarian extended-family system and have absorbed its values. The researchers also said that the more liberal parents' attitudes toward childrearing and Danish values and lifestyles, the greater the chance that their children will marry in Denmark. If parents have low levels of education, language problems, and traditional attitudes rooted in their village in the old country, the probability increases significantly that their children will marry in their homeland. The study also showed that those who marry in Denmark and whose spouses are ethnically Danish are very likely to marry people at the same level of education as themselves. This is also the norm among Danes.

And how can young people be more successful at evading family-arranged marriages in their ancestral homelands? The researchers concluded that only more education can, to a certain degree, protect young children in immigrant families from fetching marriages.

Denmark has its own version of Ahmed's family tree. In 2000, Eyvind Vesselbo mapped out the marriages of 145 Turkish men who came to Denmark around 1970 and their descendants. All of the 145 men brought wives over from Turkey, and after getting divorces some of them brought even more wives over from Turkey. Nine out of ten members of the second generation brought spouses over from Turkey. In the third generation, the rate of fetching marriages was 97 percent. By the year 2000, the original group of 145 men had multiplied almost twenty times over the course of thirty years into a group of 2,813 persons.[23]

In the Netherlands, the marriage patterns of over 81,000 first- and second-generation Moroccan and Turkish men and women were studied. Only four percent married ethnic Dutch people, eighteen percent married individuals of the same nationality in the Netherlands, while 75 percent brought spouses over from their homelands.[24] There's no data on whom the remaining three percent married, though there's reason to assume that most of them married someone in the Netherlands with another national background. The pattern is thus almost identical to that found among Turks and Moroccans in Norway.

In Britain, 71 percent of Pakistanis enter into fetching marriages. One study shows that 90 percent of the fetched spouses are cousins.[25] Since 1997, about 150,000 new immigrants have arrived in Britain every year. These figures do not include asylum seekers or refugees.[26]

In 2005, 53,000 spouses immigrated to France. There are no general statistics about these people's national backgrounds. For many years, marriage has accounted for most of the immigration into France.[27]

The internationally known British professor and demographer David Coleman claims that the fetching of spouses has been responsible for most of the immigration to Europe since the 1970s: "Originally, family reunification was a term that meant reuniting families, meaning that an already married person – usually a mother with children – immigrated to a country where her husband had already been working, often for several years. But today, as a rule, it involves newly created families. That is, a young man or woman, who was born in or has lived most of his or her life in Europe, travels to the family's homeland and fetches a person as a spouse, who – perhaps – he or she knows a bit from the family's vacations in its homeland."[28]

It's often said that it takes time to change traditions. This is a partial truth. In countries with family-arranged marriage, it's geneally accepted that the bride will move in with her bridegroom and his family. Had Mina acted in accordance with this norm, of course, she would have moved back to Pakistan and resided there with her husband and his family. But this once-firm tradition has been modified, and there are two major reasons why. One is that the huge economic differences between European and non-Western countries make it lucrative for the groom to move to Europe. The other is that immigration through a family-arranged marriage to a European cousin, close relative, or stranger is – quite simply – legal.

Plenty of examples

I would estimate that in the last fourteen years I've met 150 to 200 individuals face to face who have been assaulted by the people with whom they were united in immigration marriages. Most of the encounters came about because I was a journalist, but I also met some of these persons through acquaintances in various communities. Most often I've been sought out as an expert, either directly by the affected person, by his or her friends and family members, or by government employees who have been trying to help the individual in question. After I started working for Human Rights Service, the referrals continued.

Most of the people whom I've met have been young; a few, like Mina, have been well into adulthood. The affected individuals have come from three continents – Africa, Asia, and Europe – and from the countries of India, Pakistan, Afghanistan, Iran, Iraq, Turkey, Syria, Lebanon, Ethiopia, Somalia, Morocco, Gambia, Macedonia, and Albania. The overwhelming majority had been married off to cousins. And there were very few who didn't have dramatic accounts of assault.

Take Hera, age nineteen. I met her when she was being kept under lock and key in her father's home in Pakistan. A friend of hers in Norway was worried about her, and sent her a text message saying that Norwegians – meaning me and two colleagues – were on their way to the region of Pakistan where she was living. This pleased Hera, who asked us to visit. When, as arranged, I turned up with my colleagues at ten in the morning, her father was sitting at his house's entrance gate. Hera had asked us to say that one of us was her former teacher. With a gruff expression, the father led us into the large, two-story house. Alone with us in the living room, Hera told us in a hushed voice that she was being raped every day – with her father's permission – by the cousin she had been forced to marry. The story was this: Hera hadn't managed to earn enough income to fulfill the legal requirement that would allow her to bring her spouse to Norway.[29] When the spouse's application to be reunified with her had been rejected, Hera's father had taken her back to Pakistan. The idea was for her to get pregnant. If they had a child, Hera's father figured, her husband's tie to Norway would be strengthened and he might, for that reason, be granted a Norwegian visa so that he could live with his wife and child. Hera's father, she told us, pointing at a door, stood guard outside her bedroom every evening. Her life was restricted by the house's four walls. She wanted to flee, to run far away – all the way back to Norway, if she could. But what would happen, then, to her mother? What suffering would Hera's demand for a decent life cause her mother? She knew the answer. So it was that this nineteen-year-old girl, born in Norway, sat behind mental and physical lock and key in the house in the village while the cousin who had been forced upon her by her father endeavored every night to impregnate her against her will.

Then there's Shahid – a sturdy guy, nearly thirty years old, who for three years struggled against his family's pressure to bring back to Norway the cousin he'd been forced to marry. When he went to Pakistan on vacation in the summer of 2003, several of us who were friends of his told him jokingly: "Now don't come back and tell us that you've been forced to marry a cousin, too!" He laughed heartily. So did we – fully believing that he was only going on a vacation.

Four months later he came back – scrawny, head bowed – after a vacation that had been extended for one reason: because it had taken time to break the will of this man who was in love with somebody in Norway. But what could Shahid do, in the end, when his father simulated heart problems and had to go to the hospital, when his mother alternated between tears and accusations that his father's "deadly illness" was Shahid's fault, and when his brothers stormed and raged and threatened physical reprisals should their father die? What could Shahid do when his "weak and sick" mother said that she wouldn't be able to keep house and take care of the family in Norway any longer without the help of a daughter-in-law? Would Shahid force his own mother to return to Pakistan and live with servants she didn't know? Finally he caved in. The past three years of his life, during which he's lived in a marriage with a cousin from his village, could easily fill a book. The most burlesque detail is probably how he, after two years of intense pressure, finally climbed into bed with his cousin – while his satisfied mother enjoyed her triumph in the next room.

Then there's a Turkish-Kurdish girl named Avin. When she was eleven, her family sent her from Turkey to live with an adult cousin in Norway. Avin was supplied with identity papers belonging to an Iranian woman of eighteen. She had children in a hospital when she herself was a child, and the medical staff didn't ask her a single question about herself. Had anyone tried to speak with her, however, they wouldn't have received an answer – for her husband was constantly at her side, ready to speak on her behalf. From the time she was thirteen years old, Avid had various jobs in the public sector; but she chose not to reveal her age to anyone because she had been told by her cousin that if she did so, Norwegian authorities would send her home – where death awaited.

Cousin marriage – a hindrance to integration

I could continue to recount individual cases, page after page. But let's put away the faces and the names. Why is marriage between close relatives so common in many immigrant groups? And how much choice do the partners in such unions have? Key sources of mine who are immigration officials working with forced marriages among Norwegian-Pakistanis believe that up to 70 percent of the cases that reach their desks fall into the same category as the situation that Mina was locked into – marriage between cousins.[30] Are there any major features of cousin marriages that cause them to be particularly involuntary and to hinder integration – a state of affairs that we've observed with blinding clarity in the saga of Mina's extended family?

No one in Scandinavia has done a more thorough job of collecting and analyzing data on the involuntary nature of cousin marriages than Anders Hede of Denmark. Hede is a project leader for the weekly publication *Ugebrevet Mandag Morgen,* and he's published his material in a work entitled "Baggrundsnotat om spørgsmålet om et forbud mot fætter-kusine ægteskaber" ("Background notes on the question of a prohibition of cousin marriages"). This work had a major influence on Denmark's introduction of new immigration rules in the autumn of 2003. Under the new rules, marriages between close relatives – that is, first and second cousins – would be treated in the immigration application process as forced marriages and would therefore be regarded as invalid grounds for immigration. The presentation of cousin marriage in the following pages is mostly drawn from Hede's work. His findings and analyses are entirely consistent with my own observations.

First, some general facts. Cousin marriage is common in large areas of the world. Around 18 percent of the world's population lives in societies where 20 to 50 percent of the marriages are between cousins; 47 percent live in societies where one to ten percent marry cousins; 17 percent live in societies where the percentage is below one. For the remaining 18 percent of the world's population there are no relevant data. Although such marriages are widespread, a study of 564 cultures around the world shows that no fewer than 277 of them forbid cousin marriages. And studies in the U.S., Australia, and Norway estimate that only two to six out of one thousand marriages in the majority population are between first or second cousins.

Cousin marriages occur in all large religious groups. But there are no key religious texts in Islam, Judaism, or Christianity that address this form of marriage, either positively or negatively. Today it's unquestionably most common among Muslims. This may be related to the fact that the nephew of Muhammed, the prophet of Islam, married Muhammed's daughter. When one marires away one's children to their cousins, then, one is following Muhammed's example.

Pakistani statistics estimate that 30 to 60 percent of marriages in that country are between cousins. Among Kurds in Turkey, 11 to 31 percent marry cousins. In Iraq, the percentage is between 46 and 57 percent, in Sri Lanka 7 to 20 percent, in Morocco 29 percent, and in Bangladesh 7 to 20 percent. (The figures aren't entirely comparable, since some studies include second cousins and some don't.)

Several studies indicate that the rate of cousin marriage among immigrant groups in Europe increases from the first to the second generation. This pattern has been demonstrated among Turks in France and among Turks and Moroccans in Belgium, where it's been concluded that the marriages are an immigration tool and that families in the immigrants' homelands exert considerable pressure upon their relatives in the West to submit to cousin marriages. Cousin marriage is also more common among second- than first-generation Pakistanis in Britain. In Bradford, it's now estimated that up to 80 percent of new marriages among Pakistanis are between cousins.[31]

A study that attracted attention in Britain in 2005 indicated a high rate of deformities among newborn babies of Pakistanis. The Pakistani population accounts for 3.4 percent of the country's births, but fully 30 percent of the birth defects registered among newborns occur in children of parents with Pakistani origins.[32] In Norway, Camilla Stoltenberg of the Norwegian Institute of Public Health recorded that every twentieth child born of Pakistani parents in Norway between 1967 and 1993 was born with defects. The risk of deformities in newborn babies quadruples when the parents are closely related. When a cohort of children reaches five years of age, the rate of deformities in that cohort increases. Among children of parents who are related to each other, the risk of dying in the first year of life is also two to three times higher.[33]

At regular intervals, debates erupt about cousin marriages, with the main focus usually being on the degree to which such marriages are voluntary. A number of factors suggest that such marriages are thoroughly involuntary. Mina was eighteen when she was married. She was young, which is typical in cousin marriages. Her parents had arranged the marriage without consulting her. There had not been many candidates, since the number of available male cousins was naturally limited. They found no good reason to put off the wedding; doing so could increase the risk that Mina would grow independent and start making her own decisions – or, even worse, might lose her virginity.

To refuse to marry a cousin usually brings on family conflicts and punishment. To try to win support within one's family for an effort to escape such a marriage is essentially futile. Mina had nobody to support her when she tried to avoid marrying her cousin. "Whom should I cry to?" she asked me. Almost all of her siblings were married to cousins. Why should they support her rebellion? She knew, too, that if she put up any resistance she'd become an outcast, and perhaps risk physical danger.

Few young people in Muslim communities dare to gamble on a love match. Most of those who do marry for love become outcasts. A leading Norwegian-Pakistani lawyer, Abid Q. Raja, has told *Aftenposten* (6 August 2005) about the fight he waged to get his family to accept his marriage to the Norwegian-Pakistani woman he loved. His family wanted to marry him off in Pakistan.

Conservative Party politician Ashan Rafiq has also told, in *VG* (6 January 2004), about the serious threats she faced from her family because she wanted to marry the Norwegian-Pakistani Oslo politician Aamir J. Sheikh, also a member of the Conservative Party. The two of them fought for several years to win acceptance for their love. Sheikh himself has told about being forced to marry in Pakistan. (He divorced in 2003.) The couple, then twenty-eight and thirty-three years old, decided to defy all the threats. They married while Rafiq was a member of Parliament.

Yes, one can safely say that the Norwegian-Pakistani reality is far from the bliss-filled world of Bollywood.

The Sikhs' success

Conflicts of interests between immigrant parents and their children occur with particular frequency in cases of cousin marriage and fetching marriage. If the young people involved were able to choose for themselves, they would prefer a spouse who grew up in the West. In my experience, it's especially the girls who have this dream. A girl expects that a man who has grown up in an environment reasonably similar to the one in which she grew up will treat her with greater understanding and respect than one who grew up elsewhere.

Mina was expelled from her extended family. She was thereby also set free from the spider net. Her children, she says, will be allowed to choose their own spouses. Mina is liberated; her children are liberated. But she doesn't think that the other children in her extended family will be able to avoid following their parents' footsteps back to the village. For the purposes of integration, this is obviously a very negative state of affairs.

Probably the most striking example in Europe of the significance of marriage patterns for the success or failure of integration has been provided by Anders Hede in his studies of the situation in Britain. The Sikhs in Britain come from the Punjab region of India, while many Pakistanis in Britain come from the Punjab in Pakistan. In short, they have their origins in areas very close to each other. Yet while Sikhs in Britain are an integration success story, Pakistanis have become an obvious underclass. Thanks to their successful integration, Sikhs exhibit an entirely different level of mobility on the labour market. As a result, they weren't affected in the same way as Pakistanis by the downturn in British industry.

Why?

In large part, the reason for this dramatic difference is that Sikhs have a cultural prohibition against marrying relatives. This means that an Indian Sikh woman who marries moves into the home of a strange family. She'll therefore be more likely to try to get her husband to agree that they should move out and set up their own home. The Sikhs have thereby established a more dispersed residential pattern, which has had more positive consequences for the children, in that it enables them to befriend British children and learn English. Very many Sikh children do better at school than British children, and Sikh women, on average, earn more than British women. But when a Pakistani Muslim woman moves in with her husband's family, she's also usually moving in with her own relatives. Most likely, she lives a largely isolated life among her own people, outside the labour market, and has many more children than a Sikh woman does. Her children grow up in a ghetto-like environment, and many do badly in school because they speak inadequate English.

Once Sikhs, too, fetched spouses from their homeland. But these marriages functioned poorly, especially when the husbands were imported. Those husbands often brought with them a patriarchal village mentality. Today virtually all Sikhs marry partners from Britain or from other European countries. The young strongly oppose fetching marriage. They dare to take on their parents, and they win. Why? Because they know that their parents don't have obligations to relatives in their homeland; the practice of marrying outside the family frees the parents from having to use their children as living visas for their relatives back in India.

The pressure on parents to marry off their children to poorer relatives in Pakistan is decisive. Some British Pakistani families try to duck this pressure by wedding their children to cousins in Britain. But this usually leads to complaints by relatives in Pakistan that they're egotistic and evil – in such marriages, after all, two visas are tossed away.

Most Sikhs today lead integrated lives in their new surroundings. Few retain intimate connections to the Punjab region of India. Even so, they manage to maintain their distinctive cultural and religious traits. By contrast, as we've seen in the case of Mina's extended family, Pakistani Muslims still live with a gaze turned constantly toward Pakistan. They buy residences in Pakistan and travel "home" frequently. Money is prioritized for these purchases rather than for acquisitions in Britain. The preservation of traditional marriage patterns is thus a crucial factor in failed integration. The Sikhs, on the other hand, are a striking example of what happens when immigrants embrace an open marriage market and act independently of pressure from relatives in their homeland.

It's extremely interesting to see which groups in the West have practiced cousin marriage for generation after generation. They're the most inward-looking and isolated groups, the least educated, the ones who live in the past, the ones in which the status of women is low and the ideal of virginity at its strongest, the ones in which many children are born and in which the children are shielded from the influence of mainstream society. These groups seek to live the way their forefathers did for centuries – outside of a society of laws and outside of modernity itself. This is the case with the Amish people and the Mennonites (no fewer than 85 percent of whom marry cousins); the Hutterites (who have the highest level of inbreeding in North America); the Tinkers, also called The Travelling People (among whom, according to Anders Hede, the level of inbreeding is about 70 percent); and the Romany people in Europe.

Is romantic love a Western concept?

Among the native peoples of a modern, well-functioning welfare state such as Norway, the percentage of cousin marriage is microscopic. The families of Western citizens in Norway almost never play a role in their choice of spouse. Romantic love is the norm.

Some make the argument that romantic love is a Western idea that large parts of the world haven't adopted. But this is nonsense, as anyone who has visited countries like Pakistan or Turkey knows. These countries are seething with longing for romance and love – a fact reflected in their films, their poetry, and their folk songs. In all these genres, the recurring question is this: will the two lovers end up with each other – against all odds? The hindrance consists in the fact that marriage is a family matter that operates in accordance with strict norms regarding who can be accepted as a new family member. Hede found extensive support for the notion that romance and love are universal phenomena in the results of a study performed by William Jankowiak and Edward Fisher. Examining 168 cultures, Jankowiak and Fisher asked four questions: Are there love songs? Do young people run off together? Do people tell of an especially loved person for whom they long? And is there folklore about romantic relationships? In up to 90 percent of the cultures they studied, the answer was yes across the board. The researchers had strong suspicions that the same was the case in the remaining cultures, but anthropological data was insufficient to make a definitive determination. They thus concluded that if social conditions make romance and love possible, these phenomena will occur, for they're as universal as pain, joy, and hunger.[34]

"Love match" is an expression I've heard many times among young Norwegian-Pakistanis and Norwegian-Indians. When two lovers both living in Norway win approval to marry, the news is spread around the communities like wildfire. Young people with expressions of longing on their faces talk excitedly about "the great thing that has happened." These same young people are brought up watching Bollywood movies on DVD and satellite transmissions. There's little they want more than a love match, but few dare to believe they'll win that lottery. Most are resigned, fatalistic. For them, it's a long way from Bollywood to Norway.

It's also worth noting that every single well-known and well integrated Norwegian-Pakistani has broken with the tradition of family-arranged marriage. I'm thinking of Shazad Rana, who founded an IT firm, of comic and writer Shabana Rehman, of college teacher Nazneen Khan-Østrem, and of Labour Party politician Lubna Jaffrey. All have found partners outside their own ethnic groups. They live on the free "marriage market."

And our consultant at Human Rights Service, Jeanette, married her husband, Audun, on 29 July 2006.

For years, intellectuals and politicians in Norway, both Norwegian and non-Western, have spoken warmly about family-arranged marriage. In the non-Western communities and extended families, parents and older people issue stern warnings against romantic love. Marital friendship and acquaintanceship develop into "real" love, they say, while "Western marriages" usually end in divorce, precisely because they're based solely on intense feelings that will always eventually fade. It's unreasonable to pretend that this doesn't in fact happen in many cases, as Western divorce statistics confirm. But it's scarcely bold to predict that if women in family-arranged marriages were financially independent, the divorce rates for those marriages, too, would shoot up dramatically.

The opposition to love matches is entirely logical. Romantic love threatens parents' and elders' power and privilege, such as the right to be waited on by a devoted daughter-in-law who's also a close blood relative. Love threatens the effort to bring relatives still living in the family's ancestral homeland to the Norwegian welfare state through marriage. Love threatens the extended family's and clan's ability to strengthen its power and influence by bringing new members to the country and thereby preserve and pass on feudal values in Europe. Love threatens the caste system. And it threatens the male's power position, in that it may destabilize traditional sex roles. Love is also a threat to marriage arrangements that were entered into when the potential bride and groom were small children.

Mina's fate was exclusion from her family. This exclusion propelled her out of the family's restraints and into romance – namely, a passionate attachment to a man who shared her ethnic background and who had scuttled his own family-arranged marriage.

What would happen if our new non-Western immigrants wed outside their families – either to partners of their own choosing or to partners selected by their families? Without a doubt, it would be easier for them to resist pressure, because it would be easier for their parents to withdraw from negotiations and agreements with strangers. Parents and children would have much stronger shared interests in seeking out a compatible mate with a comparable level of education. Spouses would be more likely to come from nearby areas. Thus non-Western men in Norway would be under considerable pressure to get an education and find work to strengthen their value as marriage candidates. The women's age at the time of marriage would rise – and as a result the amount of time she'd be able to devote to an education would increase. The married couples would probably also form nuclear families, independent of their extended families, as many British Sikhs have done.

In time, this would lead to the dissolution of the ghetto-like immigrant neighbourhoods. It would thus be far easier for individuals to live *as* individuals: they'd be able to participate in mainstream society as integrated citizens without having to surrender their distinctive cultural and religious practices, just as Sikhs in Britain have done. It's precisely for this reason that education and the labour market aren't topics in this book – for the key to integration lies in a changing marriage pattern.

Of course family-arranged marriages to non-relatives won't automatically be free of force. But over time, people's ties to their homelands will grow weaker; integration will improve. And when the clan, caste, and tribal mentality is weakened, bondage and force will become less prevalent.

Let me make one thing clear: I don't mean to suggest here that living in a family-arranged marriage is necessarily synonymous with lifelong tragedy. Many young people will be inclined to think that such marriages are right for them because they've been brought up to think so.

Given this fact, they'll do the best they can to order their daily life in such a way that their marriages will work out. They'll seek to lead friction-free lives within extended-family structures. Outside the home, they'll work; inside it, they'll live with relatives in varying degrees of contentment.

And it's true, of course, that many people in Norway live in unhappy marriages to people they chose themselves – marriages in which the love has died. Many try to keep things going for practical or financial reasons, perhaps especially for the sake of the children. I nonetheless believe that the key point here is that people in the West are generally free to make the attempt – and to err. Hardly anyone wants to give up this freedom. Those who have experienced the intoxication of falling in love and the passion of romance can't deny that love is the greatest thing of all.

Creative cheating, physical assault

A friend of mine was forced at a young age to marry a close relative in Pakistan. Today she's divorced. During the last two years, she's received offers from three different men to be wife number two. All her suitors are Norwegian-Pakistanis between twenty-five and thirty-five years old. And all are married to cousins from their parents' hometowns back in Pakistan. All three are locked into emotionally barren marriages. They can't divorce without causing colossal conflicts within their extended families both in Norway and in Pakistan.

One of these men was forced to marry relatively recently. His wife, who is also his cousin, has not yet been brought over to Norway. He's trying to talk his parents into releasing him from the marriage. He hasn't yet managed to do so. He has also attempted to strike a compromise with his lover, who is my friend: would she marry him if he promised not to bring his wife to Norway? Under Norwegian law, this isn't permitted: you can't have a registered wife living in Norway and have one or more other wives in one's homeland, even if polygamy is allowed there. My friend recently told me:

> I've said yes, and I'll tolerate him going to the village once a year to stay with his wife there. I'll also tolerate him having kids with her – otherwise his family will make a lot of

trouble for both of them. But I don't think I'll be able to handle it if he brings her here. Then she'll be his real wife – the one who's in his home and whom he's together with in social situations. I'll be the wife who's hidden away and without privileges, and I'll be uncertain and jealous when he's with her. There'll be a daily competition to do the best by him in order to get as much time with him as possible. And the children will suffer in both homes because both I and the other wife will do everything we can to ensure that our children have the strongest bond to him. There's no doubt that it'll be much harder for me than for him. I'll lie alone at night knowing he's sleeping with her. But he won't have to share me with another man.

She also pointed out that, as wife number two, her legal position would be weaker. If he died, she would have no right to inherit anything, since her marriage, solemnized in a mosque, would not be formally registered. She'd be the "invisible wife." If he got sick and was hospitalized, his family might deny her the right to visit him. She'd be, in many ways, a non-person.

She hasn't given up hope that he'll succeed in wriggling out of the marriage to his cousin. She and her lover have a last card to play – a card that, according to her, has been used successfully by many people she knows: you take an overdose, just enough so that it'll result in hospitalization. The hope is that your family will then wake up and understand how serious the matter is. For the shame of losing a child through suicide is far greater than the shame of calling off a marriage process that's already underway. I, too, am familiar with such cases.

Does polygamy enhance one's status in the Muslim community in Norway? There's no answer to this, since the various groups are so diverse. A rule of thumb is that the more widespread polygamy is in a given ethnic or national group in a given country, the more accepted it is among immigrants from that country in Norway. My Pakistani-Norwegian friend believes that polygamy neither enhances nor reduces one's status among

Pakistanis in Norway. Since forced marriage is so widespread, polygamy has become widespread, too; she thinks that "people are beginning to get used to this becoming the solution for many people."

My friend thinks that polygamy will increase in the second generation, a hypothesis I find realistic:

> More and more people [in the second generation] are reaching marriageable ages, and forced marriage is widespread. Since it's so important to parents that their sons not divorce, the young people will see no alternative other than polygamy. Our mothers had no opportunity to choose love marriages. But many of us second-generation girls want love. And the boys do, too. But first we have to do our "job." The boys' "job" is to fetch a caregiver and maid for their parents. And since the boys, moreover, are supposed to live at home and provide for their parents, it can be hard to divorce. Many of us girls can divorce more easily, for when the husband who is brought over has gotten a residency permit of his own, we've done our "job." You can say that the boys' "job" is lifelong, while the girls' "job" can be over once the residency permit is secured.

This last point has been impressed upon me over and over in conversations I've had with young women, lawyers, and immigration officials. They tell me that if a girl feels she can hold out for three years, she may make a deal with her parents that doesn't oblige her to live with her spouse in a real marriage and that permits her to divorce after three years.

Another young woman I've known well for seven years was forced at age fifteen to marry a close relative in Pakistan. After three years she got a divorce. She then fell in love with a man of Pakistani origins. He's married to his cousin who was brought over from Pakistan, has two children with her, and doesn't want to take on his family by asking for permission to divorce. Last year he and the young woman married at a ceremony in a mosque. This practice, although illegal, appears to be widespread.

Each of these young women could compile a list of names of other young women they know who have been married in mosques to men who already had wives. Most of these young women, at the time of their mosque weddings, were divorced from husbands whom they'd been forced to marry, while some are non-Muslims of Norwegian or other Western ethnicity.

It can justifiably be said that these two young women have landed in a thoroughly undesirable situation. Other people practice polygamy actively. At one Norwegian embassy, I was told in confidence about men in Norway who have imported up to six wives apiece. At another embassy I heard about men living in Norway each of whom has brought five wives over from his homeland. The pattern is the same: after three to four years of marriage to an imported wife, the man divorces formally under Norwegian law, then travels to his homeland to marry a new wife who is then shipped to Norway. Only the length of the man's life limits the number of wives he can bring over in this fashion. Immigration authorities say that the men engaged in this practice are overwhelmingly Muslim.

From various sources I've also heard about children who spontaneously volunteer that their fathers have several wives. In many cases these wives all live in the same apartment house. Such information often emerges when a child points out his or her half-brothers or half-sisters at a day-care centre or at school.

Evidence that this practice is widespread can also be found at social-security offices. On several occasions, the social-security department has asked me to deliver lectures. Their problem is that many of their clients are single women who are breadwinners but whom it is difficult to find jobs for and who are difficult to integrate.[35] The women are mostly divorced, and some have been separated from their husbands for several years. Yet many keep having children. How widespread this phenomenon is, nobody knows. But what's this about? And what can be done?

During my lectures, I learned from frustrated social-security employees that when they ask such a woman who the father of her newborn baby is, they are typically told either that the child is a result of "a slip-up" between her and her ex-husband or estranged husband or that she doesn't know who the father is. The truth, in most of these instances, is probably that the woman is living in a polygamous set-up with a Muslim husband and that they have been divorced or separated under Norwegian law while their Muslim marriage contract has remained in force. For believers, this pact, whether oral or written, is far more binding than a Norwegian marriage license. Financially, such a divorce or separation is highly favourable because the woman, by passing herself off as an unmarried breadwinner, qualifies for a number of social-security benefits.

Also, when new children are born and the father is listed as unknown, the husband doesn't have to pay child support. Under current rules, it's hard to stop this practice. Under the law, the state has no right to subject children to a DNA test when their mother claims not to know who their father is. Nor is there any limit to how long one can stay separated, and under Norwegian law, of course, it's not illegal to have children out of wedlock.

Another topic related to marriage immigration – and one that has hardly been mentioned in the Norwegian debate – is the marrying off of handicapped and mentally deficient children. As a doctor told me: "They're going to be married off, as long as they can lie horizontally." Or as an immigration official wrote to me: "We have a number of, quite simply, backward Norwegian-Pakistanis who marry completely healthy people. I've had Norwegian-Pakistani girls in for conversations who don't even know what month it is, who are mentally at an eight- or nine-year-old level, and who can document it with a doctor's certificate. They want to bring their spouses to Norway, and it's the families that are pressuring them. It's clearly a form of tyranny."[36]

The first time I came across such a case was in 1997, when a Moroccan at the Oslo Red Cross International Centre was married by phone to a woman in Morocco. Marriage by phone was permitted until 2004. She didn't know anything about her husband's medical condition before she met him at the Oslo apartment of his extended family. The man was both mentally and physically handicapped. The family's motive for the marriage was to get him a nurse – i.e., her.

In the late winter of 2006, I asked a Pakistani acquaintance if he was familiar with such nuptials. He came up immediately with three examples. One of them involved a young Norwegian-Pakistani woman who suffers from an extreme case of mental retardation. She can hardly take care of herself. When she was called in for an interview with immigration officials in connection with her spouse's application from Pakistan for reunification with her, she was accompanied by her father, who presented her case to the police. Her spouse got the visa. There are no legal grounds today for stopping this practice.

The pattern is one-sided. Healthy people are brought over to marry sick people in Norway. I have yet to hear about the opposite happening.

I think it's very nice if mentally deficient people find love and marry each other. Among Norwegians, the parties to such marriages would ordinarily both be mentally deficient, and would themselves make the decision to marry. This is entirely different from a family-arranged marriage between a mentally deficient person and a person of normal intelligence living on another continent, the motive for which is immigration.

Another practice that has also received little public attention is the so-called cross-divorce. Immigration and social-security officials report that in Norway this practice is most often found among Chinese and Vietnamese immigrants. It works this way: a couple in Norway divorce. At the same time, the husband's brother in China or Vietnam divorces. The divorced spouses in Norway marry the divorced spouses abroad. In short, two brothers switch wives. The new marriages provide a basis for family reunification. Since the new "married couples" usually live under the same roof, it's difficult for the authorities, under current rules, to prove that the arrangement is pro forma, and thus deny the new arrivals residency permits. After the two newcomers have secured permanent residency, the couples divorce again and remarry their real spouses.

Several other thought-provoking new developments have been noted by police and immigration officials. One of them wrote this to me:

> It is common that a young Norwegian-Pakistani man who wanders from the straight and narrow is quickly married off to a "decent" Pakistani girl from Kharian [the city from which most Norwegian-Pakistanis come] in hopes that she will straighten him out. These girls are always young and poorly educated, and often end up in a nightmare of violence. Both their spouses and their in-laws harass them and beat them.[37]

Many young people behave differently with officials after undergoing forced marriages. As an immigration official points out, the change is particularly obvious when they've been married off to a cousin who is to be brought over to Norway:

> A few years back, these young people were often open about being forced to marry, and told us through tears about the situation. Now the trend is that they smile and claim not just that the marriage is voluntary but that it's a love match. The community has become so big now, a full parallel society alongside the mainstream community, and the internal justice is so strong. The young people see no way out, for where will they go? They've given up fighting against it.[38]

The official adds:

> We often see two or more siblings being married off at the same time, or within a brief period, to two or more

members of another group of siblings (for example, three sisters are married to three brothers who are their cousins). Even so, the parties will insist that all the marriages are love matches....Family reunification between married cousins is in reality the reunification of an extended family, and doesn't primarily serve the spouses' interests. Many of the marriages aren't real in any way: they're forced marriages that are never consummated, and they're entered into with the sole intention of helping a cousin come to Norway. Among those who employ this stratagem – entirely without conscience – are Norwegian-Pakistanis whom we'd prefer to think of as well integrated: law students, medical students, and so on. Almost nobody admits to being in a forced marriage. Most say that their parents "suggested" it, and that it was "fine" with them.

Forced marriages and immigrant politicians

Forced marriages and the deception of immigration officials are, in fact, common among people who in many respects can appear to be well-integrated. I have in my possession documents showing that leading immigrant politicians have been directly involved in the perpetration by their extended families of forced marriages, and that they've broken the law and infringed on individuals' rights in order to bring family members to Norway. Partly out of concern for their children, I won't name names.

This situation is important for several reasons: When leading immigrant politicians, of their own volition or in response to a greater or lesser amount of force exerted by their relatives, themselves contribute to illegal immigration and the infringement of individual rights, it underscores just how deeply rooted these practices are. It also illustrates why it's so hard to have an honest, fact-based debate about these issues when major participants in the debate are themselves also active participants in the illegal activity and refuse to acknowledge the extent of this illegality.

This game-playing has not only harmed the debate. What's far more serious, in my view, is that this double-dealing is also a major reason for the general impotence that has prevailed in the field of immigration. It is outrageous that people who are deeply involved in the violation of immigration rules are in positions of power from which they serve up misrepresentations of reality that have misled a succession of Parliaments and governments – and have done so at the cost of the most vulnerable individuals of all, namely immigrant youth.

It is also outrageous that authority, knowledge, and credibility are automatically ascribed to immigrant politicians simply because of their cultural and ethnic backgrounds. I've often marveled at our leading national politicians' continued failure to understand that politicians with close ties to extended families and ethnic communities marked by a feudal caste and clan culture can't easily adopt independent opinions in isolation from the power structures into which they were born. Few considerations trump the loyalty to "one's own."

Some day, I believe, documentation will come to light revealing the corrupt misuse of personal connections in major national institutions by leading politicians with immigrant backgrounds.

4

Born into Freedom, Stripped of Freedom

Today there is a steady stream of new spouses entering Norway. But there is also significant traffic in the other direction. This traffic is even less controlled than the traffic coming in. It is also far more deserving of criticism in a nation of laws.

I am speaking here about parents who send their children back to their homelands. The motive: to shield them from Norway's democratic value system, from dating, and from the opportunity to choose their own spouses in accordance with the dictates of their hearts. The idea is to bring them up in such a way that one day they'll allow their families to marry them off.

Samira from Tromsø

Her name is Samira. It's her real name. There's no reason to give her a pseudonym. She has nothing more to lose: she's already lost everything.

At thirteen, however, Samira won the lottery. She got to move from Somalia to Norway – from one of the world's worst countries for children to grow up in to one of the best. Settling in Tromsø with her parents and siblings, she embraced her new opportunities in life eagerly. Indeed, she did what our political leaders dream out loud about in speeches: she integrated herself – and in record time. In school, Samira didn't have to be asked twice what she thought about women's lives in Somalia. She was herself a victim of one of the worst imaginable traditions. Like almost all girls in Somalia, she was genitally mutilated. No one at the school was left in any doubt as to how horrible Samira thought genital mutilation was. But she went further than that: she criticized the religion she had been born into, Islam. She took for granted her right to criticize it, for she had seen Muslim girls and women denied the right to speak and act as free human beings.[39]

Samira had not lived long in Tromsø before she threw off her hijab and dressed the way other girls in Tromsø dressed. She held her head high, and was always quick to flash her teasing, laughing smile. About the everyday costs she was paying at home for her choices, she said little, and only to her very closest friends. They knew very well that her life was troubled, and that Samira's father was deeply dissatisfied with his daughter's behavior. Samira's behavior challenged his honour. She would not submit to his will. Unlike Samira, he couldn't walk with his head held high when he met his countrymen for prayer in the mosque. What should he do with this unruly youngster?

The summer vacation of 2002 was approaching. Samira had just turned fifteen. She and two girlfriends, who also enjoyed their lives in Norway, made a deal: if one of them went on summer vacation and didn't return in time for the start of the fall term, the others would alert the school.

Samira's uncle came for a visit from Stockholm. One day he walked into Samira's room and said, "Samira, you have to pack all the clothes you have. Everything. We're going on vacation to London, just you and me. We'll have a good time. I have a lot of money."

She was startled that she was supposed to pack *all* her clothes. But she did as she was asked. She said goodbye to her friends, and boarded the flight to London.

Samira wasn't back for the start of the school year. Her friends, as agreed, notified the school. The school, in turn, notified the police, Barnevernet, and the social security department, and called Samira's father in for a conversation. Samira, he told them, was in Ethiopia, with a grandmother and her three siblings. She's fine, he said. Samira herself had decided that she'd prefer to live there: "She does what she wants, that uncontrollable girl."

Could her teacher speak to Samira on the phone? Could her teacher send her a letter? No, the father had no phone number. He had no address. Meanwhile Samira's mother told others that the girl was in London. Later she said that Samira was in a certain town in Ethiopia. And later still she said that Samira was in another town in Ethiopia with her sick grandmother.

The police had a talk with Samira's father. He stuck to his story that Samira was fine and was in Ethiopia with her grandmother. Nobody did anything more. But Samira's friends and teacher were in despair. They were sure that Samira had been taken back to Somalia – but they hit a brick wall every time they knocked on the doors of government offices. So they contacted organizations – and ran into the same wall. Finally the teacher got in touch with Human Rights Service. We started working together with Samira's helpers and friends.[40] Our goal was clear: to bring Samira back home to Norway.

The school wrote a letter to the office of the Ombudsman for Children in Norway, which did nothing other than wish them luck.[41] The school sent a letter to the Parliament, which did not reply. The father was called in to a new conversation at the school.[42] The only thing the conversation accomplished was to make us even more convinced that he wasn't telling the truth. And why should he? Samira's unannounced disappearance had not caused him the slightest problem, aside from a couple of uncomfortable encounters with the authorities. Among our conversation topics was the fact that Samira's passport had been confiscated by Norwegian police stationed in Dubai only two months after Samira had left Norway. The passport had been used by a young Somali woman who had been headed for Norway. No, the father said, he didn't know anything about that. The Norwegian police let the issue die. So why should the father be anxious? The social-security office was still depositing his monthly payments into his bank account.

Letters to the Norwegian embassy in Addis Ababa, Ethiopia, which was the Norwegian foreign ministry's nearest outpost to Somalia, yielded no hope. The offer from the embassy was this: if Samira turned up at the embassy, they'd be able to help her get home. Turn up at the embassy? A girl of fifteen, alone, in a part of the world where it's very dangerous for girls to be alone? Where there's a war going on? But one comfort – if you could call it that – was that the embassy was at least able to confirm that Samira wasn't officially registered as having entered Ethiopia.

Perhaps the government would help? No, they wrote back saying that nothing could be done. Samira would have to go to the embassy herself.[43]

What about the Red Cross's tracking service?[44] We shared with the Red Cross our suspicion that Samira had been sent to her parents' hometown of Garowe, Somalia. In the summer of 2003 the Red Cross replied by letter. Samira had been found in Garowe, where she was under guard around the clock. She was attending Koran school, and was accompanied to and from school by a guard – which made it impossible for the Red Cross representative in town to speak with her. For this reason it would also be futile for us to try to visit her in Somalia.

Human Rights Service sent a twelve-page report to the police in Tromsø.[45] In it we noted that Samira might have been forced to marry, perhaps while she was still under sixteen. We pointed out that she was being held prisoner, that she was being denied her legal right to schooling, and that, in the worst-case scenario, her life might be imperiled. The police took the case out of the drawer again, and concluded, with apologies, that they could do nothing.[46]

Samira's friends were now at the breaking point. Feeling that she had no more to lose, they publicized the case. Local newspapers and the TV news program *Dagsrevyen* told her story in November 2003.[47] Norwegian authorities remained silent and perplexed.

And Samira stayed in Somalia.

At a meeting with Human Rights Service in September of the following year, cabinet member Erna Solberg agreed to look into the case.[48] We never heard another word from her about it.

Samira was truly out of sight, out of mind – for the government, that is, but not for the rest of us. Had she been married off? Had she had children? Or had she held her head up high and spoken up and been killed? An endless list of questions, but no answer. After two and a half years we all gave up.

But Samira remained firmly in our thoughts. In a meeting with the Oslo police in November 2005, about an entirely different subject, I mentioned Samira and our worries about her well-being. The police officer said he would see what he could find out. Four days later he reported back: Samira was living with her grandmother and siblings in Garowe.

So she was, in any case, alive.

Denmark's Samira

The same summer that Norway's Samira disappeared, a Danish girl named Samira also went missing. Same name, same country of birth, and almost an identical story.

Denmark's Samira underwent family reunification with her father and mother when she was seven years old. They were very strict and violent. At thirteen she discovered that her parents weren't her parents at all. The man she had been told was her father was, in fact, her uncle.[49] When she discovered that she'd been deceived, she rebelled. She took things into her own hands and lived like other Danish teenagers. In short, she integrated in record time – just like her Norwegian namesake. The rebellion became too much for her uncle. He held out to the girl the prospect of meeting her real mother during a month-long vacation in Somalia. Samira became happy, very happy, and went on the trip in the summer of 2002.

During long stretches of her stay in Somalia, Samira was kept isolated and subjected to brutal violence. Twice she managed to make contact by telephone with her friends in

Denmark. They went to the media – and got immediate results.[50] Denmark's then integration minister, Bertel Haarder, made contact at once with local authorities in Samira's home municipality in Denmark and arranged to work with them to bring Samira back. To the press, the minister said: "Samira is a terrible story. She is the quintessence of successful integration – an integration she has been punished for. Her parents should bring her home as fast as possible, or we will withdraw their social support – and the Danish state, which has been kind to a fault, will not pay for the tickets. If the parents don't do so, we will withdraw the amount from their child-care allowance."[51]

The municipality contacted Samira by telephone, and as a result of pressure by the authorities and media she was brought back to Denmark a little over a month later. Her "parents" had to pay for the trip. Samira was placed in a foster home.

Neither the Norwegian Samira nor the Danish Samira was a citizen of her new homeland. The Danish Samira didn't even have valid grounds for residency in Denmark: the fact that her "father" was really her uncle meant that she'd been granted family reunification on false premises. Nonetheless, the Danish government acted immediately to bring her home.

Was the Norwegian Samira a problem for Norwegian authorities? Was that why perplexity reigned? I have documents showing that Norwegian officials, in both the then and preceding governments and departments, as well as the Ombudsman for Children and other official agencies, were very well informed about the "Samira case" as early as 1991. In 1992, a then sixteen-year-old Norwegian-born girl gave me a stack of copies of letters she had written to a friend in Norway from her parents' homeland. They were heartbreaking cries for help. She was being held prisoner. She was to be married off to a man of around forty who was closely related to her. Her friend had shown the letters to her own father. He, in turn, had asked officials for help. No one could help, came the answer – both orally and in writing. After a year of the worst kind of imprisonment, the girl returned to Norway – unmarried. A

95

quarrel had arisen in the family as to who should get to use her as a living visa. The disagreement had not been resolved, however, and finally she had been sent back.[52]

I can document similar – and far worse – cases, up through the 1990s, of which Norwegian authorities have been fully informed but on which they have refused to act. The standard reply from cabinet ministers and others has been that parents have the right to decide how their children are raised. Yes, of course cabinet ministers and bureaucrats have to obey laws and regulations. But when the map no longer corresponds to the terrain, one would expect the map to be updated.

Sent "home"

The treatment of young people like Samira can justifiably be described as kidnapping and imprisonment. What is far more common is that children and teenagers are sent to their parents' homeland and kept there for years. How many such cases are there in Norway? Officials don't know.[53] How many of these kids are alone abroad, without their parents? Officials don't know. Are they attending school? Officials don't know. How many attend madrasses (Koran schools) and receive no other schooling? Officials don't know. Who's taking care of them? Officials don't know.

But if you ask officials how many Norwegian children live in Spain – yes, that you can get an answer to. Authorities have all that data in hand. They also know almost everything about who's taking care of those kids and where they're going to school; they work closely with Spain's child-protection authorities and have even set up a special social-security office in Spain. They've even drawn up materials, designed especially for Norwegian families living in Spain, that provide them with necessary information about these matters.[54]

The parents who send their children back to their homelands include both refugees and immigrants; they include people from Gambia, India, Iraq, Morocco, Pakistan, Somalia, and Turkey. The group that sends the most children out of Norway is the Pakistanis.[55] And the practice is spreading.[56]

Why do parents do this? The answers, as supplied by the parents themselves as well as by the young people who are "sent home," are many. The most common reason is that the parents want their children to "learn about our culture" or "learn about our religion." A few of them elaborate on the meaning of the words "our culture." Some say that it means children will learn "respect" for authorities, parents, and teachers. The children will learn discipline, for in the parents' view discipline in Norwegian schools is terrible. As they see it, the lack of discipline in Norwegian schools causes children and young people to lose respect for adults – and this, in turn, can lead them into crime. They also say that there's too little education about Islam in Norwegian schools. A few parents admit candidly that they want to ensure that their children don't absorb "Norwegian" values. When asked to elaborate on the word "values," they usually point to the sexual freedom that girls and women enjoy in Norway.

When you send your child to live with your relatives in your homeland, that child is much easier to keep under supervision. The people doing the day-to-day supervision are many: the relatives themselves, school employees, neighbours, and so forth. And the child, it is explained, acquires a "safe" identity, viewing him- or herself, first and foremost, as "Gambian" or "Pakistani." What only a few parents will openly admit is that they've sent their children back so that they can unlearn everything Norwegian. They don't admit that girls are sent abroad so that they won't be able to live on equal terms with males and enjoy the right to choose their own spouses; they don't admit that girls are sent abroad at puberty to be prepared for marriage – to be prepared, that is, to be good wives who live up to the demands and standards set by men in their families' homeland.

Nor do they openly acknowledge that social-security payments are sent out of the country along with the children. Some parents admit that boys who have gone astray are sent "back," while many say that boys are sent abroad to prevent them from ending up in criminal gangs. Parents are also open about the fact that it's financially advantageous to park their children in their homelands, where costs of living are low. Most of the parents, moreover, already own a residence there, which is often empty anyway, or partly occupied by relatives or servants.

A first-class school

Let's travel to Pakistan and take a look at these children's living situations – what kinds of schools they attend, what they're taught, and what sort of culture they're brought up in.

In certain areas of Pakistan, it's easy to find schoolchildren with Norwegian passports. Most of Norway's Pakistanis are from the heart of Punjab – to be specific, from four cities that are like a string of pearls: Jehlum, Kharian, Lala Musa, and Gujrat. The most "Norwegian" city in Pakistan is Kharian, and the most "Norwegian" village is Mehmet Chak.[57] This region is popularly known as Little Norway.

In February 2004, along with Human Rights Service director Rita Karlsen and *Aftenposten* journalist Halvor Tjønn, I took a trip around the area.

Near Gujrat is a Koran school that's recommended by the Idara Minhaj ul-Quran mosque in Norway. It's a boarding school, and some of the students are girls from Norway.[58] The brick building, measuring around two to three thousand square feet, stands near one end of a field and looms over it. There are no windows, just vents directly under the roof. When we arrived and stepped out of our car, there were no students in sight, only a couple of male guards at the school gate, who immediately went inside to get the principal.

He came out, we introduced ourselves, and he told us about his own high professional qualifications and the school's high standards. He said that all of the children at the school were taught English, in addition to a wide range of other subjects – among them computer science, which was taught in the special computer room. He added that the school followed British teaching plans.

Some girls, ranging in age from around eight to ten, appeared beyond the gate. One of them stood out from the others. She was quite plump, while the others were very thin. She was also better dressed, and both she and her clothes were cleaner. They all appeared to be scared of the principal – except for her. In English, we asked the girl her name. She didn't understand the question, and looked confusedly at the principal. The question was repeated. Again, the girl looked confusedly at the principal. The principal blushed. The same question was asked in Punjabi, and the girl answered with a smile: "Rabia." The principal, very displeased, explained that these children were so young that they didn't yet understand English well. He stammered, and made an obvious attempt to wind up the conversation. He prevailed upon the guards to chase the children back in behind the gate – all except Rabia. For Rabia was his daughter.

"Is it possible to have a look behind the walls?"

The principal shook his head, and said that it would be necessary to secure permission from the government for such a visit.

"But isn't this a private school?"

Now it was the principal who suddenly spoke very little English.

"Are there foreign students here?"

"No, absolutely not," he answered quickly. Norwegians? No, he insisted.

The conversation continued, and the smiles we directed at the principal grew increasingly friendly and good-natured. We smiled so much that finally he agreed to let one of us in.

The school was dark and cold, and the first room large and empty. A small door in one wall led to a cramped room, a sort of cloakroom in which several little children were sitting. Some of them were excited and curious at the sight of a foreign visitor; others looked uncertain and hid themselves.

The principal acted quickly, and the fast-paced tour continued as he switched on the light in a long, narrow corridor. Portions of its ceiling were grated, and this grating formed part of the floor on the story above. Through it, dozens of children looked down on the foreign visitor from upstairs.

At the far end of the corridor, the principal opened the door to a small classroom furnished with wooden chairs – no desks, no blackboard. Just under the roof was a tiny window with bars on it. Otherwise the room was totally empty. The next room was just like it. And so was the one after that.

Perhaps some of the children understood Norwegian? But no, a few gentle, friendly words in Norwegian drew no attention. Yet these words sent the principal into a near-panic. He didn't understand what was being said, and obviously feared that somebody would answer. Leading his visitor along quickly, he opened the door of a room in which there were seven to nine teenage girls. This room, too, lacked desks or blackboards. There was a little peephole at the top of the wall, just under the ceiling, through which a few rays of light shone in.

Before the principal could stop her, the visitor asked: "Is there anybody here who speaks Norwegian?" In reply came a single syllable that could have been a Norwegian or Danish "hei" or an English "hi."

Brusquely, the principal said the girls had to concentrate on their studies. He closed the door. Then, abruptly, he concluded the tour. Enough was enough. Fearing that any protest might cause problems for the girls, his visitor gave in to his wishes at once.[59]

The visit inside "the walls" was unsettling. The place was filthy, dark, and cold. There were no educational materials in sight other than some heavily thumbed-through books, and not a single female employee. All day and night, adult men and girls were together behind those walls.[60]

At a nearby school, officials confirmed that Norwegian children were registered at the Idara Minjah ul-Quran Koran school.

100

Hundreds of Norwegian children

The "capital" of Little Norway, Kharian, has a guarded, sealed-off military sector that is its own wonderful little world, with well-kept lawns, long, tree-lined avenues, and no noisy traffic. In this sector one can, if necessary, live one's entire life. It is here that the well-off have their homes; there are stores and schools and most of the facilities one needs on a day-to-day basis. Also located here is probably the largest colony of Norwegian-Pakistanis in Pakistan.[61] For though the neighbourhood was intended for military personnel and their families, in recent years "ordinary people," mainly those with Western money, have been given the opportunity to buy into the area. By Pakistani standards, they pay enormous sums just for empty lots, on which they build resplendent houses.[62]

Among the pupils at one of the schools in this sector are two Norwegian-born girls of eight and twelve. They can speak only Punjabi, plus a little English. The older girl says she attended school in Norway for three years before being sent to Pakistan. All of her siblings who are under the age of eighteen are living in Pakistan with their mother, while the siblings over eighteen are in Norway with their father. The younger girl doesn't remember when she came to Pakistan; nor does she recall anything from the time when she lived in Norway, though she has vacationed in Norway a couple of times. She lives with her mother and her under-eighteen siblings. Both girls say they'll return to Norway when they've completed school in Pakistan. The older one says with a careful smile: "And then we'll be there for good."

During our conversation, two other girls turn up. One of them is ten years old, the other fifteen. Only the younger one has a Norwegian passport, but both have families in Norway. "We're going to Norway when we grow up," they say. But how can the older one move to Norway without a Norwegian passport? Shyly, she explains that she has a cousin in Norway who wants to marry her. The principal, who is present during the entire conversation, breaks in and confirms the girl's plans: "This isn't special in any way. After the children finish their education, the parents decide whom they'll marry. It's very often a cousin. In this way, more and more young people in the same family get a visa and residency in the West. And it's been working this way since the emigration from this area began thirty to forty years ago."

The largest school building in the military sector has 1700 pupils and is very popular, the principal says. Most of the pupils have foreign passports. To ensure that their children will have a place in this school when they reach school age, according to the principal, parents register them when they are newborns.

When the school bell rings for the last time this day, a Norwegian-born pair of siblings are picked up by their father. He's an Oslo bus driver, and has five children aged seven to thirteen. Two of them are standing at his side, a girl and a boy. The girl, aged thirteen, has attended school in Norway for a couple of years. Neither the girl nor the boy can speak Norwegian.

"That doesn't matter," says the father, who is here on a visit for a couple of months. "Norwegian is very easy to learn. They'll learn it fast when they come back to Norway."

The children won't return to Norway until they're pretty much grown up.

"It's easier to get a good job in Norway," he says, and emphasizes: "They *are* Norwegian citizens."

"But why should Norwegian citizens grow up in another country?"

"In this area everything is safer. My wife can shop here alone," he says pensively, and explains how well organized and orderly everything is, and that discipline in the school is strict. The children become "proper Pakistanis."

"What does that mean?"

"They have to learn about Pakistani culture and learn Islam in a proper way," the father explains. But it takes money to keep the children in Pakistan.

"The school costs money. The books cost money, the uniforms, the private teacher – yes, everything costs money," he says, and adds: "While in Norway everything was free."

"Is it worth it?"

"Yes, it's worth it. Even though they also took away the child benefits. We get a lot more for the money here. I earn well. Yes, even if I'm sick, I get paid."

The school as waiting room

In a village near Kharian, a frustrated and dejected man runs a school that lacks most of the supplies and resources it needs.[63] This straight-talking principal was educated in the West and is eager to fill his students with knowledge. But he's banging his head against the wall. The "wall" is the children's awareness that they already have visas to the West awaiting them.

Almost all of the children at the school have parents abroad, while the children live in villages, most often with their mothers. Most of the children come to Pakistan when they reach school age, at around five years old. The principal explains why: it's about money – the cost of living here is low – and about preparing the children for marriage.

The pupils, the principal feels, are unmotivated. He literally characterizes the school as a "waiting service before marriage." The principal explains this description as follows:

"When the pupils are ready to marry, they marry a cousin and go back to the West," he says. "I ask them: 'What are you going to do there? Without education you'll end up washing dishes or sweeping streets.' But they don't care. They're just waiting to marry and go back to the West. Those pupils here who don't have parents in the West already have a visa in their pocket, because they're engaged to a cousin with citizenship in the West. And for them, too, the school is just a waiting service before marriage."

The principal is clearly in despair about the situation, and he says in a worried tone: "I *could* have educated them."

Most of the pupils in the schoolyard confirm that they have Western passports – from Norway, Sweden, Denmark, Germany, or France. Some of the girls dream aloud about becoming doctors or lawyers. Several tell us they'll study in a Pakistani city – Islamabad, Lahore – before returning to the West. They all think it'll be unproblematic to go back to Norway without being able to speak Norwegian or knowing anything about Norwegian society. The boys don't dream aloud about their future jobs. But what about problems *they* might have in Norway because they can't speak Norwegian? "There's a lot of Pakistanis in Norway," answers one boy.

Overhearing the pupils, the principal says: "This is typical. The girls dream about getting a good, respectable job, preferably as a lawyer or a doctor, or in finance or computers, but very few of them will get the opportunity to do so. They'll be married off and will have children. The boys, on the other hand, have much greater opportunities to get such an education, but they don't want to be bothered."

In Pakistan without mother and father

Enrolled in an elementary school in another village in Little Norway are two Norwegian-born sisters, aged five and eight. They're living alone in Pakistan with relatives, and have been separated from their parents for over two years. They also have a little sister in Norway who is a few months old. The little sister has already been signed up for the same school.[64]

The Norwegian-born girls are very shy, and neither of them can speak Norwegian – though they were, they say, able to speak a bit of it when they lived in Norway. Only the older girl remembers the name of the Norwegian town where she was born. The younger one tells us that she remembers little from Norway. The older one says warily that it was her parents who thought it was best for them to go to school in Pakistan. She and her little sister look forward to returning to Norway. They may go to Norway on vacation this year or next. They don't know for sure. Nor do they know if they'll be visited by their parents this summer.

The principal tells us about the school and the subjects the children study. Pretty much all the books are in Urdu. Education in Islam is important here. Therefore, he explains, they also incorporate Islamic instruction in, for example, the language lessons in Urdu and English. All the education takes place outdoors. The younger pupils sit on the ground, the older ones on benches. The pupils are actively used as teaching assistants; physical punishment is common. The pupils even punish one another – as we discover when a girl with a stick in her hand bends over another little girl who's reading aloud.[65]

We make a week-long tour of schools in Little Norway, and along the way meet several dozen Norwegian-born children. Not one can hold a conversation in Norwegian. This doesn't mean that no Norwegian-Pakistani children in Pakistan can speak Norwegian. But my overwhelming impression is that very few can. The children are mostly members of the second generation, the progeny of people who immigrated to Norway. Even if they marry someone in Pakistan, their own offspring will be considered the third generation. Perhaps their Pakistani spouses will want their kids to follow the same practice of living in Pakistan for a long period. Yet even if those children do spend a long time in Pakistan, they won't appear in Statistics Norway's immigrant statistics; they'll be regarded as having become Norwegian – even if they don't know a word of Norwegian or know anything about Norwegian society.

Paradoxically, many of their great-grandparents – that is, the actual immigrants who were the first in the family to come to Norway – may speak better Norwegian than their nominally Norwegian children, grandchildren, and great-grandchildren.

How are the schools?

Pakistan is a very poor country with major problems at all levels of society. This is reflected, of course, in its educational system, which suffers from a serious teacher shortage, a lack of qualified teachers, wretched equipment, miserable educational conditions, corruption, physical punishment, and a high drop-out rate.[66] Barely two percent of the national budget goes to education, while half goes to the military.[67]

There are six times more public than private schools. My impression is that a considerable majority of the Norwegian-Pakistani children in Pakistan attend private schools. One can easily be led to believe that the private schools have a far higher standard than the public schools.

And, yes, at private schools the conditions are generally better (with the pronounced exception of the religious schools). But as experts note, the private schools minimalize expenses by not distinguishing themselves in a significant way from public schools. Only around 10 percent of the private schools have fully qualified and fully manned teaching staffs. A press investigation revealed that over 85 percent of the private schools in Punjab did not hold to an acceptable standard in regard to teaching personnel and equipment. In the upper-class city of Islamabad, 86 private schools closed in 2003 because of low standards.[68]

UNESCO claims that as a result of the low quality of education during the first five years of school, pupils lack basic reading, writing, and arithmetical skills. Pakistani education experts are concerned that pupils who complete the first five years of school also lack the ability to think independently. Pupils are given an extremely limited exposure to major social issues, and consequently have little knowledge thereof. In 2002, a group of independent Pakistani experts concluded that the overwhelming majority of both public and private schools offer an extremely poor education.[69] The contents of the schoolbooks remain pre-modern and full of stereotypes – especially about sex roles. Education in traditional Islam is given much more emphasis than education in social and individual rights.

At none of the schools we visited in Little Norway was it possible to get access to teaching plans. Surely they must exist, but they weren't "available" at that particular time. The principals told us that the main subjects were Urdu, English, mathematics, computers, and *Islamiet*, the study of Islam. No one mentioned social studies, history, or religious instruction. But everyone emphasized that it was a major task to raise children to be "good Muslims."

Pakistan has undergone a significant degree of Islamization in recent years.[70] When I visited Little Norway for the first time in 1993, I cannot recall that I saw a single woman in hijab or niqab. Today this is a common sight. In the most "Norwegian" village, Mehmet Chak, even the female schoolteachers were wearing niqab. Covered women have also become a familiar sight in the streets of major Pakistani cities. Islamization and the covering of women in public areas go hand in hand, and the recent histories of Afghanistan and Iran bear witness to this indissoluble relationship. Until a few years ago, hijab and niqab were virtually non-existent. The women dressed in the cultural and religious attire known as shalwar kamiz, with the accompanying dupatta. The outfit consists of a tunic and wide pants, and a scarf that either hangs loose over the hair or is draped over the shoulder and breasts. In the most conservative areas, what is most often worn is the burka, which consists of a wide coat and a veil that covers the entire head and face. The hijab and niqab are thus part of an escalation of religious politics.

When Pakistan was founded in 1947, the idea was to create a secular state (Mumtaz and Shaheed, 1987:8). The father of the country, Muhammed Ali Jinnah, was far from an obedient Muslim. He drank alcohol, ate pork, could rarely be seen in a mosque, and married a non-Muslim. As a Muslim man, he should have married a Muslim, Jew, or Christian. Rattanbai Petit, whom he married, belonged to the ancient Persian religion of Zoroastrianism. Today Jinnah is presented as a God-fearing, almost pietistic Muslim who considered Pakistan an Islamic state.[71]

The key factor in the Islamization of Pakistan during the last quarter-century has been the shaping of a monolithic image of Pakistan as an Islamic state and of Pakistani citizens as Muslims.[72] To this end, national educational plans and schoolbooks in major subjects have been revised, and are today permeated with religious and national propaganda. History is falsified, and India and Hindus are the objects of what could almost be called a hate campaign. An atmosphere has been created in which non-Muslims are regarded as second-class citizens who have fewer rights and privileges, whose patriotism is suspect, and whose contributions to society are ignored.[73]

History books published prior to the beginning of Pakistan's full-blown Islamization presented India, Hindu belief, and the first great civilizations on the subcontinent (such as the Indus culture) respectfully.[74] Children's schoolbooks treated pre-Islamic Hindu kingdoms and non-Muslim political leaders such as Mahatma Gandhi with admiration and esteem. This is no longer the case. Teaching about the subcontinent's history has been replaced with teaching about the history of Muslims on the subcontinent. Pupils learn nothing about the region's pre-Islamic history. The facts of Pakistan's origins have also been rewritten. For example, the Islamic leaders who were bitter opponents of the nation's founding are presented as heroic "creators of the state of Pakistan." In reality, they were very hostile to the idea of a separate Muslim state, which for them was at odds with the goal of a worldwide caliphate.

Islam and nationalism figure centrally in the instruction of most subjects. Second graders, for example, can read in their Urdu language primer that "Pakistan is an Islamic country. Muslims live here. Muslims believe in the unity of Allah. They do good deeds." Children, the instructional plans make clear, are taught that the Islamic way of life is superior to other ways of life. They're also taught to love jihad and martyrdom.[75] In social studies, English, and Pakistani history, too, the essence of the instruction is the same: children are instilled with the national ideology – and, along with it, a hatred of Hindus and Indians.

The Human Rights Commission of Pakistan (HRCP) has cautioned against this hatred and against the general distancing of Pakistani students from all non-Muslim societies. In a newsletter entitled "Teaching Hatred" (25 April 2004), HRCP warned that Pakistani education was still promoting jihad and a narrow view of religion. The newsletter was based on a Pakistani government report on this topic, which revealed that schoolbooks around the country preached differential treatment of and direct discrimination against religious minorities, and encouraged hate by presenting a distorted historical picture of the history of non-Muslim societies. HRCP accused Pakistani officials of sowing the seeds of militant extremism and intolerance, and feared that the situation would only worsen.

Reigning social values

In what kind of society do the Norwegian-Pakistani children in Pakistan grow up?

To understand social and cultural conditions in Pakistan, one needs some knowledge about the country's political development. It's no coincidence that a saying often heard in Pakistan is this: "The fact that the country of Pakistan still exists is the best proof of Allah's existence." Pakistan has never had a long-term democratic government;[76] it has been run alternately by military dictators and political despots. Its government is riddled with corruption; it lacks such democratic institutions as a well-functioning legal, health-care, or school system; and it has no welfare system at all. Recent years have seen the increasing prominence and political power of anti-democratic, fascistic religious forces.[77] The confidence of the general public in the established order has long been on the verge of breakdown. Pakistanis can hardly trust anyone other than themselves and their kin. And the (so far) consistent lack of democratic development has been especially instrumental in the perpetuation of antagonism toward equal rights, freedom of expression, and religious liberty. The instability of the social and political structures also contributes to the suppression of the individual and the stimulation of a broad-based conformity.

Pakistan is a country dominated by feudalism and the master-slave mentality. An individual's value is strictly determined by his or her family background, caste and tribal identity, religious affiliation, and (especially) financial and political power, the latter two of which tend to be bound up with each other. A vivid example of the distortion of power relations in Pakistan is the institution of slavery. Rich people buy up whole families to work for them under the worst imaginable conditions, and pay them wages that guarantee they will spend their lives in debt. In Pakistan, these families are called "bounded labour" and occupy roles very similar to those of serfs in the era of Scandinavian feudalism. In the Punjab, it is especially common to find enslaved families working at brick factories. And among the slaveowners are a number of people with Norwegian citizenship

For example, the largest palace in the village of Alam Pur Gondelan, near Kharian, belongs to a Pakistani who officially resides in the Norwegian city of Drammen. Near his palace is a brick factory that he owns. A few years ago, he purchased an extended family from Pathan, the members of which – adults as well as children – work at his factory. The working conditions are exceedingly wretched, and he pays his slaves wages on which they're unable to live.[78] As a result, their debt to him is gradually increasing – and consequently they're growing even more firmly bound to him and his factory. When their time comes, the children will take over their parents' debt. No one can say with certainty how many slaves there are in Pakistan. The highest estimate I've seen is 20 million. For major Pakistani human-rights organizations, fighting slavery is a banner issue.

I've mentioned the distinctive role played by hatred for India and Hinduism in Pakistani society. In Pakistan, as in so many other places in the Muslim world, one also encounters a similar hatred for Jews.[79] In a variety of circumstances – and even in the best social circles – I've overheard extremely imaginative conspiracy theories and terribly disturbing comments about Jews. It's said that the Jews rule America and

110

that their goal is economic and political domination of the world. The Jews were behind the bombing of the Twin Towers on September 11, 2001 – their motive being to turn the West against Muslims. Jews are evil through and through; they're hardly human beings. These attitudes are widespread.

In the 25 May 1995, issue of *Aftenposten,* the author Salman Rushdie described his relationship to Pakistan in this way: "I come from an Indian Muslim family, but I experience India as a very pleasant country, whereas in Pakistan I feel ill at ease. You would think it should be the reverse. But in spite of its many defects, India is a rich and open society, while Pakistan is culturally an impoverished and closed society."

Culturally impoverished and closed, says Rushdie. Pakistan is especially impoverished in its view of girls and women. Among the comments most frequently heard from intellectuals, politicians, and human-rights activists is that "in Pakistan we treat our women worse than cattle" and that "every woman is regarded as a prostitute."[80]

Pakistan is one of the world's most patriarchal countries. The low status of girls and women also has a good deal to do with the dowry system. While a son's marriage enriches his family, a daughter's takes money out of its coffers in the form of the obligatory dowry. The dowry and caste system in Pakistan is a tragic inheritance from Hinduism. In Islam there's a bride price, which means that the husband pays for his bride.

In Pakistan the rule of thumb is that the closer you get to India, the more Islam is influenced by Hindu tradition and practice, and the closer you gets to Afghanistan, the weaker the Hindu influence.

The lack of a welfare system also bolsters anti-female attitudes. A woman who opposes the widely accepted views of her sex risks, at the very least, being made an outcast. Since there's no government department to take care of her if that happens, she's entirely dependent on the good or ill will of her extended family, clan, or tribe.[81] Yet the picture isn't entirely bleak. There are a few brave women and men who run private crisis centres where women can get different kinds of help, including legal aid. Some of these organizations receive economic and moral support from Norway.

In Pakistan, so-called purdah – the separation of the sexes – is a fact of daily life. It's practiced not only in public but also in ordinary people's homes, where the women of the house are hidden from male visitors. In public, it operates at most levels of society. Thanks to purdah, it's tremendously difficult for friendships to form naturally between men and women. Generally speaking, people automatically assume any man-woman friendship to be sexual. As a male Pakistani friend of mine in Islamabad said: "Pakistani men can't image a platonic relationship with a woman."[82]

According to reports by both Pakistani and foreign researchers, violence toward girls and women in Pakistan is widespread. And it's not abating, either: on the contrary, it seems to be increasing, a conclusion that's supported by the annual reports of human-rights groups.[83] Various estimates put the percentage of women in Pakistan who are abused in their homes at 70 to 90 percent. A report by the respected organization Human Rights Watch puts the rate of domestic violence against women at 90 percent.[84] When the Human Rights Commission of Pakistan also issued an estimate of around 90 percent, it drew criticism from people who considered it too low.[85]

Violence has a variety of faces and involves a range of actions. Pakistan leads the world in the number of registered honour killings of women, with around a thousand such murders a year. There is reason to assume that this number only represents the tip of the iceberg. Throwing acid in women's faces, burning them to death or to the point of unrecognizability, cutting off their noses, selling girls in order to end conflicts between families or tribes, kidnapping young women for gang rapes, stripping women and parading them naked through villages – all these practices have become more common.[86]

It's often said that Norwegian-Pakistanis have been stuck in a pre-modern era ever since they emigrated – the implications being that Pakistanis in Pakistan are far more modern today than they were thirty to forty years ago, and that women in Pakistan are far freer now than they were then. For example, young Norwegian-Pakistanis, in particular, tend to claim that in Pakistani cities marrying for love has become quite common.

This is untrue. In undemocratic, feudal regimes, there will always be an intellectual and economic overclass that lives, in whole or in part, outside the social code. In Pakistan, this elite makes up a microscopic fraction of the total population of 162 million.[87] I would claim, on the contrary, that Pakistan was a more liberal country when the first large wave of Pakistanis came to Norway in the first half of the 1970s – that is, when the democratically elected and very woman-friendly prime minister Zulfikar Ali Bhutto ran the country. My female friends in Pakistan, who were young in the 1970s, say that in those days they could dress in short-sleeved blouses and short skirts without a problem. To wear such clothing in public today can be characterized as a highly dangerous extreme sport.[88]

The Norwegian-Pakistani children in the heart of Punjab, which in Pakistan is viewed as an area that is particularly rooted in tradition and conservative in its values, grow up in an environment suffused with feudal values – a place where human worth is determined by caste, tribe, and sex, where intolerance of other cultures, religions, and societies reigns, and where free critical thought is an alien concept. It's in such a setting that Norwegian-Pakistani children are "educated."

I've often asked myself this question: don't Norway's Labour and Socialist Left parties still consider uniform schooling a fighting issue – an essential cause in the struggle for social and educational equality, for the formation of basic democratic values, and, yes, for the socialization process? Why, then, is there such striking silence from those quarters about the distressing conditions I'm discussing here?

Norwegian authorities, then, don't know how many Norwegian children are, at any given time, "back home" in their ancestral homeland. But it's possible to come up with a

113

reasonable guess. The Norwegian embassy in Pakistan estimates that at any given time between four and five thousand Norwegian-Pakistanis are in Pakistan. Of these, the embassy suggests that as many as 90 percent may be under sixteen years old. But it must be emphasized that these are highly uncertain figures.[89] The embassy in Morocco has reported a serious increase in the number of Norwegian-Moroccan children in that country. Norway's foreign station in Gambia has reported a similar rise, which is confirmed by a Norwegian-Gambian friend of mine. He visits Gambia annually, most recently in the late winter of 2006, and tells me that "there are so many people who have their children here now; there are just more and more of them." Members of various communities in Norway – among them the Somali, Iraqi, and Turkish communities – also acknowledge that more and more people are sending their children "home" to go to school. I personally know Somali families with five or eight children all of whom have been shipped back to Somalia while their parents remain in Norway. When a Norwegian-Pakistani father who works at a pub in Oslo was asked whether his children were in Norway or in Pakistan, he said: "Only the losers' children go to school in Norway." He had sent his wife and their four children to Little Norway. And he laconically added: "It's me they're sorry for – I'm the one who has a long, expensive trip to work."

All this suggests that it's hardly an exaggeration to estimate that four to five thousand children are at any given time on long-term stays in their parents' homelands. But why can't the Norwegian government put the exact figures on the table? The answer emerged after a series of disagreements between the second Bondevik administration and Human Rights Service. We claimed in June 2004 that four to five thousand children might be out of the country. The government argued that this had to be a gross exaggeration. Statistics Norway (SSB) was therefore asked to look into the situation – whereupon SSB explained why the exact figures could not be arrived at.[90] Curiously enough, the reason had a good deal to do with Norwegian ship owners. How so? Well, in order to prevent the ship owners' tax flight from Norway, the Norwegian parliament changed the national register law in the 1980s. Those with so-called "strong ties" to Norway, such as children or a spouse living here, are still registered as residing in Norway even if they actually live in another country. The law was changed in this way so that Norway could continue to tax the ship owners. The consequence for children with immigrant and refugee backgrounds, alas, is that if they have a parent or sibling in Norway, they're still registered as living in Norway. Only if the parents actively report the children as having moved abroad will their absence be recorded by the system. And the fact is that very few parents with immigrant or refugee backgrounds let the government know when they send their children abroad. Why should they? The children and their mother (if she accompanies them) will return to Norway when the time comes – that is, at the latest, when "the red book" (that is, the Norwegian passport) gives them and their spouses the right to live in a welfare state. It was no surprise, then, that Statistics Norway's study showed only around 1200 children with Pakistani, Moroccan, and Turkish backgrounds registered as having been sent abroad.

Plainly, this was only the tip of the iceberg. Yet after the study results were released, the second Bondevik government publicly claimed that the exact number had finally been put on the table. Professing relief, the government maintained that only around a thousand or so children in Norway had been sent "home."[91] Why the government misrepresented data that it had ordered itself will have to be explained by someone other than me. There is little reason to believe anything other than that the number of children sent abroad is somewhere in the several thousands – and that the likelihood is high that the number will continue to rise.

In Denmark, when Human Rights Service issued a comprehensive report expressing concern about children who are sent out of the country, it was taken very seriously. The Danish government immediately set a research project in motion, and in June 2006 a full set of measures was adopted, in which the main focus was on employing all available means to keep children in Denmark – where, after all, they would be living their adult lives.[92]

While our report led the Danish government, then, to take effective action, the response of Norwegian leaders to the same report was to do nothing. It's hard for me, as a Norwegian citizen, to react to this contrast with anything other than numbness and shame.

Rights and obligations?

There can be little doubt that for the great majority of children who are sent for long periods to their families' homelands, the situation is highly unfortunate for their future integration in almost every way. Their foreign stays are also often in conflict with – and, indeed, may well totally violate – a number of laws, rules, and international conventions regarding children's rights. It's also quite worrisome that children are being educated in countries where human rights generally, and women's rights in particular, are often in a terribly feeble state. Another concern is the question of who, exactly, is taking care of these children – especially those who have been placed in boarding schools run by religious organizations. That these children have very little opportunity to develop their powers of critical reflection, to develop an individuality and independence that will equip them to stand up for their own needs and desires (for example, when choosing a spouse), is also unsettling.

In my view, these children are, practically speaking, virtually without rights. Is the doctrine really what it seems to be – namely, get your children across the Swedish border and you can do what you want with them without the Norwegian government stepping in? Yes, this is how it works – at least if the children have immigrant backgrounds.

As for the level of educational these children receive, I think it's especially important to listen to Hege Faust, an advisor at Hellerud upper secondary school in Oslo. Faust has many years' experience with Pakistani youth who return to Norway to continue their education after having attended school in Pakistan. Faust told *Aftenposten* on 31 March 2004 that an estimated eight out of ten of these students don't manage to make up the knowledge gap between them and their agemates who have been schooled entirely in Norway. Her experience was that most of those who are sent "home" return to Norway when they're about to start eighth or ninth grade – and thus enter upper secondary school with a weak educational foundation: "The reality, unfortunately, is that this kind of student hardly ever catches up in any subject. As we know, Asian schools put plenty of emphasis on mathematics, but we scarcely notice it. In English they're often beginners when they come here. And they hardly have any knowledge of Norwegian....Even if they work hard, it'll be difficult for them to get good grades. This is because Norwegian schools demand critical reflection from students if they want to be rewarded with A's or B's."

Faust also emphasized that students who are sent out of the country become accustomed to social patterns very different from those prevailing in Norwegian schools: "Girls who come back from Pakistani schools are particularly shy."

It may only be a question of time before some young adult with a minority background who hasn't had proper schooling, and who is at best functionally illiterate, slaps the Norwegian government with a damage lawsuit. Nor do I think it'll be long before others who have been neglected for years by the Norwegian government, and who have suffered psychological damages as a result, will also sue for damages. It's likely, too, that young people whose families have deprived them of their freedom for years with the full knowledge of government bureaucrats will someday drag the Kingdom of Norway into court on the grounds that they've been denied human rights and legal protection. Eventually the number of damage lawsuits that have been filed by other "old" minorities, such as the Tatars, as well as by Norwegian children who were neglected in their childhood homes, may be vastly outnumbered by damage lawsuits filed by our "new" minorities.

5

A Baby Can't Tell Tales

I suspect that most people in Norway associate Egypt with vacations, sunshine, heat, sand dunes, diving, and the spectacular pyramids. Only a very few, I think, connect Egypt with the world's most widespread tradition of assaults on girls and women. But it's true: nearly 90 percent of Egyptian girls and women are mutilated. Their external sex organs are entirely or partly cut – a custom that is said to have begun in the Nile valley almos six millennia ago, in the time of the pharaohs. From Egypt, the practice spread along the caravan routes and took root in a belt across central Africa, in parts of the Arabian peninsula, in some countries of the Middle East, in parts of Kurdistan, and also among Muslims in Malaysia and Indonesia. Genital mutilation is now culturally entrenched in over thirty countries. The World Health Organization believes that perhaps as many as 140 million girls and women in today's world are affected. A minimum of two million girls in these countries are mutilated annually.[93]

But this is only half of the truth. When people migrated to Europe, they took the pharaonic tradition with them – so that it now also exists in Norway.

In Norway today, over nine thousand girls under nineteen years old have roots in countries on the African continent where genital mutilation is practiced. Almost seven thousand of these girls are from what I would call high-risk countries – that is, countries where at least 80 percent of the girls are mutilated.[94] The most vulnerable national group, namely Somali girls, is also, by a considerable margin, the largest group, consisting of around 4300 girls. Several experts believe that nearly half of the girls who either move here as still unmutilated children, or who are born here, end up being mutilated. Some experts believe the figures are even higher.[95] This means, in any case, that at least 3000 to 3500 girls in Norway today are affected by this custom that dates back to the pharaohs – a statistic that will continue to rise unless the Norwegian government changes its policy.

What is genital mutilation?

Female genital mutilation (FGM) is an umbrella term for various kinds of operations on the sexual organs. The World Health Organization describes four types of FGM. Type 1, which involves the removal of the foreskin of the clitoris, is also called Sunna circumcision, because Muhammed is said to have recommended it. Type 2 includes the removal of the foreskin as well as the clitoris. In addition, the labia minora are wholly or partly cut away. This type can also be described as Sunna circumcision. In Type 3, the clitoris and the labia minora and majora are entirely or partly removed, after which the vaginal opening is sewn up until it is the size of a pinhead. In an unknown number of cases, the clitoris is not cut away, but hidden away under the skin when the vaginal opening is sewn up. This type is called an infibulation, and the victim is often described as being "sewn up" or "closed." (It also goes by other names, such as "Pharaonic circumcision," since it is supposed to have been the type of genital mutilation that the pharaohs prescribed.)

All kinds of female genital mutilation that don't fall under any of the other three categories are called Type 4. For example, the clitoris and/or the labia may be pierced, perforated, or cut; the clitoris and the surrounding tissue may be burned; the tissue around the vaginal opening may be scraped away; the vagina may be cut; or cauterizing agents or herbs may be placed in the vagina to cause bleeding or to tighten up or narrow it.

120

Types 1 and 2 account for 80 percent and Type 3 for 15 percent of all genital mutilation.[96] Type 3, the most extreme variant, is especially common in the Horn of Africa and parts of southern Africa.

The age at which girls are genitally mutilated varies from country to country and from tribe to tribe. As a rule, the operation takes place well before puberty. According to the World Health Organization, girls are usually mutilated between four and ten years of age. But some, especially in West Africa, are mutilated as infants. In Somalia, the procedure is most often performed when a girl is between five and seven years old.

In Norway, female genital mutilation was forbidden in 1995 by a special law that prescribes a jail term of eight years – not only for those who carry it out but also for those who aid and abet it.[97]

My first encounter with mutilated girls

My first encounter with young women who had been genitally mutilated was at a café in downtown Oslo early in 1997. I made contact with them through Uteseksjonen, a governmental agency that had established a support group for Somali girls who wanted to discuss mutilation. Two of the girls I met had been mutilated as children in Somalia. The third was a girlfriend of theirs who had escaped the razor blade. I requested the meeting because I suspected that the custom of genital mutilation had been imported into Norway.

Although the meeting took place nine years ago (at this writing), the things that the young women said, and the images they placed in my mind, are as vivid to me now as they were then. One of them said: "It's better to get drunk than to have sex." Another said with undisguised sorrow: "I wonder so much what it's like to have sex if you're not circumcised." A third said: "I feel a little left out because I'm not circumcised. I usually tell the people close to me that I'm circumcised. Then they don't look down on me – they don't think I'm loose."

Both of the girls who were mutilated had undergone the procedure at age seven. Both were sewn up. The result is a buttonhole of an opening, which makes it hard to urinate and menstruate – and of course will make it difficult and painful to have a good sex life in adulthood. So both girls had had their vaginas opened up by a doctor in Norway. But they had to keep it secret. As one of them explained, "If others know that I've opened myself up, they'll think immediately that it's because I want to have sex." The other put it this way: "When you're sewn up and you pee, it takes at least ten to fifteen minutes to finish. Because it just drips out in little droplets. When I'm at Somali get-togethers and I have to go to the bathroom, I sit on the toilet for a long time and just pee very carefully. No one must know that I've opened myself up. That would mark me as a whore."

The words I set down in my notebook that day seemed unreal. But this is the reality of young women living in Norway today. It's not fiction.

And what about these three girls' younger sisters? Only one of them, in fact, had younger siblings – two sisters. Both had been taken back to Somalia by their mother in 1991. One of the girls had been six years old at the time, the other seven. A young cousin of the girls had also been taken along on the journey back to the country from which the family had "fled" only a couple of years earlier. During that visit, all three had been genitally mutilated in the traditional way. This didn't lead to any consequences for the parents, though it resulted in lifelong consequences for the children.

My conversation with the three young Somali women took place while I was working on my book *Hellig tvang (Holy Force,* 1998). That book's main focus was on marriage-related barriers, pressure, and force that young people encountered in their families and communities. Unquestionably, genital mutilation falls under the topic of love and marriage. But I chose not to cover genital mutilation in that book. At that time, it hadn't yet been revealed that children were being sent out of Norway to be mutilated; the fact that such mutilations were taking place had considerable news potential in itself, and might have taken the focus off of the book's main topic, forced marriage. I also thought that the issue of genital mutilation was so serious and important that it deserved to be investigated in depth before it could be publicly mentioned – especially if I wanted to ensure that government officials responded not just with words but with practical policies. So I chose to place the information on hold.

I now think this was the right decision. After publishing *Holy Force,* I was contacted by someone from the TV2 program *Rikets tilstand (State of the Nation)* who had read the book and noticed my coverage in it of a probable honour killing, that of Shazia Saleh from Grimstad. Shariz had died in 1995 in her parents' home village in Pakistan, where she had refused to marry her cousin. With this event as our starting point, we made several programs in the autumn of 1999 about forced marriage and the importing of spouses to Norway. Reactions by both the general public and politicians were overwhelming. The then cabinet minister who was responsible for such matters, Karita Bekkemellem, quickly formulated a new action plan against forced marriage. I was therefore in no doubt that a TV program revealing the genital mutilation of girls in Norway would result in political action.

By January 2000 the source list was complete. Saynab Mohamed and Kadra Noor, two Norwegian-Somali girls, would be involved in the project. I also had specific information about other children with Gambian backgrounds who had been mutilated while living in Norway. And *State of the Nation* didn't have to be asked twice to collaborate on the program. I also wanted to use a hidden camera to record statements by major Muslim leaders, in order to avoid a problem that had been tied up for years with the issue of forced marriage: in public, these leaders explicitly distanced themselves from the practice, while minimalizing its extent; privately, however, they more or less endorsed it. The grotesque practice of mutilating defenseless children would not be brought to an end by a paralyzing debate.

It was something that needed to be actively addressed before it was too late.

The programs that were broadcast on TV2 in the autumn of 2000 were so remarkably successful in placing the issue on the political and public agenda that I don't need to enlarge on that topic here. I will simply point out that one leading politician after another made bold and specific proposals. Opposition politician Odd-Einar Dørum proposed requiring medical examinations of girls' genitals to prevent and uncover cases of mutilation. Cabinet member Karita Bekkemellem characterized genital mutilation as "terror," and wanted the Director of Public Prosecutions to bring charges against imams who supported it. Cabinet member Hanne Harlem also used the word "terror" and suggested that government financial support for Muslim congregations that promoted mutilation be reconsidered.

Karita Bekkemellem was the cabinet member whose portfolio included responsibility for genital mutilation. In record time, she introduced a comprehensive action plan that involved an outlay of fifteen million kroner to prevent FGM by distributing information and by providing medical help to those already mutilated.

I was disappointed. You can't eliminate a several-thousand-year-old custom with an information campaign. You can't just wait around hoping, in the name of humanism and humanity, that "things will get better over time" as long as children are being mutilated here and now. The problem has to be addressed resolutely. That was my position then, and it's my position now. I think that the genital mutilation of defenseless children who were born on Norwegian soil or who have grown up in Norway is one of the great scandals of our time. It's scandalous that we know this is going on and silently permit it. I believed then – and I believe even more strongly and with even more foundation now – that there's just one way to bring this form of ritual abuse under control: by requiring regular medical check-ups of all children's and young people's genitalia, and by punishing parents and others who are found to be responsible for any mutilation that is uncovered. Only by responding to this practice with legal action can we fight it successfully.

Sweden was the first country in Europe to pass a law specifically addressing genital mutilation. It was introduced in 1982, but only one case has ever been tried – and the trial occurred in June 2006, during the writing of this book. A father with a Somali background was found guilty of having arranged for his eleven-year-old daughter to be mutilated during her stay in Somalia. He was sentenced to nearly four years in prison and had to pay the girl damages of almost 350,000 Swedish kroner.[98] Britain has had a law that specifically addresses, and punishes, genital mutilation since 1985, but no one has ever been prosecuted under it. Other major European countries with laws that cover all kinds of mutilation of children have never tried a single criminal case of genital mutilation. Norway, then, isn't alone in its failure.

It's France that is in a class by itself where the prosecution of genital mutilation is concerned. More correctly, there's one department in France that's in a class by itself. And there are two women whose commitment is largely responsible for the existence of this "French example": Linda Weil-Curiel, a lawyer, and Emanuelle Piet, a doctor.

Milestones in France

Linda Weil-Curiel probably has France's most comprehensive press archive of cases of genital mutilation in that country. When I visited her in Paris in 2003, I looked through her archives and took notes. In 1979 the first case went to court – which is to say that it was heard by a lower court that handles child abuse. An infant had bled to death in Paris. The focus in the trial was on the fact that a child had bled to death, and that this was not the intended result of the action. The *cultural* practice received almost no attention. The person who had performed the circumcision was given a one-year suspended sentence.

But then, all at once, France awoke. In 1982 a three-month-old baby named Bobo bled to death after a home mutilation on a kitchen counter. The circumciser understood that she'd made a wrong cut and that the child was at risk of bleeding to death, but the father, who was of Malian extraction, refused to call for help, because he knew he'd been involved in something illegal. Bobo died. But what could they do with a dead infant? They had few alternatives, since Bobo had been born in France and, like all children in France, had been closely followed up with infant check-ups. The baby's corpse was put in a diaper and taken to the hospital. At first the medical personnel couldn't ascertain the cause of death: all the internal organs were intact. Then they took off the diaper. It was full of blood. The autopsy showed that there was hardly a single drop of blood left in Bobo's body. The baby's death stirred broad debate, and has become a milestone in contemporary French cultural history.

Over the next two years, two new tragedies occurred – also involving babies who bled to death. The deaths were the impetus for preventive and investigative work as well as for lawsuits. French and African women organized a movement against mutilation. In 1991, for the first time, a circumciser was given a prison sentence: a Malian woman went to jail for five years for mutilating six girls in the same family. And in 1993, for the first time, a parent was sent to jail: a thirty-four-year-old Gambian woman was given a four-year sentence, plus a year's suspended sentence, for having mutilated her two daughters. In the same year, two fathers were sent to jail. One of them was married to a circumciser.

"I want to sit up there"

In February 1999, judgment was pronounced in the most extensive lawsuit about genital mutilation in French legal history. A woman known as Mama Greou received an eight-year sentence for having mutilated forty-eight girls in Paris. The court also sentenced a mother to prison for two years, while twenty-six other parents were given suspended sentences ranging from three to five years.

One of the aspects of this lawsuit that made it a milestone is that for the first time, a victim of FGM had lodged a complaint against the perpetrators. Mariatou Koita, then twenty-three years old, filed charges against both her own mother and Mama Greou. Mariatou had been mutilated by Mama Greou when she was eight years old. At the trial, she was the prosecution's chief witness.

Mariatou had been born in Paris in 1975. The next year came her sister Sira, and the year after that a third girl, Koudjeta. Ten months later the mother had twins, a girl and a boy. They were born prematurely, and the twin girl, Mariatou, and Koudjeta were temporarily placed in a French foster home in the same village.

Five years later the girls were flown back to their parents. Shortly after their homecoming, the mother took them to Mama Greou. When Mama Greou began to cut Maritou, the girl screamed: "Why are you doing this to me?" A few days later Mariatou tried to tell a social worker about what had happened, but was stopped by her parents.

The sisters came to believe that all of them would be mutilated. Not until she was in her teens did Mariatou fully understand what had been done to her: in sex-education class, her teacher talked about genital mutilation. At around this time, Mariatou's mother had yet another baby girl. Mariatou tried desperately to talk her parents into sparing her. It was in vain: a year later the girl was mutilated by Mama Greou. In fact, Mariatou's mother allowed her own bedroom to be used by Mama Greou for her "work" – not just on her own children but on others'. One baby after another was brought to the family's house and mutilated with a razor blade. At eighteen Mariatou ran away from home, unable to live in the house any more knowing what damage was being done there to children. By this point, Mama Greou had already been given a suspended sentence for mutilation. She knew, then, that her actions were criminal.

Mariatou reported both her mother and Mama Greou to the police. The investigation revealed that Mama Greou had mutilated children ranging in age from newborns to ten years old. As payment, she took 250 to 500 kroner for each baby she mutilated. She had probably performed several hundred mutilations in Paris and its suburbs. Forty-eight of them were documented. When the verdict was pronounced, the lawyer Linda Weil-Curiel asked if Mariatou, who was then studying law, if she wanted to be a lawyer. "No, I want to sit up there," she said, and pointed to the judges.

No law against genital mutilation

But let's return to little Bobo, who bled to death in 1982. After her death, several people called for the introduction of a law specifically banning genital mutilation. Weil-Curiel was totally against it. She felt in principle that there should not be laws specifically directed at people of foreign origin – an "ethnic legal code," as it were. She felt that everyone should be subject to the same laws, and that there already were laws on the books in France that made it a crime to damage body parts. (Norway, too, already had such laws in effect when FGM was specifically outlawed.) Weil-Curiel's view prevailed, and France still has no law specifically banning FGM. She also succeeded with her argument that genital mutilation should not be treated under the law as child abuse, which is handled in lower courts. Mutilation consists of the destruction and removal of a body part, and leaves a lasting wound; it should therefore be prosecuted in the higher courts, where serious acts of bodily harm are prosecuted and where the possible punishments are far more severe. She made this argument: these are children who are victims of an obvious act of physical disfigurement; they should have the same rights as a white child who has been permanently maimed. Her argument carried the day.

Most of the mutilation lawsuits in France have ended with the defendants being given suspended sentences. Weil-Curiel considers this a victory for the defendants, who persuade the court to accept the argument that in mutilating the child they had no intention of doing harm or inflicting pain. But Weil-Curiel doesn't agree with this reasoning. The intention of those who mutilate a girl's genital, she argues, is to destroy the sexual desire of the housewife she will grow up into. Many parents insist that they've had their daughters mutilated to ensure that they conduct themselves in a seemly manner. Some say explicitly that mutilation ensures that a woman will calm down sexually and be able to get along without sex if her husband is away for a while – thus freeing her husband from the worry that his wife will be unfaithful. Others maintain that a woman who isn't mutilated will be too sexually demanding for a man. Since FGM destroys a woman's sexual organs, it's the ideal biological safety belt.

Linda Weil-Curiel also says that parents often claim to be unfamiliar with the French law against FGM. If they'd known about it, they say, they wouldn't have mutilated their children. Weil-Curiel rejects this claim. The topic has been widely discussed, and a well-organized information campaign has been in operation since the 1980s. For my own part, I can quote a Norwegian woman who was married to a Gambian from a tribe in which all the girls were mutilated: "If people didn't know this was forbidden, they'd ask the government to perform the operation for free at the hospital, just as they ask for their boys to be circumcised at government expense." The reasoning is absolutely logical.

A trial in France

The lawsuits in France have concerned mutilations performed both in France and in immigrants' homelands. While in Paris in 2003, I attended a trial on mutilation. It was an epochal experience.

The accused, a mother named Mariya Kante, was thirty-eight years old. She had supposedly come to France from

Mauritania as a new wife at the age of sixteen. Her husband, Mohamedi Kante, age sixty-nine, was her cousin.

Together they had seven children – four girls and three boys. The mother was charged with having been a co-conspirator in the genital mutilation of the three older girls, Coumba, Fatomata, and Kama. The crimes were uncovered as a result of the abuse of one of the children, the girl Hawa, whom Mohamedi Kante had with another wife. Kante's two wives argued a great deal, and for this reason the husband sent his Malian wife and their daughter Hawa back to Mali. A couple of years later he brought Hawa back to Paris. She had been abused, and in the hospital doctors checked to see if she had also been genitally mutilated. The answer was yes. During the police interrogation, Mariya Kante admitted that three of her own children, too, were mutilated.

At first the Kantes were given an eighteen-month suspended sentence for extremely grievous abuse of Hawa. The reason for the suspended sentence was that they had no previous criminal record.

A mother in the witness box

Mariya Kante enters the witness box in a colourful African robe. She is wearing large pieces of gold jewelry in both her ears and around her neck and wrists. She is illiterate and has a translator. The judge asks Mariya several times if she understands why she has been charged – that genital mutilation is extremely serious and damaging, and that it is forbidden by French law. She does not answer the questions, and declares herself not guilty of the charge. She says that he has done nothing wrong. Circumcision is her tradition. Besides, she says, she didn't know that her daughters were mutilated.

Mariya claims to remember little. The session almost devolves into a cultural tragicomedy: she doesn't know when she came to France; nor does she remember when she visited Mauritania, where, she maintains, the girls were mutilated, one after the other. But she insists that she only went to Mauritania to show the newborns to her family there. Her own father, a poor farmer, supposedly paid the airfare, and her husband supposedly knew nothing about these trips. "Are you saying this to protect your husband?" the judge asks. She says no. Nor can she explain why she never took a newborn son to Mauritania.

Mariya Kante's mother is the village circumciser. Mariya says she herself was in another village at the time when the mutilations of her children must have taken place. Not until after she had returned to France, she says, did she notice that the girls were mutilated. The prosecutor attempts several times to get an idea of how and when the circumcisions took place – unsuccessfully. But how could she leave her children with a grandmother who was a circumciser? Not even in response to this question does Mariya manage to come up with an even remotely logical answer. Not even when it's documented that all the children were included only on her husband's passport – meaning that they couldn't have traveled to Mauritania with her alone – does the prosecutor manage to engage her in a reasonable dialogue. Everything she says is imprecise, incomplete, and inconsistent.

The judge asks: why didn't she mutilate the youngest daughter, Tiguidé, born in 1992? Mariya says that it was not until Tiguidé was born that she was told at the Child Health Centre about the prohibition.

The judge makes a determined effort to get Mariya to clarify where she stands on the prohibition: "After you understood that genital mutilation is forbidden, why wouldn't you keep doing it?"

"Because it's forbidden."

"But do you understand *why* it's forbidden?" continues the judge.

"Because you go to prison," she replies.

"Have you understood *why* one goes to prison?"

"I respect the law," she replies.

The judge changes the question radically.

131

"Do you think that it's good or not good for a child to be genitally mutilated?"

"I think circumcision is best, because if you don't do it, there will be complications when you grow up. Those who aren't circumcised can have intimate contact with everybody."

The judge asks further: "Does this mean that for you, everybody who isn't genitally mutilated is lost? Is it so categorical for you?"

"Yes, that's how it is," replies Mariya. She says that she fears daily for the future of her youngest daughter, Tiguidé, who isn't mutilated. She is afraid that "the devil will take her daughter."

"But for heaven's sake, I'm French!"

Muhamedi Kante enters the witness box. He, too, is traditionally dressed – he's wearing a green robe with embroidery on the collar and has sandals on his feet. A retired cleaning worker, he speaks very good French. The judge asks him why his wife has never worked and why she can't speak French. "She still can't take the subway alone because she can't read," says the judge, who wants to know why Kante's wife is so poorly integrated. Kante explains this by saying that she has to take care of the children.

"So when you brought your young wife to France, it was just to keep your bed warm?" the judge asks. Kante doesn't reply.

"Are you against genital mutilation?" the judge asks.

"It has something to do with Islam," Kante replies. "I don't know whether I'm for it or against it."

Kante says he first became aware of the law against genital mutilation in 1995, when it was revealed that his daughters were mutilated.

"Do you know why it's forbidden?" the judge asks.

"No," Kante replies.

"Have you tried to understand *why* it's forbidden?"

"No," Kante says. "It's religion. It's something all Muslims do."

"When your wife went to Mauritania with the girls, was genital mutilation something you were aware of?" asks the judge.

"I don't know," Kante says.

"Do you know that your wife is genitally mutilated?"

"Yes."

"Have you had sex with a woman who isn't genitally mutilated?"

"I don't know."

"Is it of interest to you how women experience sex?" the judge asks. Kante shrugs.

"Is it positive or negative that your daughters are genitally mutilated?"

"I don't know."

Like his wife, Kante isn't interested in helping to clarify when the supposed trips to Mauritania took place, who bought the tickets, or how the children were able to travel when their names didn't appear on his wife's passport. In the end, the prosecutor almost manages to establish that the reason why the Kantes are throwing a smokescreen over these matters is that all the girls were in fact mutilated in Paris. The judge, obviously furious over Kante's unwillingness to cooperate, asks him why he doesn't go back to Mauritania now that he's retired.

"But for heaven's sake," Kante replies indignantly, "I'm French!"

Witnesses and experts

A series of experts now enter the witness box – psychiatrists, doctors, social workers, school personnel, and police officers. Mariya Kante's half-sister also testifies.

Several doctors describe the process of mutilation the girls went through. It involves clitoral amputation and removal of the labia minora. This requires at least three or four rounds of cutting. Because of the violent pain and the inevitable strong resistance by the child, it takes two or three people to hold the victim down. As a rule, the child doesn't recall the operation when she grows up, either because she was an infant at the time or because the experience was so painful that the memory is repressed. All of Kante's daughters have been examined and discovered to be mutilated. "You don't need to be an expert to tell whether a girl or a woman is genitally mutilated," says pediatrician Mselati Jean Claude. "It's impossible not to see it with the naked eye." The girls don't remember being mutilated; they've told the pediatrician that the mutilations were done for their future husbands.

In her testimony, Emanuelle Piet says that "everyone knows mutilation is illegal. The news of the verdicts spread from home to home." The great majority of the mutilations, she says, take place in France. She explains that the mutilations themselves, which almost without exception are performed without anesthesia, inflict such violent pain that the shock in itself can cause a child to die.

A psychiatrist who has examined Mariya describes her as a pleasant, poised, loving and caring woman. How can she accept genital mutilation? The answer, believes the psychiatrist, is this: she's bound by her ethnic tradition. The obligation to mutilate her daughter's genitals is non-negotiable. By mutilating her children, she has also repeated her own history – she's done to them what her own mother did to her. This "ethnic law" supersedes French law, and internal justice within the ethnic group is extremely strong: it's all but impossible to violate the "ethnic law" and continue to live as a member of the group.

A Senegalese-French woman who is a social worker describes the way in which a young person typically discovers that she has been genitally mutilated. She visits a social worker and says she believes she isn't normal. A medical exam is performed, and reveals that she has been mutilated.

This is new to her, and she reacts to it with intense sorrow and despair. The social worker says that she talks to young women whose boyfriends have left them because they don't function sexually. Young people, she says, support the law against mutilation and the prescribed punishment. But Kante's now half-grown girls don't feel mutilated, and neither the girls nor their parents can understand why genital mutilation is a punishable offense. The one possible exception is the youngest of the girls, who is now fifteen years old. She says that she doesn't think she'll want to mutilate her own children.

School officials describe the girls as well integrated. A principal who has known the family for fifteen years characterizes them as the best integrated African family at the school: "I'm very surprised at this case. This is the last family I would have expected to have this problem."

Linda Weil-Curiel, who has assisted the victims in almost all of the criminal cases involving genital mutilation in French history, shows excerpts from a documentary about genital mutilation in order to ensure that the judge and jury understand the nature of the operation. Mariya Kante leans forward to get a better look at an infant who's being held down by three women while a fourth woman cuts the child's sexual organ several times with a razor blade. The screaming and the sight of the bloody, writing little body are indescribable. For the first time during the trial, Mariya Kante seems interested. She follows the film intently and doesn't so much as wince.

Weil-Curiel believes that the Kantes already knew in the 1980s that genital mutilation was forbidden. It was in 1982, when little Bobo died, that Mariya had her first daughter. And she was told about the law during her children's medical check-ups.

Summing up the prosecution's case

The prosecutor sums up the case; the members of the jury are warned against letting themselves be seduced by the defendants' cultural background: "We're talking about an extreme mutilation. As described by the experts, it's a criminal act. We cannot close our eyes to this violent crime in which there is proven amputation of the clitoris. French society used to overlook rape. We don't do that any more. Rape is punishable. So is genital mutilation."

The prosecutor maintains that when Mariya took the girls to her mother, who is a circumciser, she must have known they would be mutilated, and that it's impossible "to ignore this point." He adds that whether the procedure took place in Mauritania or in Paris doesn't matter: in either case, Mariya has contributed to an act of mutilation. The prosecutor believes that "a cultural view" of the circumstances shows that if the girls were in fact taken to Mauritania, it was so that they could be mutilated. (The boys had no need for the trip, because they could be circumcised legally in France.) At the same time, the prosecutor argues that the genital mutilation undoubtedly took place in Paris.

The most important point, in the prosecutor's view, is this: Mariya Kante knew that genital mutilation was against the law, but her fealty to tradition led her to ignore the prohibition.

The prosecutor supports this claim by pointing out that Mariya Kante's half-sister in Paris already knew about the law in 1982: "She is accused because she knew what she was risking. The only thing she feared was prison. This shows how important it is that we put the law into practice."

He points out that there are several thousand West Africans in France. Many of them continue to practice FGM. In these communities, the ethics and practices of the homeland hold sway and are passed on from generation to generation. "Only when there's talk of prison or of children dying of genital mutilation," says the prosecutor, "do the communities seem to react."

As for the family's good character references, he says: "What is inside people and what is a façade can be diametrically opposite." He points to the harsh abuse of Hawa, which went on for two years.

Mariya Kante is given a three-year suspended sentence and three years' probation for mutilating her daughters in Paris. In addition, the youngest daughter, eleven-year-old Tiguidé, who is not mutilated, will be regularly examined to prevent her from being mutilated. Mariya Kante is also sentenced to pay 15,000 euros in support to the youngest of the mutilated daughters, Kama, age fifteen. The sum is to be paid out when the girl turns eighteen. The two other girls won't receive payments, since the legal condition for support is that they must be underage.

An indelible impact

The two-day trial had an indelible impact on me. The most striking impression was produced by the French-Senegalese social worker when she talked with warmhearted sympathy about the shock, sorrow, and deep inner pain with which teenage girls receive the news from a doctor that they've been mutilated for life – girls who, up to "the last moment," have no inkling of what was done to them when they were little. As babies, they hadn't known what was being done to them – and hadn't been able to report it to anyone. A baby can't tell tales. This is, indeed, often the main reason why these operations are performed on infants: parents migrate to a country where mutilation is forbidden, and choose to have the job done when their daughters are too young to serve as witnesses. So logical – and so grotesque.

The Kantes' almost total uncooperativeness on the stand, and their unwillingness to recognize the nature of the injustice to which they'd subjected their children, also made a deep impression on me. The father, who had lived in France for over thirty years, had worked full time until he reached retirement age. He spoke fluent French. Yet when it came to fundamental values, he seemed almost totally unintegrated into French society. Ditto his wife. Neither of them was willing to make the slightest effort to cooperate on any level. When the videotape showing the mutilation of a little girl was screened, there was hardly anybody in the courtroom who didn't turn away or close his or her eyes. The little body struggling desperately to escape the razor blade, the strong adult hands making sure that she didn't have a chance of escaping the ritual abuse, the baby's screams – it was all horrible. And Mariya Kante leaned forward with interest and studied the images without so much as a wince. For the first time during the entire trial, Mariya Kante was "present."

The teacher's and the principal's surprise that this "well-integrated" family had "this problem" reminded me of all the young children I've met in Norway who superficially seem very well integrated but whose families may subject them to the same amount of pressure to marry as the parents of young women whose low level of integration is easy to recognize. Appearances can be misleading.

After the trial, Linda Weil-Curiel told me that some parents regret having mutilated their children. They simply didn't realize how cruel genital mutilation was – didn't realize what kind of pain and damage they were inflicting upon their children. They were, they say, only motivated by custom and by the legal traditions of their own ethnic communities. During the trial, they realize what a terrible injustice they've subjected their children to, and they regret it deeply. Other parents, however, don't change their attitudes at all: they neither regret what they've done nor feel that they've done anything wrong. M. and Mme. Kante, Weil-Curiel believed, fell into the latter category.

For me, the most gratifying part of the verdict was the protection that was given to the youngest girl, Tiguidé – the assurance that she would be examined annually until she grew up in order to prevent mutilation. Weil-Curiel also pointed out that the compensation awarded to the child would have an extremely important preventive effect. Kante and other immigrants are highly motivated by financial factors. Awarding compensation not only hurts – it says something about power: the one who has a right to money has power.

On the way out of the courtroom I run into one of the doctors who testified, Emanuelle Piet. She has some terribly interesting experiences to relate. She is a doctor in the

138

department of Seine-Saint-Dénis, which is northeast of Paris and has a sizable West African population, and she works particularly closely with the health stations. In the mid 1980s, she warned that small children were being mutilated in the department. In 1987, therefore, she initiated a study to map five hundred West African girls under six years old. All of their mothers had been genitally mutilated. Piet put several measures into effect. Some of the parents whose children were mutilated were prosecuted. She informed the parents thoroughly about the damaging effects of the procecure and about the law against it. And she introduced systematic medical check-ups of all children's sexual organs, regardless of their sex or ethnic origins, beginning with their first check-up as newborns and continuing until they reached school age. She included all children in the check-ups, because some instances of sexual abuse can also be discovered through such check-ups. These check-ups, it is important to point out, are simply a matter of so-called clinical observation: as the pediatrician in the case against Mariya Kante put it, it's impossible not to notice genital mutilation with the naked eye.[99]

Ten years later, Piet carried out another mapping of five hundred West African girls under six years old at the health station. Only seven girls proved to have been mutilated. A new round of lawsuits followed, and the information work and medical check-ups continued. In 2000, Piet performed a third study of five hundred West African girls in the department. Hold on to your seat: not a single girl was mutilated. One might be led to believe that the reason for this gratifying result was that parents who still wanted to mutilate their children had stopped taking them in for medical check-ups. "No," said Piet, "the turnout at the health stations is just as good as before. Especially because *money talks*." For in France, you see, you have to display your child's health card, with a valid stamp from his or her last medical check-up, in order to get an increase in your child benefit allowance. It's that simple.

It's therefore not the French state itself that has the right to call itself the jurisdiction in Europe that best protects girls against genital mutilation. That honour belongs to the department of Seine-Saint-Denis. And those who deserve the credit for this distinction are an unrelenting lawyer and human-rights champion, Linda Weil-Curiel, and an equally determined advocate for children, Dr. Emanuelle Piet.

Will Norway learn its lesson?

France's experiences were a crucial inspiration to those of us at Human Rights Service when we argued – and produced documentation to support our argument – that Norway should introduce medical check-ups and actively enforce current laws. We did this under the second Bondevik government, which was a minority government – meaning that the real power lay in the Parliament. We had conversations with all the members of the Committee on Local Government and Public Administration, which is responsible for integration. The committee members represent parties from one end of the political spectrum to the other, and all of them responded enthusiastically to our proposals.

But how to get them to take meaningful action? How to convince them to follow Weil-Curiel's and Piet's example?

With financial support from the organization Fritt Ord (Free Word), we invited Weil-Curiel and Piet to Norway. At a February 2005 meeting with the committee, they described their work to an audience that listened carefully and asked good questions. Three months later, on 29 May, a majority of the members of Parliament, including members of the Labour, Progress, Centre, and Socialist Left parties, adopted a resolution instructing the government to discuss how medical check-ups, that is to say "clinical observation of all children's sex organs," could be introduced in Norway in order to prevent and uncover genital mutilation, how parents could be held responsible, and whether the check-ups should be made obligatory. The government was specifically referred to Weil-Curiel's and Piet's work in France.

Yes, we at HRS were jubilant.

But our joy didn't last long. The government completely locked up – revealing just how illogical and inhumane "good-thinking" people can be. The cabinet member in charge of integration, Erna Solberg, and her parliamentary secretary, Cathrine Bretzeg, spoke harshly about our proposals in one national media organ after another. In their view, the clinical observation of girls' sexual organs would be "demeaning for tens of thousands of girls" and "enormously insulting." They said that "it is extremely surprising that … all girls should have to show their sexual organs so that a small group in society will be reached," and that "the public health service will become a threat and an enemy."[100] Referring to their own daughters, the government's representatives insisted that they personally would not do anything to bring the health service into line with contemporary reality – namely, the fact that children are being genitally mutilated and sexually abused.

The fact that boys' sexual organs undergo routine check-ups, which don't just involve "the naked eye" but the palpation of their scrotums to ensure that their testicles have descended, was overlooked. So was the fact that health authorities recommend regular checkups, until puberty, of the testicles of newly immigrated boys.

The statements by Solberg and company were a nearly incomprehensible reminder that the grim taboos of earlier times with regard to girls' and women's sexual organs were still alive and well.

And what had become of the idea of solidarity with the most vulnerable among us?

Despite the government's repugnance, however, they were now obliged to discuss the Parliament's resolution. After the government had made clear its opposition, the question was this: Will the government use any tactic to forestall the resolution, including arguing that no new cases of mutilated girls in Norway had been identified in recent years? That was absolutely a possibility.

Trip to Gambia

Two months after the 2005 parliamentary resolution, then, I'm in the living room of a Norwegian citizen on Africa's West Coast, in Koto, Gambia. Through sources with close ties to the Gambian community in Oslo, I know that this man belongs to the Serahule tribe, in which almost 100 percent of the girls are mutilated. He has six daughters under eleven years old, all born in Norway. The four oldest girls were sent to Gambia two years ago without their parents. He and his wife have been separated for five years, but he's had three more children during this period, in whose entries in the national registry he's named as the father. I was told before the trip that he has two additional wives in Gambia. He's here on summer vacation.

The man sitting opposite me has been convicted of cheating the social-security office. He also belongs to a congregation whose imam totally supports mutilation. There's good reason to assume that all of his four daughters have been mutilated during their time in Gambia. The man knows nothing about my suspicions on this score, or about my knowledge of these other unimpressive facts about him. With us in the room are the journalist Astrid Meland, who wants to cover this story for *Dagbladet*'s website.[101]

The oldest girl speaks very good Norwegian, while the two youngest, aged five and eight, don't speak it at all. The youngest is a charming beauty and seems to be lost in her own thoughts. Let's call her Awa. I put little Awa on my lap and stroke her back and chat with her. Awa sits as still as a lit candle.

Her father is an intense, nervous, restless person whose glance wanders around the room as we talk. He speaks decent enough Norwegian after nearly twenty years in Norway. He says that the girls are in Gambia to learn about Gambian culture. What this actually means, he is unable to explain. The girls will be there for a few more years, he says, but he won't specify how many. The two youngest girls back home in Norway – one of the four months old, the other two and a half – will also come to

Gambia when they get a little bigger. The plan, he explains, is to bring them to Gambia when the four other daughters are sent back to Norway.

The two-story house contains more than a hundred square meters of floor space. By Gambian standards, it's a palace. But it's stifling, gloomy, and sparsely furnished – indeed, quite simply, empty. The man, we learn, has three other such houses.

The father tells us proudly that all his girls attend Koran school four days a week; in fact, they're going to school tomorrow morning. Meland and I ask if we can accompany them to the school. It's agreed that we'll meet them early the next day.

Something about the Norwegian-born girls doesn't seem right. Neighbour children – some of whom are in the house with us, some of whom are playing out in the street – are lively and spontaneous, like most Gambian children. But "ours" are withdrawn, and it doesn't seem to be a matter of shyness. The oldest girl, especially, seems to me clenched and sceptical. During the many hours' long visit, I notice that not once does the father or his second wife direct any sign of affection toward the children – not a single loving smile or glance. Nor do the children invite affection – not in any way at all. What's this about?

In response to a discreet question, someone in the house confides in me that the Norwegian-born girls are circumcised. It's impossible to know whether this informant actually has specific knowledge about the matter or whether this person simply takes it for granted that all Serahule girls in Gambia are mutilated. This source's explanation for the girls' mutilation is this: "All girls have to be circumcised in order to be able to marry."

With so many people around who understand a little or a good deal of English, and because the two oldest Norwegian-born girls, aged nine and eleven, can speak a bit of English, it's hard to inquire further.

The next day Meland and I knock on the door again. From the first minute, the girls are, if possible, even more reserved than they were the day before. It's impossible to get an ordinary conversation going. They seem totally out of contact. Little Awa, age five, is the exception. She comes immediately over to me when we enter the backyard. Without a word, she presses up tightly against my left side and looks out into space. Not a word, not a glance. With her whole self, however, she's asking for something. She wants more cuddling.

An imam teaches the children at the Koran school. He says that the circumcision of girls is "a good thing." Several of the oldest girls, aged around thirteen to fifteen, tell us with utter candor whether they're circumcised or not, how old they were when they underwent the ritual, and whether they're for or against it. In Gambia, FGM is so common that there seems to be nearly total openness about whether one is mutilated or not. For example, one mild-mannered girl of thirteen says that she's circumcised, but doesn't remember when it happened because she was so young at the time. It was her parents, she says, who told her it had been done to her. The youngest girls, particularly in these conversations, are about the same age as the oldest Norwegian-born girl, who is eleven. Since similar conversations with the Norwegian-born girls seem to be absolutely impossible, given their reserve with us, we don't even try.

Three generations of mutilation

Who are these women who mutilate small children? What are they thinking? In a visit to the town of Sangang, not far from the capital, Banjul, we got a picture of the kind of person in whose hands Norwegian-born girls can end up.

In this town almost everyone belongs to the Mandinka tribe, in which virtually all the girls are mutilated. Among the inhabitants is a thin woman of sixty or so named Binta. Sitting on a slanted, worn-out chair in her very mean house of no more than twenty square meters, Binta talks about her work. Once a year, in the month of January, a number of girls – ten, fifteen, maybe twenty of them - are brought together to be mutilated.

144

They're taken out into the jungle where she does the job with a razor blade. She claims to use a new razor blade for every girl in order to avoid causing pain. The payment is about six kroner per girl. She maintains that no girls have bled during the fifteen years she's worked as a circumciser. Everything about what goes on in the jungle is secret, she says with a raised index finger: only the girls who are to be mutilated and women who are already mutilated are allowed to be present when the ritual takes place.

Binta took over the job as circumciser from her own mother, as is traditional. Her family has been in the business for countless generations, or, as Binta says, "Always." On the bed nearby sits a young woman in her mid twenties. She is Binta's daughter. Binta confirms without hesitation that she took a razor blade to her own daughter. On the daughter's lap is the circumciser's nine-month-old granddaughter, who was circumcised by Binta six months earlier. Three generations of women in the room, three generations of mutilations.

The circumciser's daughter confirms that she will take over the job when her mother retires. Both mother and daughter have great problems understanding such questions as: Do they think that one day circumcision will stop? They look at each other with surprise. They seem to consider the question totally absurd. Absolutely unthinkable. Girls must be circumcised. That's how it is. To make the girls "pure," Binta explains. And if parts of the sexual organ are not cut away, it becomes "narrow and it becomes difficult to give birth," she continues.

"But what about women in the Woloff tribe? They're not circumcised, and they don't have problems giving birth?"

Neither the young nor the old woman seems to grasp the problem.

Meeting Binta, her child, and her grandchild made me feel powerlessness – period. Plainly, Gambia has a long way to go before girls will be able to escape being the victims of one of the world's worst customs. This means that Norwegian-born girls of Gambian parents may, for many years to come, have their futures sealed by ladies like Binta.

"Completely disciplined"

But what about the four sisters from Norway? What has happened to them? Almost entirely by accident, some important information emerges only hours before our return trip to Norway. The source is someone in the girls' neighbourhood. The information is so sensitive that I have to keep the source's identity hidden, since that person might be in mortal danger if his or her identity were disclosed.

The source says that the man had two wives in Gambia until last year. The other wife, who is the girls' mother, is the first wife. She is furious that her husband has married several women. In 2004 she managed to force him to divorce wife number two, called the "middle wife" in Gambia, the wife he had back in his hometown. The first wife, in Norway, also tried to get him to divorce the third wife, called the "last wife" (the one we met during our visit to the home in Koto); but then the man sought help from a sorcerer who "saved" him. The man has two children with the middle wife, the one from whom he is now divorced; they live with his parents in the village. These children, under Norwegian law, have an absolute right to Norwegian citizenship because their father is a Norwegian citizen. The man, then, has nine children altogether.

The last wife has responsibility for the four Norwegian-born sisters in Gambia. The source says that she doesn't care about the children, which the source ascribes to the unfriendly relationship between her, the last wife, and the girls' mother, who is the first wife. The last wife wants to take over the role of the first wife – that is, she wants to be the one who gets to live in Norway. The source expresses deep concern for the four girls, and says that when they came to Gambia in the summer of 2003, they talked only Norwegian among themselves, and could only speak a little of their tribal language. At that time, they had been outgoing and talkative. Not now. During their first visit to Gambia they reacted negatively to a number of things; they turned down the Gambian food they were served, and refused to sit on the floor and eat with their fingers. Their father felt they had become too Norwegian, and should become Gambian girls; so he "disciplined" them severely, the source says, and refused to allow them to speak Norwegian. The source says the man is "a bad man and a bad father," and describes the first wife, back in Norway, as "a hard woman."

The source adds that the father has told other people in Gambia that the circumcision of girls is forbidden in Norway. After our first visit to his home in Koto, says the source, the father threatened his daughters with physical punishment if they should tell anyone that they were genitally mutilated.

According to the source, the mutilation occurred early in the autumn of 2003. All of the girls were taken to their parents' hometown in the interior of Gambia. They came back after about a week. The girls had been "completely disciplined," as the source said. There was no resistance left in them. In accordance with tradition, the genital mutilations were celebrated in a ceremony in the house in Koto.

Reported for genital mutilation

Human Rights Service filed complaints against the parents of the four Norwegian-born girls for a number of actions that were or might be against the law in Norway: contributing to genital mutilation; violation of the Education Act (on the grounds that the girls' schooling did not satisfy the Norwegian school system's subject requirements); violation of the Child Benefits Act (since we assumed that the parents did not tell social-security officials in 2003 that they had taken their two smallest children, then three and five years old, out of the country); and violation of the Convention on the Rights of the Child (since Norwegian officials weren't given the opportunity to find out from the children how they felt about being separated from their parents). We filed a complaint against the parents for violating the criminal code regarding parents' obligations to children, on the grounds that they had actively prevented the children's integration into Norwegian society. And we filed a complaint against them for possibly deceiving the social-security office, since there was every reason to believe that the separation between the man and his first wife was a sham that had been concocted for financial reasons and that the couple really lived together.

The police in Oslo immediately sought to take the girls into custody, but ran into a wall. The children were outside of Norway, and the Children Act is not valid beyond Norway's borders. Nor had the police found a reason to arrest the father.

The investigation is still underway. Out of consideration for the work of the police, I can't say anything more specific here than that the girls' father, who was to have returned to Norway in September 2005, remained in Gambia. As of 1 August 2006, the mother of the girls is still safely lodged in a large public-housing unit in Oslo. She is supposed to have six children, but only two small children are living with her now. She is registered with the social-security office as a single provider and still collects payments on this basis, just as she did before we reported the family to the police.

A source in Gambia told us as late as the spring of 2006 that the children still suffer from a lack of parental care on the part of both the father and his second wife.

I'll admit that I've often wanted to visit the mother in Oslo and tear her to bits verbally. She knows very well that her daughters are having a rough time of it in Gambia. She's the one who holds the cards, because she's the one who is the family's sole provider. If she turns off the money tap from Norway to her husband in Gambia, there's little he'll be able to do. She can demand that the children be brought home to Norway. But she knows very well that if she does so, she risks a damning conviction for having contributed to her daughters' genital mutilation.

Better to allow one's innocent children to remain in their prison in Gambia, then, than to go to jail in Norway oneself for one's sins?

Some nights I have painful dreams about little Awa. I admit that I've often fantasized about going back to Gambia, taking the law in my own hands, and bringing all those girls home.[102]

Silence reigns

The 1995 Norwegian law against genital mutilation has been sleeping soundly for eleven years now. Only a couple of complaints filed, not one indictment, not one charge, not one conviction – even though there's good reason to fear that thousands of girls (in a country of just under 5 million people) are affected by this custom.

How many more thousands have been mutilated in Sweden, Denmark, Britain, Germany, the Netherlands, Belgium, Italy, France, and Spain? Where is the EU? Why this silence? And what about all the girls who are mutilated in other parts of the world – approximately two million a year? Where is the UN? Why this silence?

Is the EU silent because the children in question have non-European roots? Are their parents being treated differently because of their "different cultural and religious background"? Or does the EU refuse to act because the very brutality of genital mutilation makes it uncomfortable to take on? Does the UN hold back because the children are girls – and because girls' sexuality has always been subordinated to boys' sexuality?

In Gambia, where little Awa now lives, the country's president, Yahya Jammeh, has publicly threatened people or organizations that actively oppose genital mutilation. Why is the international community taking such a passive attitude toward such a head of state? Why hasn't he been charged with crimes against humanity? But perhaps the most important question is this: Why don't they take a zero-tolerance approach to such a horrible crime?

6

It's also about Islam

Mina, Samira, little Awa, and all the children, young people, women and men with immigrant background whom I've mentioned in the previous pages, whether named or unnamed, have one thing in common: they all have roots in the Muslim world. To a greater and greater degree, the public and private debate on immigration and integration is a debate about Islam. We rarely discuss challenges related to the integration of Hindus, Sikhs, Jews, or Buddhists; nor do we often witness debates on integration in which the persons involved refer to themselves as Hindus, Buddhists, Jews, or Sikhs.

The picture is the same throughout Europe. Why is it Muslims and Islams that are at the centre of this public discussion? What is it about Islam that creates conflicts on so many levels of society?

Islam doesn't just have one face. It's a highly diverse religion that is practiced and interpreted differently from country to country and from one ethnic group to another. In Islam, culture and religion are woven together. Customs that existed before Islam's introduction into a culture either fade away or are strengthened by Islam; meanwhile new practices are established and legitimized in Islam's name. With Islam, it's impossible to distinguish categorically between religion and culture. And it's wrong to claim categorically that cultural practices such as family-arranged marriage, genital mutilation, honour killing, and the oppression of women do not also, generally speaking, have something to do with Islam.

There's good reason to assume that the father of little Awa would emphatically justify the mutilation of his daughter as being rooted in both Islam and culture, just as orthodox Christians in Ethiopia defend it with reference to *their* religion. It's also probably safe to assume that Mina's father used Islam and culture as arguments for marrying off his daughter, just as well-off people in Norway once used their religion as an argument for marrying off their innocent young daughters.

Similarly, many Muslims claim that honour killings, such as the murders of Anooshe and Fadime, are legitimate on both religious and cultural grounds, just as executioners in the Middle Ages invoked divine sanction when they burned witches at the stake. Most likely the father of Samira in Somalia sees Islam as his beacon, just as a certain version of Christianity is the guiding star for parents who withdraw their children from public schools and enroll them in conservative Christian academies.

Part of the explanation for Muslims' conflicts with a secular democracy like Norway can be found in the pillars of the religion. A key factor, especially in the context of this book, is Islam's teachings about women and sexuality.

Two works in particular have helped me to understand Pakistan, other Muslim countries, and Muslims in Norway and Europe. One of them is the 1992 study *Den muslimske familie: en undersøkelse av kvinners rett i islam (The Muslim Family: A Study of Women's Rights in Islam)* by Tove Stang Dahl, a late Norwegian professor of women's law. The other, written by the internationally famous Moroccan professor and sociologist Fatima Mernissi, is *Beyond the Veil: Male-Female Dynamics in Modern Muslim Society* (1985). Both Stang Dahl and Mernissi went to the historical sources of Islam to investigate Islam's view of women and its regulation of relations between women and men, as well as the laws and norms that regulate life in the Muslim family.

When Muhammed began his missionary work among the tribes on the Arabian peninsula in the seventh century A.D., women had a great deal of power to make decisions about their own sexuality. A woman didn't belong to her husband; she and her children were part of a tribal community. She could have several husbands; she could divorce; and she could decide which man was to be considered the father of her child. The children belonged to her and to her tribe; the men came and went with the trading caravans. It was thus impossible for a man to exercise day-to-day control over his wife. A tribe's honour and prestige were not tied up with women's sexuality. At that time, in fact, Arabs were highly promiscuous.

During this period the Arabian peninsula underwent considerable social changes. Commerce blossomed, leading to changes in the social structure. This bred social unrest and insecurity, especially in population centres like Mecca, where Muhammed began his missionary work. The reason for the insecurity was that tribal leaders were beginning to forsake the role of material and financial benefactors and protectors. The increasing prosperity awakened the tribal leaders' desire for financial and material gain. Women and children had no right of inheritance at that time, but women did receive their small portion of the tribe's goods and treasures. As the financial and social system began to crumble, women and children, in particular, grew vulnerable.

It was at this time that Muhammed came along with his new project: the family as a substitute for the tribe. Muhammed's success in conquering the Arabic peninsula over a period of about twenty years can be explained largely by these changes. Making the family as the new backbone of society restored norms, values, and security.

Muhammed was especially preoccupied with controlling women's sexuality. The prospect of securing control over women's bodies increased the likelihood that Arabic men would accept the family as the new social unit. With the family as a fundamental unit of society, a man could pursue an independent career and achieve financial self-sufficiency.

For a man, therefore, it was decisive to ensure that his wife's children were his full progeny, children who would someday be his heirs. The key question thus became: how to regulate fatherhood? One answer became Islam's explicit prohibition on sex outside of marriage. The second became the rule that a woman, after her divorce or upon her husband's death, would have to wait for a period of four months and ten days, the so-called *idda,* before she could marry again, in order to avoid uncertainty regarding the fatherhood of any child she might have.

But how to satisfy the social needs that were so important to the Arab tribes? Muhammed replaced the tribal community with the community of the faithful, the so-called *ummah.* All those who accepted Muhammed and his doctrines, no matter what their former religion or their tribal or racial identity, could become a part of the ummah. The shared feeling of community in the ummah was strengthened by faith and by the common struggle for expansion – i.e., holy war.

Bottom line: when the family became the new backbone of society, women's sexual and marital freedom disappeared.

The sexually dangerous woman

Islam warns against love and affection between man and woman. Why? Because a man who loves a woman risks failing in his most important duty: total devotion to Allah. For Allah has a sole and exclusive right to a man's attention. As Mernissi says, the Muslims' God "is known for being jealous" (1985:175). Everything that can come between the believer and devotion to Allah is therefore a threat.

Islam views women's sexuality as powerful and therefore dangerous. The woman is the tempter, the man the victim. Therefore she must be separated from men and closed out of activities beyond the home. The sexual power that Islam ascribes to women constitutes the entire basis for Islam's regulation of relations between women and men, and between women and the Muslim community as such.[103] For Muhammed, control of sexuality was also the key needed to lock the door to the sexual liberation of pagan Arab culture.

153

In Christian history, there is a deep-seated tradition of viewing sexuality as sinful; since the time of Jesus, celibacy has played an important role in a wide variety of faith traditions. In more recent times, Western culture has tended to view men as sexually active and women as sexually passive, a perspective that is strongly antithetical to that of Islam. Freud, who of course had a great influence on modern Western thinking about these matters, conceived of women's sexuality in a way that contrasts profoundly with Islam's basic view of the subject. He described women as passive, masochistic, and inclined to be frigid, and viewed female passivity as destructive. Muhammed and early Muslim theologians also regarded female sexuality as destructive – not, however, because women are passive but, as Mernissi explains (1985:34-41), because they're very much the *opposite* of passive.

Abu Hamid al-Ghazali (1050-1111), who is considered the most important and influential theologian in Islam's history, claimed that no power is a greater threat to Muslim society than women's sexual power, and that women and Satan are therefore two sides of the same coin. Mernissi believes that Ghazali's work reflected the essence of what Muhammed had done several centuries earlier: Muhammed created the necessary circumstances for men's devotion to Allah by establishing optimal control of "the temptress," and also ensured that men had optimal access to sex (1985:33).

In Islam, it's a husband's religious duty to satisfy his wife sexually in order to keep her from committing adultery. Ghazali provided detailed sexual guidelines – for example, a man must have sex with his wife at least every fourth night. Why every fourth night? Because, according to Ghazali, a man can have four wives.[104] A husband must also be sure to give his wife the time she needs to achieve an orgasm.

What about the man's satisfaction? The Muslim man has full right to have his sexual needs satisfied within marriage. Thus a wife can't refuse to sleep with her husband. If she refuses, he can punish her by refusing to support her, and she will also be punished in the hereafter. Ghazali even suggested that a man's right to sexual satisfaction extends so far that he can have sex with his wife even if she's menstruating. But since intercourse during menstruation is viewed as unclean and is thus forbidden in Islam, Ghazali proposed that a menstruating wife cover herself between the navel and the knees and masturbate her husband.[105]

Belief in a man's absolute sexual rights is, in my experience, very much alive today in Islam, even among the Norwegian-born children of immigrants in Norway. An example: two teenage Muslim sisters, both born in Norway, were married off against their will at a double wedding. That same evening and in the same house, the marriages were consummated. Years later, in reply to a question I asked them, they said that at no time since then had either of them ever denied her husband sex. They said the very idea was almost unthinkable. The message they'd been given by their mother before marrying was that they "must never deny your husband what he wants." Jeanette, who works for Human Rights Service, was told the same thing when she was married off at sixteen in Pakistan. Not even when she was repeatedly raped by her husband did her parents support her. Her husband, in their view, was entirely within his rights.

There are verses from the Koran as well as the *hadith*, the collections of sayings attributed to Muhammed, that affirm the wife's absolute subordination to her husband. For example, sura 2, verse 223, reads in part: "Your women are a field for you, so go to your field as you wish...." This Koran verse is interpreted by many to mean that a husband has the absolute right to satisfy himself sexually whenever he wants. Stang Dahl comments as follows on this verse: "One goes to one's cornfield as one decides, when one wants, and one tills it as one wishes. One has full dominion over it" (1992:146).

Why does Islam focus so intently on male sexuality? Because once a man is sexually satisfied, it's much easier for him to give himself entirely to Allah. It's also easier for him to concentrate on developing his intellect – a virtue in Islam. As both Mernissi and Stang Dahl point out, polygamy and simple, fast divorce were introduced to create a situation ideally designed to provide a husband with sexual satisfaction.

As for Muslim women's subordinate sexual role in marriage and the demand for absolute sexual obedience, it's appropriate to point out that it wasn't until 1974 that rape within marriage became a "visible" offense in Norway. Not until that year did a Supreme Court decision clearly state that the possibility of rape can't be excluded just because the parties are married or living together.[106]

Islam doesn't preach equality between woman and man. A girl is subordinate to her father; a wife is subordinate to her husband; a fatherless widow is subordinate to her brothers or sons. The person ordering the widow around may be a brother who's younger than her, or her own young son, as I've witnessed myself in both Pakistan and Norway. After a woman of my acquaintance was divorced in Norway, for example, her oldest son, aged twenty-one, took over as head of the household; he made the financial decisions and assumed authority over his mother and his two sisters.

The social and marital freedom women generally enjoyed prior to Muhammed's revelations can't be found in any Muslim country today. On the contrary, a woman who wants to divorce without her husband's blessing can expect to be punished, or even murdered, which was Anooshe's fate. Since the time of Muhammed, the idea that a woman should be able to decide who should be considered the father of her child has been unthinkable. Muhammed introduced the severest possible punishment for sex outside of marriage. I also want to comment on what appears to be a widespread myth – namely, the claim that Islam gave rights to women that raised their social status. This is only a partial truth. Yes, women received inheritance rights, which in fact amount to half of a man's inheritance rights, and Muhammed also condemned the practice of buring infant girls alive, to name a couple of points that are often brought forward as "evidence" for the improved conditions of women under Islam. But women also lost the right to make decisions about their own bodies and their children. And the separation of the sexes strongly limited women's ability to have a life outside the home. A striking example of this is Muhammed's first wife, Khadija. When Muhammed married her, she was a rich widowed businesswoman in Mecca – a status that speaks volumes about the kind of freedom Arab women enjoyed in pre-Islamic times. I can also mention a friend of mine in Lahore, the fashion designer Yasmin Khan. She lives day and night under armed guard for which she herself pays. Islamists regard her as a threatening example to other women because she's unmarried and financially independent. Other women, they fear, might follow in her liberating footsteps.

Thanks to Muhammed's elevation of the family as an institution, his introduction of curbs on sexual behavior, and his establishment of polygamy and easy divorce for men, women's right to make independent decisions about their lives was severely reduced.

The obedient woman

One indication of the strong position of polygamy in today's Muslim world is that only Turkey and Tunisia forbid it. The acceptance of polygamy by the European Council for Fatwa and Research (ECFR), which instructs Muslims in Europe about Islamic law and morals,[107] reflects the nearly unanimous theological agreement about this practice on the part of Muslim scholars.[108]

The scholars' position is almost entirely supported by the example of Muhammed. Muhammed lived polygamously, and the Koran justifies polygamy. Today, however, secular Muslim feminists reject this justification, noting that the Koran only allows a man to marry up to four women *if hen can treat them all equally*. With this stipulation in mind, they quote sura 4, verse 128: "You will not be able to handle your wives equally, however much you attempt to do so." The Muslim feminists argue that when you put these two Koranic injunctions together, they add up to a prohibition on polygamy. Alas, feminists' interpretations of Islamic scripture have never been viewed as authoritative.

A woman's total subordination to her husband is characterized by both Mernissi and Stang Dahl as a master-slave relationship. The man has no moral obligation to his wife. She can't demand loyalty, but he can demand obedience. In sura 4, verse 34, we read: "Men are superior to women on account of the qualities with which God has gifted the one above the other, and on account of the outlay they make from their substance for them. Virtuous women are obedient, careful..."

Under Islam, a woman's obligation to obey her husband is an absolute commandment. For a man, it is likewise a religious duty to give his wife orders. His key religious duty, moreover, is to support and protect her. When he fulfills this duty, she should respond with obedience.

How broadly Muslims accept this rigid set of mutual obligations can be illustrated by a conversation I had with a woman doctor in Islamabad. At first we discussed her unhappy marriage. Despite the unhappiness, however, she was pleased that her husband "permitted" her to work, as she put it. In this context she also said the following: "The money I earn I put in my own pocket. For it's his obligation to support me." To this I replied that her husband's obligation to support her was accompanied by her obligation to obey him, and that accepting these strictures was not the way to get what she really wanted out of her marriage – namely, respect and a role in making everyday family decisions. This idea seemed to be impossible for her to consider. His non-negotiable obligation was to support her. "Islam says so," she insisted, and the conversation stopped there.

Another illustration of the widespread acceptance of the idea that wives owe husbands obedience is that some women, when they marry, make sure to have specific rights written into their marriage contracts. Among these rights are permission to continue one's education, to work outside the home, to visit one's family at certain times and intervals, or to shop in this or that store without a chaperone. For a young Norwegian-born Muslim woman married to a man from her family's homeland, the duty to obey can force her into a position of powerlessnessness in the face of brutal power, and compel her to succumb to his pressure to give up the education, the job, and the social life she had before he came to Norway. Religion historian Kari Vogt also focuses on the importance of obedience in marriage: "Through the marriage contract, the woman comes under the man's authority, control, and protection." Vogt also refers to the demand for "sexual availability." Disobedience and rebellion can cause a woman to lose her rights (2005:118ff).

Muslim women's subordinate position is also the crucial reason why they don't have the right to marry non-Muslims: it's taken for granted that children in a marriage will follow their father's faith, since he's the master of the home and chooses the family's religion. And it's important for children to be Muslims, because Islam should expand not only through war, but also through reproduction. It's for this reason that a Muslim man has the right to marry non-Muslims, as long as they're so-called "people of the Book" – that is, Jews or Christians.

The prohibition against Muslim women's marriage to non-Muslims remains strong among the great majority of Muslims, in Norway and Europe as well as in the Muslim world. The convert Anne Sofie Roald writes in her book *Are Muslim Women Oppressed?* that most Muslim women with whom she discussed the subject reject the idea of marriage to a non-Muslim man. Some say that such marriages are "sinful," while others say that they would risk expulsion from their communities as well as their families if they were to marry non-Muslims.

Roald says that according to her own interpretation of Islam, Muslim women can marry non-Muslim men; her argument is that "in the Koran there is no direct prohibition against marriage between Muslim women and men from the 'people of the Book,' as there is in regard to marriage with pagans" (2005:127).

In my experience, hardly any personal issue is more sensitive for Muslims than the question of marrying outside the faith. I've met Pakistani Muslim women in Islamabad who belong to the Western-educated elite, and who have married Western men with Christian backgrounds. All the men have converted to Islam, if only on paper. In cases where a Muslim man marries a non-Muslim woman, it's also quite common for the woman to convert, whether in reality or only on paper. Talking to many Norwegian Muslims, both scholars and laymen, I've encountered highly negative attitudes toward the idea of Muslim men marrying women from other religions – even though there's evidence in the Koran of marriages between Muslim men and Christian and Jewish women.

Issues of obedience and sexual availability aside, how should the Muslim man treat his wife? Answer: with respect and justice. And how can she earn the respect of those around her? Stang Dahl: "Elements that are crucial in determining whether a woman can be said to be a success in life are whether she marries, gets a good man, and has children" (1992:53).

Man – a sexual beast

Islam's view of the human male is that he's little short of a notorious sexual beast who will throw himself at any woman who isn't "decently" covered in public, and who requires optimal access to several wives and the right to a quick divorce.

This view, along with the requirement of female chastity, figures importantly in Ayaan Hirsi Ali's explanation of the developmental stagnation of the Muslim world and Muslims' integration problems in Europe. Hirsi Ali notes Muslim cultures' extreme preoccupation with girls' virginity and the demand for female sexual purity. All responsibility for sexual morality, she emphasizes, is placed on women's shoulders: "From a very young age, girls are surrounded by an atmosphere of mistrust. They learn early that they are untrustworthy beings who constitute a danger for the clan. Something in them drives men crazy" (*The Caged Virgin,* p. 21). This monotonous fixation on girls and women as temptresses and sex objects is supported by sura 24, verse 41, an oft-cited verse of the Koran:

> And tell the believing women to subdue their eyes, and maintain their chastity. They shall not reveal any parts of their bodies, except that which is necessary. They shall cover their chests, and shall not relax this code in the presence of other than their husbands, their fathers, the fathers of their husbands, their sons, the sons of their husbands, their brothers, the sons of their brothers, the sons of their sisters, other women, the male servants or employees whose sexual drive has been nullified, or the children who have not reached puberty. They shall not strike their feet when they walk in order to shake and reveal certain details of their bodies.

Sexualizing relationships

The segregation of the sexes and the veiling of women – the intention of which is to desexualize the relationship between the sexes – usually result in the exact opposite. As Mernissi puts it, sexual segregation leads to "the sexualizing of human relations" (1985:140).

The sexualization of men-women relations in Muslim cultures can also be illustrated by the ways in which unrelated men and women address one another. To desexualize such encounters, they employ kinship terms. For example, when a man of about my own age or younger waits on me at a store in Pakistan, or drives me in a cab, I call him "brother." If the man is considerably older than I am, I call him "uncle." If he is even older, I call him "grandfather." This is a means of indicating that a sexual relationship between us is impossible. Similarly, men use family titles when addressing women. If a woman is sexually harassed, she may say: "Don't you have a sister? Haven't you got a mother?" The point of such questions is to play for empathy by likening oneself to the man's immediate family; they are also attempts to desexualize the situation.

My experience in both Norway and Pakistan is that the thoroughgoing sexualization of human relations, in combination with ignorance and taboos, gives rise to tragedies. It can lead to assaults on children, and especially to abuse within extended families.

Mina's family is an example of this. During the first couple of years I knew Mina, it emerged that another daughter, in addition to the youngest one, had supposedly been sexually abused by a relative. The assailant, according to the girl, was an uncle. It also emerged that the girl, in all probability, had been abused by a male relative several years earlier during a stay in Pakistan. Some time later, in the spring of 2006, Mina contacted us again with more dramatic news: a third daughter, she said, had been sexually assaulted several times. First she had been attacked by an uncle during an overnight visit with relatives; then another uncle had purportedly raped her. This had taken place a year earlier, but she hadn't dared to report it until now, for she'd seen how her younger sister was treated when it came out that her father had sexually assaulted *her*.

After learning of this latest assault, I asked Mina whether she herself, in her childhood, had been subjected to sexual abuse by a relative. She said she had. I asked her directly about this sensitive subject because in my experience, most young Muslim women in Norway who've been in conflict with their relatives have been sexually assaulted at some time or another. Most were abused as children or teenagers by relatives, while some were abused by religious leaders or private tutors during stays in their families' homelands.

One day in 2003, two girls who were related to Mina showed up at my office. They told me they'd' been sexually abused by two of their uncles. The reason why they were telling me was that one of them, as a result of this abuse, was suffering psychological damage that was having a negative effect on her marital life.

This is very uncomfortable information to bring up in public. But it shouldn't be a surprise that sexual assaults on children take place within Muslim extended families. In the West we're accustomed to exposés of sexual abuse of women and children in closed communities rife with sexual taboos, such as the Catholic Church and various Protestant sects. In Pakistan, the abuse of children in extended families (as well as in Islamic boarding schools and other such places) is a familiar story, too.

In the mid 1990s an organization in Islamabad set up evening discussion groups for victims of assault.[109] The organizers told me that the groups had attracted a great many adults who needed to share their pain and sorrow over what they'd been put through as children. The organizers said that they'd been contacted not only by women but also by many men who'd been victims of sexual assault as children. Friends of mine in Pakistan have told me that they never allow their children to be alone with servants or outsiders because they're concerned about the possibility of sexual assault.

Several factors, I think, can account for the sexual abuse of children within Muslim extended families. One of these factors, in my view, is the sexualization of human relations. As Mernissi points out, this sexualization is a result of sexual segregation. Opportunities for normal social interaction with members of the opposite sex only occur, as a rule, within families. As a result, it's difficult for romantic relationships to spring up out of everyday encounters between men and women – since there hardly ever *are* such encounters. The sexual frustration this can lead to – especially among young unmarried men, but also among married men in unhappy family-arranged marriages – renders girls and young women in extended families vulnerable to assault.

The view of women as sex objects – sex objects, moreover, who are personally responsible for ensuring that men are not tempted by them – may also be a factor. As was true in Norway at one time, there is also a widespread lack of respect for and understanding of children's integrity, feelings, and needs, plus a generally low level of respect for girls and women.

Another part of the explanation, I believe, is the lack of respect that boys and men often have for their sisters and female cousins. The fact that boys are also subjected to sexual assaults, usually by non-relatives, can also be explained by segregation: men can easily socialize with boys who are not related to them.

I believe it would ease many people's lives if assaults, especially on small girls by their relatives, were placed on the political agenda in Norway.

Passing on traditions of assault

Islam's view of sex and of women lies at the heart of the challenges involved in the integration of Muslims and the denial of fundamental rights and human dignity to Muslim females. Islam seeks to achieve optimal control of sexuality, seeks to ensure that girls are married off as virgins and become faithful wives. It's to this end that Muslim girls are kept out of swimming classes and denied the opportunity to go camping trips and school expeditions. It's to this end that Muslim girls, especially, take part to a far smaller extent in outdoor activities than other people.[110] It's to this end that Muslim girls are sent back to their parents' homelands during the years before and after puberty. And it's to this end that the age of marriage is generally far lower for Muslim girls than for other girls.

Islam and family-arranged marriages go hand in glove, since love between men and women and pre-marital romance are seen as threats to Muslim society. There's also direct support in Islamic law for the use of force in marriage. Several "classic texts," as Kari Vogt points out (2005:116), give a father or grandfather the right to marry a daughter or granddaughter off with force.

The strict segregation of the sexes is also a major reason for the generally rock-bottom employment rate among Muslim women.[111] In most professions, and at most workplaces, they'd be beyond their husbands' and male relatives' sexual control. Plus a fact, women's employment is prevented by their obligation under Islam to obey. A man can deny his wife the right to work, in addition to which Islam imposes upon her the responsibility for keeping the home and taking care of the children.[112]

In the name of "optimal sexual control," girls are genitally mutilated. This custom is practiced in around half of the countries that are dominated by Muslims, and is not practiced by the majority population in any country dominated by any faith other than Islam. It's wrong, then, to categorically maintain that genital mutilation *doesn't* have anything to do with Islam. True, the Koran doesn't mention the circumcision of women or girls, a custom that arose thousands of years before Islam was founded; but there's a story about Muhammed instructing a woman who circumcised girls to limit the operation, and another about him describing sex as an encounter between two circumcised sexual organs, which is considered an expression of approval for the practice. FGM has indeed come to be seen as one of Muhammed's customs, part of his sunna – which is why two of the four forms of genital mulitation (as we saw in Chapter 5) are called "sunna circumcision."

The two centuries after Muhammed's death saw the formation of groups of religious and legal experts who interpreted Islam. These groups led to four schools of law within Sunni Islam. All four describe the circumcision of girls. The Shafi school puts so much emphasis on Muhammed's statements that it considers the custom obligatory. The Maliki, Hanafi, and Hanbali schools, while not regarding it as obligatory, recommend it. It's therefore correct to say that in countries where FGM is widespread, it's viewed as a matter of obeying Islam's teachings. As Anne Sofie Roald writes: "In those countries where this custom existed prior to Islam, it has been maintained by the Islamic schools of law" (2005:165).

Islam's general acceptance of FGM is also in harmony with the desire to control women's strong and dangerous sexual desire. And it's additionally underscored by the fact that the president of the European Council for Fatwa and Research

(ECFR), Yusuf al-Qaradawi, recommends the practice.[113] Al-Qaradawi, who is considered one of the leading theologians in the Sunni Muslim world, is the key figure behind one of the world's most important websites for Arabic- and English-speaking Muslims.[114] He's also highly respected by the Islamic Association in Norway.[115]

If you look at the spread of genital mutilation in the world, it's obvious that the custom has followed in Islam's footsteps. This is illustrated especially by the fact that it spread across the Indian Ocean from East Africa to Indonesia and Malaysia and became established among various peoples who had embraced Islam's teachings. When orthodox Christian Ethiopians argue for FGM, they can't seek to legitimize it with reference to Christian law or statements by Christian prophets. And if it were true, as some claim, that Islam categorically rejects FGM, you could argue with full justification that, if so, Muslim leaders have failed spectacularly to put a stop to it among the faithful.

The honour killing of girls and woman is another phenomenon that today occurs mostly in the Muslim world – and has now been imported into Muslim communities in Europe. The motives for such murders almost always have something to do with female sexuality or "disobedience" – such as Anooshe's availing herself of the un-Islamic right to divorce in Norway. Suspected adultery is another major reason for such murders.

According to classic Islamic law, extramarital sex is supposed to be punished with whipping and/or stoning to death. Islam's strong emphasis on authority also plays a role here. Muslims are enjoined to obey the oldest men in their families – and, as we've seen, the duty to obey in Muslim cultures is intimately related to the concept of honour. The duty to obey, the concept of honour, and the individual's weak position under Islam combine to create an atmosphere that's ripe for the legitimization of honour killing. Many Muslim religious leaders support honour killing; so do the laws in a number of Muslim countries, where the honour killing of

166

"immoral" women is considered valid in the eyes of both cultural tradition and Islamic theology. It's important to stress here that neither the Koran nor other Islamic writings encourage honour killing; tragically enough, however, a number of Muslims nonetheless view such killing as a religious duty – as could be seen clearly in Olenka Frenkiel's 1999 BBC documentary *Murder in Purdah,* in which men interviewed in a Pakistani village asserted that they were *obliged* under Islam to kill women in their families who brought dishonour upon them.

When a Christian woman from an Arab culture is the victim of an honour killing, it can be much harder to connect the murder to religion. There's nothing in the New Testament that legitimizes such a killing; it must, rather, be understood primarily in a cultural context – an Arab context. That the kind of honour killing which occurs in much of the Muslim world today has never existed in Western culture strengthens the argument that such executions can't easily be connected to Christianity. On the contrary, there's not one country that's dominated today by Christians in which the native Christian population practices honour killing.

In Norwegian debates about forced marriage and honour-related violence, there are constant references to the concept "medieval attitudes and values." The intention is partly to suggest that in Norway, too, our treatment of girls and women was once founded on an extremely patriarchal honour code of the sort that can be found in some immigrant communities today. But this is an unfair way of characterizing medieval Norway. Indeed, the attempt to draw parallels is absolutely misguided. In all of known Norwegian history, back to pagan times, the status of Norwegian women has never been as low as it is today in the communities and territories discussed here. This has been pointed out by Gro Steinsland, a professor of religious history, who told *Aftenposten* on November 15, 2005, that "If we look at phenomena like honour killing, the sanctioning of physical punishment of women, as well as the right to divorce, it can also seem that women's position in many respects was stronger in Norway in the year 900 than it is in some immigrant groups in 2005." When it comes to the reference to the Middle Ages, Professor Ole Jørgen Benedictow pointed out in an op-ed entitled "The Slandered Middle Ages" that Norwegian law in the Middle Ages expected that "marriages would be entered into voluntarily and with consent, and that forced marriage provides a foundation for annulment. Honour-related violence, honour killing, and forced marriage are infringements beyond any legal acceptance" (*Aftenposten,* 20 April 2005).[116]

Islamic law has also established itself on Norwegian soil. In 2003, the "Declaration from the Bridal Couple before Testing of the Marriage Terms," which all brides and grooms in Norway have to sign, was abridged to include a clause asking the bridal couple to recognize each other's equal rights to divorce.[117] The reason for this alteration is that women have limited divorce rights under Islamic law; in order to even have a reasonable hope of securing a divorce, a Muslim woman must be able to prove that her husband was impotent at the time of their marriage, that he's been mentally ill for years, or that he hasn't supported her for several years, is violent, or has prevented her from practicing Islam. Even if one or more of these conditions can be documented, it's still far from certain that a Muslim court will grant a divorce.

A Muslim bride and groom who sign a Norwegian marriage contract are also wed in the presence of a Muslim congregation and sign a Muslim contract specifying the terms of their marriage. This contract is considered binding both by Islamic authorities and by the Muslim community, and for believers it's far more binding than the Norwegian civil contract. Today, if a Muslim woman wants to divorce, Norwegian law, of course, acknowledges her absolute right to do so; but her husband can hold her to their Muslim pact, and thereby force her to remain as married as ever. The annex to "The Declaration from the Bridal Couple" is meant to strengthen a Muslim woman's right to dissolve her marriage in the face of a husband, family, and Muslim community that may oppose her decision.

A comprehensive system

As we have seen, Islam isn't only a religion; it's a set of laws, a social system, and a moral code. Indeed, it's a comprehensive system of norms that provides believers with a complete framework for life. The system of norms – sharia – is universal, in the sense that it applies to all Muslims no matter where they live in the world. Sharia is considered divine law, and far exceeds the scope of secular law, for it covers all aspects of life, including private and public conduct, religious rituals, hygiene, and approved customs. Sharia is divinely ordained, its rules and obligations having supposedly been revealed by Allah and quoted verbatim in the Koran.

In addition, there's Muhammed's so-called exemplary custom, his sunna – that is to say, both his actions and pronouncements as recorded in the so-called hadith. Sharia developed during the three centuries after Muhammed's death, and its basic elements remain essentially the same to this day.

Why is all this relevant to today's Norway and Europe? Precisely because many Muslims do indeed regard sharia as divinely ordained. Like many believing Christians, believing Muslims would place religious commandments and prohibitions above Norwegian law. This isn't essentially problematic in the case of Christians, since the Old Testament, in which brutal punishments are set down in Mosaic law, is regarded by the great majority of Christians as a historical document whose prescriptions are no longer binding. (The exception is found among very minor fundamentalist groups.) It's the New Testament message of charity that counts. Nor would it be easy to extrapolate the Ten Commandments into a full body of law.[118] Sharia, by contrast, represents a major challenge for Norway, Europe, and the Muslim world. Consider, for example, the fact that while Muhammed set down a blanket prohibition on eating pork, he didn't prohibit FGM.

Sharia also prescribes brutal punishments, such as the amputation of thieves' hands and feet and the whipping and stoning to death of adulterers – punishments that are still in force today in countries like Saudi Arabia, Sudan, Nigeria, Iran, and Afghanistan. Sharia also offers instructions and guidelines for prayer, dress, permitted and prohibited food, and much more. If you wanted, you could live by sharia in every detail of your activity from the time you got up in the morning until the moment you went to bed at night.[119]

Islam and human rights

Of Islam's three categories of law, it's family law that is central and that is followed by most Muslim countries. Family law regulates marriage, divorce, child custody, and inheritance. Women are discriminated against in every area of family law – for example, in regard to the bridal gift (*mahr*), which treats women's sexuality as a "commodity" that's paid for in the marriage contract, as Kari Vogt puts it, and that gives the man the right to full control over her (2005:118).

In addition to Islamic family law and criminal law (the latter being far less widely implemented in Muslim countries than the former), sharia includes laws pertaining to religious liberty and freedom of expression. In relation to the international community and human rights, the Islamic world's Achilles heel consists in its stands on women's rights, forms of punishment, religious liberty, and freedom of expression. When the UN's Declaration on Human Rights was drawn up, major Muslim member nations took part in its formulation. When the final version was approved in 1948, only Saudi Arabia voted against it, mainly because it guaranteed religious liberty. But in the years since, as new UN conventions on human rights have been adopted, an increasing number of Muslim countries' governments have refused to make them legally binding within their borders.

As Kari Vogt says: "They reject the laws or accept them only with drastic reservations.... The objections that are raised are always the same: everything that touches on religion and sex is controversial. This has to do with women's legal status, questions about equality before the law, plus all questions concerning religious freedom and freedom of expression. Islamic criminal law is also problematic from the perspective of human rights" (2005:112).

The Muslim opposition to the Declaration's provisions about women is summed up as follows by Moroccan scriptural scholar Muhammed Naceri: "The Universal Declaration of Human Rights was for complete equality for men and women. For us, women are equal to men in law, but they are not the same as men, and they can't be allowed to wander around freely in the streets like some kind of animal."[120]

How unwavering Muslim countries are in their view of sharia was clearly articulated in the Cairo Declaration on Human Rights in Islam, the Islamic world's own human-rights declaration.[121] It begins by maintaining that Muslim nations are superior: "God has made the Islamic fellowship of believers the best nation."[122] It further states that the "divine commandments" stem from holy books and from Muhammed, "the last prophet." The declaration includes the following statements:

- "It is prohibited to take away life except for a Shari'ah-prescribed reason."

- "Safety from bodily harm is a guaranteed right. It is the duty of the state to safeguard it, and it is prohibited to breach it without a Shari'ah-prescribed reason."

- "Every human being is entitled to inviolability and the protection of his good name and honour during his life and after his death."

- "Men and women have the right to marriage, and no restrictions stemming from race, colour or

171

nationality shall prevent them from enjoying this right."

- "Woman is equal to man in human dignity, and has rights to enjoy as well as duties to perform….. The husband is responsible for the support and welfare of the family."

- "Parents and those in such like capacity have the right to choose the type of education they desire for their children, provided they take into consideration the interest and future of the children in accordance with ethical values and the principles of the Shari'ah."

- "Both parents are entitled to certain rights from their children…in accordance with the tenets of the Shari'ah."

- "The State…shall guarantee educational diversity in the interest of society so as to enable man to be acquainted with the religion of Islam and the facts of the Universe for the benefit of mankind."

- "Islam is the religion of unspoiled nature. It is prohibited to exercise any form of compulsion on man or to exploit his poverty or ignorance in order to convert him to another religion or to atheism."

- "Every man shall have the right, within the framework of Shari'ah, to free movement and to select his place of residence whether inside or outside his country and, if persecuted, is entitled to seek asylum in another country. The country of refuge shall ensure his protection until he reaches safety, unless asylum is motivated by an act which Shari'ah regards as a crime."

- "Everyone shall have the right to enjoy the fruits of his scientific, literary, artistic or technical production and the right to protect the moral and material interests stemming therefrom, provided that such production is not contrary to the principles of Shari'ah."

- "There shall be no crime or punishment except as provided for in the Shari'ah."

- "Everyone shall have the right to express his opinion freely in such manner as would not be contrary to the principles of the Shari'ah."

- "Everyone shall have the right to advocate what is right, and propagate what is good, and warn against what is wrong and evil according to the norms of Islamic Shari'ah."

- "Information is a vital necessity to society. It may not be exploited or misused in such a way as may violate sanctities and the dignity of Prophets, undermine moral and ethical values or disintegrate, corrupt or harm society or weaken its faith."

The Declaration's last two articles state: "All the rights and freedoms stipulated in this Declaration are subject to the Islamic Shari'ah." And: "The Islamic Shari'ah is the only source of reference for the explanation or clarification to any of the articles of this Declaration."

The Cairo Declaration can hardly be called a human-rights declaration; it is, rather, a "sharia rights declaration," whose purpose is to protect God, not man. Utterly absent from it, for example, is any hint of political or civil rights. "Rights" would appear to mean the right to be Muslim – and the duty to remain Muslim. The Declaration's purpose is to specify the individual's obligations under the divine sharia.

Thus the Declaration, in its discussion of "the right to marriage," mentions religion but not race, colour, or nationality – since under sharia a woman is free only to marry a Muslim. Thus the Declaration – in accordance with sharia – forbids criticism of Islam and permits the taking of human life. Thus the Declaration threatens those who leave Islam with punishment – since sharia prohibits apostasy from Islam. Thus the Declaration says that women and men have the same dignity, but not that they're equal – since sharia imposes upon them specific roles and obligations. Thus the Declaration prohibits free thought in science and art – lest the divine sharia from be revealed for what it is: a set of rules, laws, and norms formulated by human beings in a time when there was no respect for the inviolability of the individual; a time when the individual was, indeed, only an indissoluble part of the tribe.

The UN on stagnation and lack of freedom

This unshakable view of Islam and sharia as mankind's liberation and salvation has had catastrophic consequences for individuals as well as for society. Three times since the turn of the century, the UN has published reports on development in the Arab world.[123] The reports examine the last thirty years' development, or lack thereof, in the Arab League's twenty-two member countries. The reports, written by Arabs, have shocked both Arabs and the international community, for they have shown that social, political, and economic conditions in Arabic countries were far worse than had been thought.

The UN has determined that the Arab world suffers from three basic failings: a lack of freedom of expression, a lack of knowledge, and a lack of women's emancipation, which amounts to a veritable waste of half of the population's resources. An authoritarian style of childrearing serves to suppress curiosity and hunger for knowledge, the report says. Arab society encourages collective thinking and invites passivity and a low level of social involvement. Both Islam and Arab political systems crush individuals' self-confidence and sense of independence.

The Arab countries' oil reserves are significant, and many of these countries are among the world's richest. It's nonetheless here that you'll find the world's highest unemployment rates. Economic development can't even be described as limping along, according to the UN's reports. The total gross national product of all the Arabic countries put together is just slightly higher than Spain's. One in five Arabs lives on less than two dollars a day. In the world, on average, it takes around ten years for people to double their income; in the Arabic world today, it would take 140 years. According to the UN, when it comes to the freedom of its citizens (and especially its women), the Arab region comes at the very bottom of the list, even lower than the poorest parts of sub-Saharan Africa.

A major symptom of this underdevelopment and lack of freedom is the fact that half of the young people in the Arab world want to leave it. The dream of migration is especially connected to poor educational opportunities and a lean labour market. Of 280 million inhabitants, sixty-five million are illiterates. Ten million children don't attend school. During the last millennium, the Arab world has translated the same number of books from other parts of the world that Spain does annually. Strict censorship is one reason why a bestseller in the Arab world rarely has a print run of more than five thousand copies. Only one percent of the world's scientists can be found in the Arab world. The brain drain is massive.

The UN's 2003 report says that Islam has a tradition of encouraging knowledge and tolerance. But today's Muslim world is distinguished by an alliance between oppressive political systems and reactionary interpreters of Islam with hostile attitudes toward development and progress. "Certain Muslim educational institutions," the report says, are viewed as impediments to development and modernization.[124] And then comes the criticism that is perhaps the hardest for the Arab League to take: the Arab UN reporters believe that modernity and development are *not* created by mixing politics and religion in the way that the Cairo Declaration on Human Rights does. The UN points to the need for new perspectives, such as a focus on "the creation of paradise on earth and the enjoyment of the earth's bounties."

Or, as Ayaan Hirsi Ali puts it: there must be an end to the idea that "life on earth is merely a transitory stage before the hereafter" (*The Caged Virgin,* p. x).

The report points to concrete areas in which the Arab countries need to improve: "curiosity, reason, science, the senses, vision and feelings." As for religion, the report concludes that Arabs must return to "a civilized, moral and humanitarian vision"; that religion must be given "independence from political authorities, governments, states, and radical religious-political movements"; and that "intellectual freedom" must be recognized and "the right to differ in doctrines, religious schools and intepretations" preserved. [125]

When I studied the UN reports on the Arab world, my thoughts turned several times to Pakistan, and especially to the schools in Little Norway where so many Norwegian citizens receive their education – where children are raised in religious conformity; where there's precious little in the way of intellectual curiosity and independent thinking; where visions and emotions are suppressed; where children are fed with their mother's milk on the idea that they should subordinate themselves to parents, teachers, religious leaders, and other authorities; where they're taught, both in words and by the example of what they see every day in their gender-divided surroundings, that women are second-class citizens; and where boys and girls learn that "life on earth is only a passage to the beyond," and that the only legitimate way to lead one's life is to subordinate oneself uncritically to Allah, Muhammed, the Koran, and sharia.

176

As in the Arab countries, development in Pakistan has gone in one basic direction: backwards. There has been increasing cultural stagnation and disintegration, and increasing spiritual confinement owing to Islam's growing influence on the life of society.

Reading the UN reports, I recalled what I had candidly told *Dagbladet* on 3 August 2006, in my first interview on integration problems. I explained what I saw as crucial obstacles to the integration of Muslims into Western culture: Islam's oppressive view of women, its all-embracing ideology of purity, and the sexual segregation that results from these things and that closes women out of the public square. I was far more correct than I realized at the time.

7

The Muslims' Challenge:

What Went Wrong?

In the previous chapter we saw that the Arab part of the Muslim world, in particular, has decayed in learning and is now, by pretty much all societal measures, a backwater. What went wrong?

A major explanation for this decline, the UN reports indicate, is Islam's negative view of women. This is also the thesis of the book *What Went Wrong? Western Impact and Middle Eastern Response* (2002) by the man who may be the leading expert on Islam today, historian Bernard Lewis. The following is principally based on Lewis's account of Islam's period of greatness and decline.

After Muhammed's death in the year 632, his followers conquered most of the world that was then known to Europe, including parts of Europe itself. Over the course of little more than a century, Islam subdued an area larger than the Roman Empire. The Islamic kingdom stretched from Christian North Africa in the West to Hindu India in the east. In the year 711, the Muslim army crossed the Straits of Gibraltar and captured Spain.

Islam's rapid expansion was based on the Koranic principle of jihad – in a belligerent sense, not in a sense of personal striving to follow the way of Allah and struggle against evil. The expansion also owed much to the fact that the Arab tribes had managed to come together under a single language, a common culture, and a shared political system. Everyone was held in Islam's embrace; everyone had received the calling, final and perfect for all eternity. Muslims were also motivated by the need to transcribe the Koran, collect the hadith, and interpret both. These tasks inspired immense energy and incentive.

From India, the Muslims borrowed the decimal system. They translated into Arabic the ancient Greek philosophical works of Aristotle and others. Philosophy, science, and art blossomed. There was progress in both mathematics and medicine. Islam became the world's greatest military and economic power. During these first centuries after Muhammed's death, in short, Islam was at its zenith. This era is called Islam's Golden Age, and during it large areas of Europe, developmentally speaking, lagged far behind the Muslim world.

Not until around the year 1000 did Europe start to awaken. In both Spain and Italy, the Muslims were gradually pushed back, and the Crusades, which were a response to the Muslim conquests of Jerusalem and the "Holy Land," began in 1095. The wars went on for centuries, and by the end of the 1400s Europe's Muslim rulers had pretty much been driven from the continent. These conflicts, however, are not central to this book. What *is* central to it is the question of why the Muslims declined from greatness into backwardness.

The answer has a lot to do with the previously mentioned theologian al-Ghazali. Ghazali sabotaged the close relationship between Islam and Greek philosophy – a philosophy that stands for self-realization, reason, critical reflection, rationality, and science. Ghazali believed that the Koran should be understood literally. In and of itself, this was nothing new; but when a leading figure of his caliber preached such a view, it had crucial significance. Reason was tossed out in favour of belief. Ghazali represented irrationality, force, sacrifice for the sake of the collectivity – values that, as world history has shown repeatedly, lead to oppression and dictatorship, poverty and cultural stagnation.

179

During these first centuries after Muhammed's death, Islam underwent a period of interpretation and formation at the hands of many legal scholars. But in the tenth century A.D., most scholars closed the door on further interpretation of the texts, which is known as ijtihad. They introduced the principle called taqlid – the doctrine of following one's predecessors, that is to say the classical Muslim jurists (Stang Dahl 1992:47). For Islam, this marked the end of the road. The answers to all of life's questions, small and large, both on the individual and societal level, had already been worked out for all time; henceforth, Muslims would simply echo, and live by, the divine truths that earlier religious authorities had set down once and for all. Ghazali, then, didn't put an end to ijtihad singlehandedly.[126]

Another factor Lewis points to as contributing to Islam's decline is that Muslims, during these first centuries, regarded Europeans as stupid, backward, and (not surprisingly) bestial. In addition, they viewed the countries of Europe as the lands of the infidels, where they would prefer not to travel.

"The doctors of the Holy Law for the most part prohibited such journeys," Lewis writes (2002:37). The Muslims thus had very little to do with the unconquered portion of Europe – which is to say the greater part of it. As a result, they remained largely unaffected by Europe's scientific awakening, technological progress, and journeys of discovery.

By the time of the Renaissance (which began in the late 1300s) the Europeans had made significance progress in science and art; they took over the Muslims' scientific, technological, and cultural heritage, even the Muslims' desire for knowledge from without was dying out. In the Islamic world, writes Lewis, "independent inquiry virtually came to an end, and science was for the most part reduced to the veneration of a corpus of approved knowledge" (2002:78).

Not until the 1700s, and after many military defeats and much lost territory, were Muslims' curiosity about and desire for European knowledge awakened. They wanted to catch up with Europeans' military advances precisely in order to renew their struggle against Europe's armies. They went to Vienna and Paris to learn. But for them, according to Lewis, acknowledging that the Europeans' progress was connected to "the underlying philosophy and the sociopolitical context of these scientific achievements" was highly problematic (2002:81). Relations between the sexes in Europe posed a special challenge.

The Enlightenment of the 1700s was absolutely crucial to Europe's further blossoming. It was a time of liberation for the individual and of rebellion against social oppression and dictatorship. The Enlightenment attributed critical reason and freedom to the individual. Citizens were given rights that the state committed itself to ensuring. This led, in turn, to greater freedom of expression and a growth in the life of organizations.

The child born of this long process was European democracy. The Enlightenment was also crucial for the development of women's rights.

No Golden Age for women

Muslims' view of the relations between men and women in Europe can be illustrated by an example from 1665, when a Turkish envoy visited Vienna and reported on an "extraordinary spectacle." Lewis quotes him: "Whenever the emperor meets a woman in the street, if he Is riding, he brings his horse to a standstill and lets her pass. If the Emperor is on foot and meets a woman, he stands in a posture of politeness. The woman greets the emperor, who then takes his hat off his hed to show respect for the woman. After the woman has passed, the emperor continues on his way. It is indeed an extraordinary spectacle" (2002:65).

The position of women was, according to Lewis, "one of the most striking contrasts between Christian and Muslim practice." Muslims who visited Europe spoke "with astonishment, often with horror, of the immodesty and frowardness of Western women, of the incredible freedom and absurd deference accorded to them." They also said that

European men didn't exhibit jealousy of women's "immorality and promiscuity" (2002:66).

There are three groups that according to Islamic law and tradition should not enjoy legal and religious equality: slaves, infidels, and women. In one crucial sense, women are entirely at the bottom. A slave can be freed, and an infidel can convert to Islam and become a full citizen. "Only the woman was doomed forever to remain what she was – or so it seemed at the time," writes Lewis (2002:69). When Europeans acquired strength and influence and also colonized parts of the Muslim world, they used their influence to secure rights for Christians, a change by which Jews, too, profited. The struggle to free slaves was carried out with weapons in hand. But the Europeans showed no interest in putting an end to Muslims' oppression of women; indeed, careful not to offend Muslims on this score, they followed "conservative social policies" in regard to women (2002:69). This history recalls the situation in today's Europe, where politicians fail to use their power – to use the *law* – to lift Muslim women out of their inequality.

From the perspective of women's rights, it is highly misleading to refer to the first centuries after Muhammed's passing as Islam's Golden Age. In the Muslim world, women have never had a Golden Age. On the contrary, it was during the so-called Golden Age that not only Islam, but also the subordinate role of women in Islam, took shape under the influence of the leading theologians of the day. A notorious statement by al-Ghazali that dates back to the so-called Golden Age – a statement that tells us a great deal about women's status under Islam and that is frequently cited in literature on Islam and women – is this:

> She should stay home and work at spinning, she should not go out often, she must not be well informed, nor must she talk to the neighbours, and only visit them if it is totally necessary. She should take care of her husband and respect him both when he is present and when he is away, and try

182

to satisfy him in all things. She must not deceive him or nag him for money. She must not leave the house without his permission, and if she receives this permission, she must go unnoticed. She should dress in old clothes and use empty streets and alleys, avoid marketplaces, and make sure that no stranger is able to hear her voice or recognize her. She must not speak to any of her husband's friends even in case of an emergency....The only things she should worry about are her virtue, her home, and prayers and fasting. If a friend of her husband comes on a visit while he is away, she must not open the door or answer him, in order to protect herself and her husband's honour. She should accept what her man gives her as sufficient to her sexual needs at any time.

Ghazali goes on to warn men against women, because the latter's "dissimulation is enormous and their evil inventions are dangerous; they are immoral and ill-natured ...It is a fact that all tests, accidents, and sorrows that affect a man come from women."[127]

Woman-friendly voices, but...

The earliest example of advocacy for women's rights by a Muslim was found by Lewis in an 1867 article by Namik Kemal: "Our women are now seen as serving no useful purpose to mankind other thsan having children; they are considered simply as serving for pleasure, like musical instruments or jewels. But they constitute half and perhaps more than half of our species. Preventing them from contributing to the sustenance and improvement of others by means of their efforts infringes the basic rules of public cooperation to such an degree that our national society is stricken like a human body that is paralyzed on one side....Many evil consequences result from this position of women, the first being that it leads to a bad upbringing for their children" (2002:70).[128]

Kemal's criticism didn't lead to any improvement in the situation of Muslim women. But a book published a few years later, in 1899, created more of a stir. Entitled *Woman's Liberation,* it was written by a young Egyptian jurist, Qasim Amin, who had lived in Paris and whose French lover had apparently had a certain influence on him. He wanted to improve women's position through education, employment, and social participation. His boldest suggestions were to remove the veil, reinterpret the Koran's view of polygamy, and change divorce laws that made it easy for men (but not women) to dissolve a marriage. A free society demands that all its citizens be free, Amin believed. He attempted to ground his arguments in Islamic belief, but his book led to "a very strong reaction from the traditionalist establishment in Egypt and elsewhere," Lewis says (2002:71). Over thirty polemical books were written attacking him. Amin was later called "the father of Egyptian feminism."

During this epoch, there was some positive movement in the Muslim world, largely thanks to European influences. The right to own slaves was abolished, and concubinage was forbidden in most regions. In Tunisia, Turkey, and Persia under the Shahs, polygamy was forbidden, while some other countries put limits on it.

But the most important form that progress for women took in the 1900s had to do with personal finances. According to Islam, women have a right to own property, and during this period this right was widely granted. The wars fought by the Ottoman Empire in the early twentieth century created a need for more workers, which led to the introduction of women into the workforce (just as would later occur in the West during World War II); and since the Ottoman men were at war, their wives also had to take care of day-to-day finances. As a result of all this, more and more women began to study; some also began careers as teachers and nurses. But it wasn't long before a reaction set in. Militant Islamists strongly opposed (among much else) women teachers, a concept which violated their principle of sexual segregation.

The founder of the modern Turkish state, Kemal Ataturk, spoke warmly in the 1920s of the complete liberation of women, which he saw as the route to modernity. His woman-friendly ideology went hand in hand with his republic's focus on the expansion of political rights. In other Muslim countries, however, political rights were a non-issue. Most of these countries were governed by the military or by a single dictatorial party, and in most of them, such as Saddam Hussein's Iraq, the majority of the population enjoyed very little freedom.

Women's rights have fared the worst in places where fundamentalist groups have had significance influence on the government or have governed outright, a situation of which Iran and Afghanistan are the most obvious contemporary examples. Most Muslim countries today particularly pine for technological modernization. Their motives aren't necessarily noble; often it's a matter of needing to lubricate the engines of war, or (in the most extreme cases) of wanting to commit terrorist acts.

It's precisely here that we can isolate a crucial factor in Islam's inability to adapt itself to the modern world. Western technology is accepted because it's necessary; but women's liberation isn't. Women's liberation is seen as a matter of Europeanizing, of Christianizing. As Lewis points out, conservative Muslims view women's liberation as "a betrayal of true Islamic values," as something that "must be kept from entering the body of Islam" (2002:73).

The history of Muslim attire illustrates very well the difference between what's seen as necessary modernization and what's viewed as unhealthy Europeanization. By the 1800s, Muslims had modernized their armies by equipping soldiers with Western-inspired uniforms. These changes were militarily useful: they made it harder for deserters to skip off unidentified.

Then Muslims westernized the attire of public servants. Today in the Muslim world, men in major cities and in government positions are almost always dressed in Western-inspired clothing. Only the tie is omitted, since it's seen as distinctly Western, and probably because it reminds some people of a cross. But, as Lewis says, the women are never "compelled to adopt Western dress or to abandon traditional attire.

Indeed, if the matter arose at all in public relations, it was in the form of a prohibition, not a requirement" (2002:75). In short, Western clothing on men is *modernity;* Western clothing on women is *Europeanization.* And since Europe is Christian, Europeanization is synonymous with religious decadence and falling away from true Islam. The major exception is in Turkey, where Kemal Ataturk made it illegal for women to cover up. Today it's still illegal there for female government workers or university students to wear veils. The same is true in Tunisia.

Signs of opposition to women's "Europeanization" can still be observed among the majority of Muslims in Norway. Most of the men wear Western clothing (though without a tie), while most of the women dress according to the codes of Islam and their homelands.

Scapegoats, yes; self-scrutiny, no

Muslims have found one scapegoat after another to explain their civilization's regression. First it was the Mongolians, because of their invasions in the thirteenth century. Then the Arabs and Turks blamed each other. The Persians have pointed fingers variously at the Arabs, Turks, and Mongolians. In recent times, with nineteenth- and twentieth-century French and British colonialism, Western imperialism was, naturally enough, offered up as the principal reason for Islam's decline. Lewis doesn't conceal the fact that the colonial era influenced the Arabs politically, economically, and culturally, and "changed the face of the region and transformed the lives of its people" (2002:153). But the Arabs' stagnation had definitely begun long before colonial times, and was in fact a decisive factor in the region's colonization.

In today's Muslim world it is not only political leaders who rage against the West; the commonfolk do, too. In Pakistan, their targets are the U.S. and Britain. (They look down on

Western women as well.) They accuse the U.S. of imperialism, while placing much of the responsibility on the British, as former colonial lords, for everything that's gone wrong in their country. The Muslims, who conquered much of the subcontinent by the sword only shortly after Muhammed's death, are never blamed. Westerners, they often say, treat women disrespectfully: Western women have to work and are immoral and promiscuous. They often cite the high divorce rate as evidence that Western women are the victims of cynical exploitation.

On his list of reasons for the Muslim rage at the West, Lewis also includes the Israeli-Palestinian conflict and the Western support for corrupt and oppressive regimes in the Muslim world.[129] The real reason for that rage, however, lies in the West's fundamental values, especially its secularity and its view of women. This-worldliness, capitalism, democracy, individualism, sexual equality: these are the West's true-born children, and they have been adopted around the globe. It's this fact that rouses the Islamic world to such violent ire – for these Western values are intensely antithetical to the values that are the very essence of Islam. It's the struggle for values that fuels Muslim rage against the West. It makes Muslims feel that their religion should be even more fully protected, and it leads them to dive headfirst into the role of victim. As a result, the Muslim world loses even more ground, politically and socially. And this, in turn, leads Muslims to engage in cultural self-exaltation and to scour their scriptures for answers to the challenges they face both in private life and in society generally. For if Islam holds within itself the absolute and divine truth, it must – mustn't it? – also contain the recipe for creating a good and powerful society.

The fact that the medicine that's inevitably prescribed is greater doses of Islam – and of more "correct" Islam – is also consistent with what I've experienced in countless personal conversations in Pakistan. I've discovered that even for celebrated feminists, Islam is the principal starting point for a discussion of any social problem, including the oppression of women. And in discussing these problems, they employ Islamic

187

argumentation – citing, for example, a hadith which says that "paradise lies at mother's feet." This same hadith is also served up as "evidence" of how highly Islam values women. The Islamization of society and law, especially under the Pakistani dictator Zia ul-Haq, is defined as *negative* Islamization.

We're thus meant to understand that there's such a thing as a *positive* Islamization – one that would involve a focus on other scriptural prescriptions and other interpretations of the faith as it originally existed. When you discuss social challenges with educated Muslims, only rarely do the solutions they propose not incorporate Islam. And you constantly hear this: "We're not good enough Muslims. Islam says...." – followed by a reference to *true* Islam, an Islam in which (for example) the role of women is defined more or less literally, in which moderation is put forth as a solution, where deference and humility on the part of individuals are recommended. And each point will be accompanied by specific scriptural citations.

It seems to be impossible for Muslims to acknowledge that it's precisely Islam's dominant role in their society that is the reason for its miseries. Such an admission, it appears, would be too humiliating. It's easier to blame others –the U.S., Israel, the West generally.

Today, the U.S. is the leading scapegoat in the Muslim world. Yet as Lewis puts it, the American influence in the region is "a consequence, not a cause, of the inner weakness of Middle-Eastern states and societies" (2002:153). It's striking that former British colonies that aren't predominantly Muslim, such as Singapore and Hong Kong, have thrived in the post-colonial era, while such Muslim ex-colonies as Pakistan and Gambia have not. Note, too, the contrast between India and Pakistan – two countries which were ruled by the same colonial lords during the same period.

In his book *Terror and Liberalism,* the left-wing American writer Paul Berman notes that the scapegoating of America in the Muslim world is a paradox, for "in all of recent history, no country on earth has fought so hard and consistently as the

United States on behalf of Muslim populations" as the U.S. Among other things, Berman points to the intervention in Somalia "which was intended to feed the Muslim masses" as well as "to crush the Muslim few who stood in the way" (2003:17). Similarly, a Pakistani who writes under the pseudonym Ibn Warraq points out in his book *Why I Am Not a Muslim* (2003) that the U.S. has more often intervened "on behalf of Muslims than against them. The U.S. protected Saudi Arabia and Kuwait against Iraq, Afghanistan against the Soviet Union, Bosnia and Kosovo against Yugoslavia, and Somalia against the warlord Muhammed Farah Aidid."

Even as people in the Muslim world blame its political and social wretchedness on forces beyond its borders, they churn out reams of ardent rhetoric about a return to "true" Islam. One manifestation of this enthusiasm for "true" Islam has been the recent growth of Islamist groups. For at the heart of the Islamist movement is the dream of restoring pure Islam – or of restoring (to quote the Cairo Declaration) Islam's "uncorrupted nature," which means turning away from all the values that the West stands for.

The rise of political Islam

Today's Islamism is nothing new. Islamic history offers many examples of "sectarian movements with political ambitions," and often with violent traits. By the 600s, political opponents were already being executed, and in the century following the year 1000 several "feared terror groups" were established, according to Kari Vogt (2005:239). The best known political group that was founded in the twentieth century, and that continues to be important today, is the Muslim Brotherhood in Egypt. The Brotherhood first came on the scene in 1928. The major motive for its founding was Kemal Ataturk's secularization of Turkey, which roiled the Muslim world. Ataturk's liquidation of the remains of the caliphate, the Ottoman Empire, was met with consternation by political

Muslims, especially the man who would come to found the Brotherhood, Hasan al-Banna. Al-Banna's vision, according to Paul Berman, was precisely the opposite: to resurrect the caliphate and restore the Islamic world's seventh-century Golden Age (2003:83). The Brotherhood's founding was understood as a reaction not only to Ataturk's virtually blasphemous act of throwing the caliphate overboard, but to the importation of Western values that was facilitated by British colonization. The Brotherhood believed that the sociopolitical problems of Egypt and the Arabic world were rooted in the separation of state and religion.

In addition to Hasan al-Banna, the key figures in the rise of political and militant Islam during the last century were the Indo-Pakistani Abu Ala Mawdudi, the Egyptian Sayyid Qutb, and the Iranian Ayatollah Khomeini. In the context of this book, al-Banna, Mawdudi, and Qutb are of particular interest – Mawdudi, because the politico-religious movement he started on the subcontinent before World War II was firmly established in Norway in 1974 as a result of Pakistani immigration; Qutb and al-Banna, because their heir is the leading European-born Muslim ideologue in today's Europe, Tariq Ramadan.

The Brotherhood began primarily as a missionary movement, but quickly turned its hand to "revolutionary subversion," according to Paul Berman (2003:86). Its explicit goal was a sharia-run Egypt, an Egypt in which Islam and the state would be clad in new, more modern attire. Hassan al-Banna's ideology, according to Kari Vogt, was formulated in these words: "Political power is in Islam's nature, for if the Koran provides a law, it is presupposing a state that can enforce the law" (2005:246).

Appealing as it did to a politically oppressed people with significant social needs, the Brotherhood grew quickly into a mass movement. By around 1940, it had about two thousand branches spread across Egypt, plus additional branches in other Muslim countries such as Jordan, Syria, Sudan, Iraq, and Lebanon. As a result, it gained considerable political power.

Precisely for this reason, it was banned by Egypt's secular government. In 1949 al-Banna was killed, probably by order of Egyptian authorities. Egypt's leader, Gamal Abdel Nasser, then lifted the ban, only to be assassinated. His murder was attributed to the Brotherhood, and the movement was once again banned.

From Qutb to al-Qaradawi

At about this time, Sayyid Qutb (1906-1966), an Egyptian, was studying in the U.S. In 1951, he returned to Egypt and joined the Brotherhood. Paul Berman characterizes Qutb as "the movement's leading thinker – the Arabic world's first important theoretician of the Islamist cause" (2003:85). Qutb's last and most radical book, *Milestones* (published in 1964), is Islamism's most widely read and discussed polemic. Among Qutb's accomplishments was his development of the idea of *jahiliyya,* the pre-Islamic pagan society, which he, as an Islamist, had definitely experienced in the woman-friendly, capitalistic, secular, and democratic U.S. In *Milestones* he passionately takes on all *jahiliyya* societies, including godless Communist societies and capitalist societies (which, in his eyes, were also godless).

In short, he assailed all societies that aren't founded on Islam's divine principles and toward which one therefore shouldn't show the slightest loyalty. In one work after another, he preached sharia and a literal interpretation of the Koran and explained, down to the last detail, the divine rules governing such matters as divorce, the remarriage of widows, marriage outside one's own religion, and the kind of clothing Allah prefers.

His explicitly articulated goal was to bring the whole world under Islam. And to attain Islamic world domination, it wasn't sufficient just to engage in verbal jihad; the repeal of man-made laws and the establishment of Allah's dominion on earth could only be accomplished through a combination of verbal and armed jihad. Qutb's book *Milestones* is regarded at the Brotherhood's manifesto, and is often compared to Adolf

Hitler's *Mein Kampf.* For today's terrorists, Qutb, with his hatred for the West's "moral decline," is a major inspiration.

The Brotherhood is believed to be the richest and most influential Islamic organization in the world today. It likes to present itself as peaceful, but it views violence as a legitimate political means. It goal is to spread totalitarian Islam around the entire world. Today, its ideological leader is the president of the European Council for Fatwa and Research, Yusuf al-Qaradawi. This is the same man who, as we have seen, has proclaimed fatwas about the genital mutilation of girls. He has also proclaimed fatwas to the effect that Muslim woman can only marry Muslim men, that polygamy is permitted, that the veil is compulsory, and that homosexuals should be punished in the same way that Islam punishes sex outside of marriage: with whipping and stoning to death. A much-quoted statement of al-Qaradawi's is this: "With Allah's will, Islam will return to Europe and Europeans will convert to Islam. Then they will be able to spread Islam to the whole world." He then adds these reassuring words: "I guarantee that this time the conquest will not take place by the sword but with the help of conversion and ideology."[130] Because of terrorism charges, al-Qaradawi fled from Egypt and settled in Qatar.[131]

Tariq Ramadan and Euro-Islam

Tariq Ramadan is the grandson of the Brotherhood's founder, Hasan al-Banna. He's also the son of Said Ramadan, who took over the leadership of the Brotherhood from al-Banna, his father-in-law. Said Ramadan fled to Europe in 1958, as thousands of other members of the Muslim Brotherhood did around 1960, because their political ambitions led to government persecution.

In the more than forty years since then, the Brotherhood's members have established well-organized networks of mosques, charitable associations, and other groups in Europe, with financial backing from Arab governments. Of all the European nations where the Brotherhood has put down roots, they go deepest in Germany,[132] though the organization is also well-established in both Britain and France. In Sweden, the Brotherhood is among the leading Muslim organizations.[133] And throughout Europe it has managed to forge close ties to political leaders. The examples are many. I will mention only illuminating event. In 2004, the then mayor of London, Ken Livingstone of the Labour Party, literally embraced the Brotherhood's ideological leader, Yusuf al-Qaradawi. Because al-Qaradawi supports Palestinian and Iraqi suicide bombers, he's denied entry into the U.S. But Livingstone, who is nicknamed "Red Ken," described al-Qaradawi as a religious scholar who "preaches moderation and tolerance" and said it was an "honour" to be visited by him. This happened at a London meeting that was attended by about 250 European Muslim delegates. Al-Qaradawi, the meeting's principal attraction, held a lecture about Muslim women's right to wear hijab. The visit occasioned criticism, especially by gay people, owing to al-Qaradawi's death fatwa for homosexuals; but Livingstone apologized to al-Qaradawi for the criticism and characterized it as "hysteria" – and even invited al-Qaradawi to make another political visit to London.[134]

Tariq Ramadan's father, Said Ramadan, is suspected of having had institutional and economic ties to terror networks.[135] One reason for these suspicions is that the Ramadan family in Switzerland is closely associated with the Islamic bank in that country, Al-Taqwa, which is used by al-Qaida to finance terror. Said Ramadan was, as it happens, one of the bank's founders.[136] He was also a founder of the Muslim World League in Saudi Arabia, which has sent billions of Saudi oil dollars to fundamental Muslim groups worldwide. The league seeks to spread to Europe the Saudi ideology of Wahhabism, which is extremely conservative and puritanical.[137] Said Ramadan also drew the attention of international intelligence services because of the centre that he founded in collaboration with the Brotherhood in Switzerland, the Islamic Centre of Geneva. The doctor and terrorist who is Osama bin Ladin's right hand, Ayman al-Zawahiri, is supposed to have used this centre as a base after he was released from an Egyptian prison for participation in the murder of President Anwar Sadat in 1981. Al-Zawahiri then fled Egypt.

The European-born Tariq Ramadan, then, is the child and grandchild of the Brotherhood's central figures. Educated as a philosopher, Tariq Ramadan is described by European critics as the leading European Islamist ideologue of our time. He is the founder of so-called Euro-Islam, a form of Islam that is, he maintains, a non-fundamentalist version of Islam, and that he argues will enable new generations of Muslims in Europe to practice Islam in modern secular states.[138] Ramadan has considerable political influence, and enjoys the respect of leading Muslims in Norway.[139] He is denied entry into the U.S. because he is suspected of having ties to al-Qaida.

In a number of important books and articles, leading European experts on Islamism have revealed Ramadan to be an Islamist in sheep's clothing.[140] For many observers, the single episode that most vividly illuminated his "message about European values" occurred in 2003. It began when Ramadan's brother, Professor Hani Ramadan, was suspended by the Swiss government from his position as a secondary-school teacher. The suspension was a reaction to the support that Hani Ramadan had expressed in several articles for the requirement under sharia law that adulterers be stoned to death – which, as Hani Ramadan explained, was not simply a matter of punishment but of "purification." This caused a scandal – which Tariq Ramadan took to a higher level when, in a prime-time debate with French foreign minister Nicolas Sarkozy on the TV channel France 2, he refused to reject his brother's argument.

Jens Tomas Anfindsen, a philosopher who is the editor of the Norwegian website HonestThinking.org, lives in Switzerland and monitored the broadcast on France 2. In an op-ed that appeared in *Dagbladet* on 13 July 2005, he recounted the French TV program and the reactions that followed. Sarkozy's unambiguous opposition to Islamism, as described by Anfindsen, contrasted dramatically with Norwegian politicians' – and journalists' – passivity in the face of Muslim extremists.

"It was Saturday," wrote Anfindsen, "and it was prime time. Tariq Ramadan was to meet France's foreign minister, Nicolas Sarkozy, on a popular discussion program on France 2. The newspapers had warmed up the audience for this broadcast several days in advance. Some scattered, feeble voices attempted to sow doubt about Ramadan's credibility. Ramadan, they said, was an Islamist in sheep's clothing, an ingratiating version of his grandfather, founder of the feared Muslim Brotherhood. But the great majority of commentators found these complaints monstrous: who, after all, chooses his own grandfather? Few wanted to put much weight on the fact that Ramadan's brother, Professor Hani Ramadan, had argued in several articles for stoning as a punishment for adultery, and in one specific case had actually defended the stoning of a Moroccan woman. Who, after all, is his brother's keeper? But Sarkozy had taken note of it. Sarkozy's voice boomed over several million TV sets: 'Monsieur Ramadan, your brother has defended, explained, and found good reasons to support stoning of adulteresses. Stoning a woman, is this something monstrous or not?' Three times, in slightly different versions, Sarkozy asks this question; and three times French TV viewers are able to see that Ramadan will not unambiguously reject the death penalty by stoning. What we hear him say is that he wants a temporary moratorium – a *moratoire* – for the application of Islam's criminal law. *Moratoire* is a precise legal term that means, specifically, an amnesty that applies for a period of time, but that will then be revoked. One word: *moratoire*. This word was a turning point in Tariq Ramadan's life."

Commentators, Anfindsen explains, identified Ramadan as an enemy of society: "Ramadan tried several times to convince people that he had been misunderstood, but it was useless. Even though he's since said several times that he does not think Islamic criminal laws should apply nowadays, he's always made this conditional on certain factors; he's always kept open the

195

possibility that Islam's criminal law would be applicable in an Islamic society."

Tariq Ramadan is very influential among young Muslims in Europe today. He comes across as a modern man in Western clothing and a gifted speaker who can juggle Islam and Western philosophy. He draws thousands of spectators to events in France and elsewhere, and fills auditoriums in Oslo. One of his messages is that Muslim citizens have a right – and, from a Muslim perspective, an obligation – to demand that their presence and identity to be acknowledged. And what does this acknowledgment mean in practice? This revealing statement by Ramadan appeared in the Danish newspaper *Berlingske Tidende* on 6 February 2004: "It can, in the future, mean that the content of certain laws must be re-examined. Western law is not absolute, timeless, or eternal. Therefore Muslims who are now Western citizens, and at home in the West, must involve themselves in legal questions and make proposals that will enable them to develop and shape for themselves a balanced Western identity." Such quotations are a regular part of the diet Ramadan serves up, and have induced one of his strongest critics, the Syrian-born professor and Islam researcher Bassam Tibi of Göttingen University, to issue very clear warnings about him. Tibi is especially concerned about Ramadan's political influence in Europe – for example, his role as advisor to the EU Commission. Tibi believes that Ramadan doesn't speak of an Islam that is detached from politics: "…if one listens carefully to what he says, and what he wants to achieve, it is not Euro-Islam. He speaks in a way that is supposed to mollify those who are scared of political Islam, and thus call it Euro-Islam. But European Islam involves the separation of political and spiritual Islam. And this is not the language he speaks."[141]

It has also been shown that Tariq Ramadan has close ties to a number of fundamentalist European organizations that can be found on the watch lists of various countries' intelligence services. He is, moreover, closely tied to al-Qaradawi and is a spokesman for the European Council for Fatwa and Research.

Naturally enough, Ramadan advises his followers to heed al-Qaradawi on religious questions. Ramadan's image as an ideologue is further damaged by his current membership on the board of the Islamic Centre of Geneva – a board led by his brother Hani.

I've mentioned al-Qaradawi's not very pleasant views, in particular his attitudes toward girls and women. How does Tariq Ramadan fit into this picture? Hardly anyone in Scandinavia has studied Tariq Ramadan more closely than the Danish writer Helle Merete Brix. As Brix told me in July 2006, Ramadan believes that the sexes should be separated, that Muslim women should marry only within the *umma* (the fellowship of Muslim believers), that Muslim women should wear the veil (as Ramadan's French wife does), and that polygamy is a legitimate option.

There is, in other words, good reason to believe that Ramadan views sharia as a divine and eternally valid set of laws – just as his grandfather believed and his mentor al-Qaradawi preaches. The fact that he's made his grandfather's words his own, in book form, supports this claim: "Islam's rules comprehend the whole of life – for Islam is faith and worship, fatherland and nation, religion and state, spirituality and action, Koran and sword."[142]

Ralf Pittelkow, a Danish author and political commentator, calls Ramadan a Salafist. Salafism means returning to pure, unfalsified Islam by attending directly to the holy scriptures and to Muhammed and his first generation of Muslims.[143] Pittelkow says this about Ramadan: "His reformism falls within Islam's foundational principles. Even where democracy and human rights are concerned, he doesn't attempt to alter the essential elements of the Islamic view. When he calls for Muslims in European countries to respect democracy and human rights, his argument is pragmatic: the basis for such arguments is that Muslims, according to the Koran, have an obligation to respect agreements that have been entered into. Ramadan reasons from this that a Muslim who has settled in a European country has thereby agreed to accept that country's political system and understanding of human rights. If one does not respect the country's political system and laws, this is tantamount to violating the message of the Koran, of sharia" (2002:116-118).

In Pittelkow's view, Tariq Ramadan is opposed in principle to democracy: "In principle, Ramadan is an opponent of secular democracy ('the Western model') – that is, a democracy that is founded only upon the human being and his rights without God being involved in the system of political governance."

Paul Berman, too, has taken note of Tariq Ramadan's Islamistic sympathies: "Anyone who reads Qutb, or, from our own time, Tariq Ramadan, will notice that these authors, the great Islamist theoreticians, the ultraradical and the not quite so radical, are very touchy when it comes to women's rights – clearly a sore point with them" (2003:237).

In September 2005 and May 2006, Tariq Ramadan came to Norway at the invitation of the Islamic Association to give lectures. This group was the sole organizer of the September event, while the weekend seminar in May was a collaborative effort between it and the Saudi-based Muslim World League – the above-mentioned extremist organization that Ramadan's own terror-suspect father helped found.[144]

Mawdudi

One major Islamist intellectual left both his spiritual and physical footprints on Norwegian soil. His name was Abu Ala Mawdudi (1903-1979), and he was the greatest Muslim theologian in the history of the subcontinent.

Mawdudi has left a considerable religio-political influence in today's Pakistan, having left his mark, for example, on the education of children in the schools. Mawdudi's thinking is also reflected in the religious instruction offered to children at the Islamic Cultural Centre in Norway. This mosque was founded more than thirty years ago, and has direct ties to Jamaat-i-Islami, the Pakistani religio-political party that Mawdudi himself established. Mawdudi is thus the Islamic Cultural Centre's lodestar.

Mawdudi's ideology is almost identical to that of the Muslim Brotherhood, and it arose, as did the Brotherhood's, as a religious and political protest against a society influenced by the values of the British colonial government. Mawdudi founded the Jamaat-i-Islami party, which is to say the Islamic Association, in 1941, six years before the division of India into India and Pakistan (now India, Pakistan, and Bangladesh). It is now Pakistan's largest religious party.

Mawdudi produced a good deal of religio-political literature. His book *Purdah and the Status of Women in Islam* (1939), which celebrates the veil, is considered "a masterpiece" when it comes to degrading the status of women. Among the book's current fans are Saudi theologians.[145]

For Islamists like Mawdudi, the question of women and families is central to the realization of their political vision. Kari Vogt describes the Islamic vision and women's essential role in it as follows: "In the Islamic state the family is at the centre – the family administers the true Islamic values. The issue of women was thus given great attention and is an important part of Islamic propaganda." The way women lead their lives is therefore "itself the symbol of Islamic morality" (2005:250ff). *Purdah* includes a detailed explanation of why a woman's eyes are an "erogenous zone" that can lead to prostitution. The same goes for perfume. And also her voice, which is the devil's agent, and the sound of the heels of her shoes. In my experience, with the exception of the late dictator Zia ul-Haq, nobody is hated by women's rights activists in Pakistan more than Abu Ala Mawdudi.

Sayyid Qutb and Abu Ala Mawdudi are considered the major Sunni Muslim ideologues of the twentieth century. Kari Vogt notes that both men "had a sovereign ability to formulate a simple and powerful message. They developed the idea of Islam as 'a third way' – the Middle Way between Marxism, which unilaterally addresses itself to material needs, and Christianity, which limits itself to spiritual matters. Islam concerns itself with the whole person, with 'the human in balance,' it is said. Mawdudi's motto is that 'Islam is an all-encompassing ideology.' He thereby suggests that society has not been Islamized until all of life and all social and political institutions are governed by Islamic principles. The goal is to develop not only an Islamic state with an Islamic body of laws, but also an Islamic economy, Islamic scientific theory, Islamic science, and so on" (2005:245).

I believe that the idea of Islam as a "third way" between purely material Marxism and spiritual Christianity is what draws so many converts to Islam. Trond Ali Lindstad and Lena Larsen are former members of Norway's Workers' Communist Party who became Muslims. Anne Sofie Roald is another far leftist who went over to Islam. One after another of these converts has exchanged an extreme political ideology – but one that lacks a key element, the spiritual – for another extreme, which embraces both the material and the spiritual. In the preface to her book *Are Muslim Women Oppressed?*, Roald writes this about her conversion: "The strict limits on what is permitted and what is forbidden, how one should think and how one should not think, were also attractive....One of the reasons I became a Muslim was 'the Islamic system' with its fixed limits" (2005:9-10).

Since its establishment, Jamaat-i-Islami has had extremely limited electoral support. Not until after the most recent national election in Pakistan, in 2002, were they even represented in the National Assembly. This happened as a result of the merging of the religious parties under the umbrella group Mutahida Mujlas Aamal. This alliance now governs the North-West Frontier Province, and has prohibited all music in public transportation and advertisements that include photographs or drawings of human beings.

Now, as in his own time, Mawdudi's ideas have had a major impact in Pakistan, especially among politicians and religious leaders. His influence manifested itself in a truly catastrophic fashion under the Zia dictatorship. As Vogt writes (2005:244), "General Zia ul-Haq's comprehensive Islamization process during the years 1977-1988 was the first attempt to realize

Mawdudi's vision of an Islamic state." Zia's Islamization process became especially violent with the introduction of the Hadood Ordinance – a criminal law, based on the Koran and hadith, that prescribes amputation as a punishment for stealing, whipping as a punishment for drinkers and gamblers, and whipping or stoning as a punishment for prostitutes. Under the Hadood Ordinance, a woman's testimony counts for half as much as a man's.

It's important to emphasize that neither amputation nor stoning as a means of punishment appeals to the soul of the Pakistani people. No amputations have ever been carried out; no doctor has ever wanted to step up and do the job. Nor has anyone been stoned to death. Whipping, however, was frequently employed during Zia's regime.[146]

Nevertheless, the Hadood Ordinance remains firmly entrenched today and has had particularly ghastly consequences for Pakistani women. Under this law, a woman who reports a rape has to supply four honourable male Muslim witnesses.[147] If she can't, she'll be prosecuted for extramarital sex – since by making the accusation she's admitted to having sex outside of marriage.

It's in the very nature of such cases that the evidentiary requirements for proving rape are virtually impossible to meet. As a result, about 75 percent of the females in Pakistan's prisons are there because they've confessed to extramarital sex – most of them being rape victims. There was thus widespread celebration on 8 July 2006, when President Pervez Musharraf let out on bail 1300 Pakistani women who'd been imprisoned for alleged infidelity. They were released as the result of a change in the law that made it possible for women to be bailed out of prison.[148] It's clear that the president wants to repeal both the Hadood Ordinance and other holdovers from Zia's regime, but conservative religious forces have prevented it.

According to Vogt, Mawdudi argued that "Islam stands for democratic ideals" (2005:250). Given that he was the godfather of the Hadood Ordinance and the author of the female apartheid manifesto *Purdah,* one must conclude that his "democratic ideals" are on a full collision course with what the UN, Norway, Europe, and other parts of the world define as democratic ideals.

Jamaat-i-Islami's basic goal is not to strengthen democracy, but to carry out a worldwide Islamic revolution. The party is fighting to introduce sharia at all levels of society, and opposes every attempt to repeal the Hadood Ordinance. It actively supports polygamy, and argues that a wife should subordinate herself to her husband in every regard – that, for example, she can never deny him sex unless it's physically impossible for her to perform. The party also vigorously opposes any liberalization of Islamic family law, especially laws designed to improve women's divorce rights. Similarly, they oppose the use of contraceptives. In accordance with Mawdudi's spirit of sexual apartheid, moreover, Jamaat-i-Islami firmly advocates the covering of women.[149]

Several key figures in the party also argue that parents have the right to refuse to let a daughter marry, if her choice of spouse conflicts with their interests. Not surprisingly, the party strongly opposes the incorporation of the UN's Women's Convention into Pakistani law.

The party's base in Norway, the Islamic Cultural Centre (ICC) mosque in Oslo, has 2077 members. Statistics from the regional commissioner for the municipalities of Akershus and Oslo show that the mosque received something over a million kroner in government support in 2005. An examination of the literature and other materials available at the mosque's library leaves little doubt as to its ideology. The library contains items that were published at the main headquarters of Jamaat-i-Islami in Pakistan and that reflect Jamaat-i-Islami's views of women, martyrdom, and jihad. In these materials, Mawdudi is the central figure, along with the party's highly regarded leader in Pakistan, the Islamist Qazi Hussain Ahmad. Some of the literature – for example, a Mawdudi-influenced pamphlet entitled *Polygamy in Islam* – was published in Norwegian by the mosque itself. None of the literature available in the library is critical of the ideology of Mawdudi or Jamaat-i-Islami.[150]

The ICC is not alone in this regard. Take the Oslo-based Idara Minhaj ul-Quran (IMQ) mosque, which is characterized by a somewhat milder and more spiritual ideology, has 3898 members, and in 2005 received over two million kroner in Norwegian government support. It is part of a worldwide religio-political network that is based in Pakistan and has branches in about seventy-five countries, including the Scandinavian kingdoms.[151] The movement also has its own political party in Pakistan, Awami Tehrek, whose leader, Tahirul Qadri, is also the head of the Minhaj ul-Quran movement.[152] Qadri and Jamaat-i-Islami's leader, Qazi Hussain Ahmad, have virtually identical views of women, as you will find out if you visit the IMQ's Oslo library. Here you can read the traditional view of why women should not have divorce rights equal to men's, why hijab and polygamy are correct from the perspective of Islamic law, why Islam preaches the necessity of sexual segregation, and why Muslim women should not marry non-Muslim men. There is no literature at the library that reflects other views.[153] In 2000 it became very clear just how closely tied IMQ is to Tahirul Qadri when the congregation's imam was fired. Why? Because he didn't follow Qadri's philosophy down to the letter: "Dr. ul-Qadri in Pakistan is our religious leader. We follow his philosophy, use his books and videos, and we cannot accept an imam with another philosophy."[154]

In today's Norway there are just under 100 Muslim congregations.[155] I haven't found a single one that preaches sexual equality. Not one congregation or imam in the country has ever publicly questioned the Koran's dictate that Muslim women can only marry Muslim men.[156] None has ever publicly questioned the severe sharia-dictated limitation on women's right to divorce. Yes, some Muslim community leaders say that forced marriage is forbidden and contradicts Islam's teachings. But these same leaders won't say publicly that they believe friendly social contact between the sexes should be permitted, let alone suggest that it's a good thing and a prerequisite for the community's growth and development. On the contrary, they encourage Muslims to practice sexual segregation – which, as we've seen, creates the conditions that lead to involuntary marriage.

The kind of Islam that's practiced in Norway, indeed, mirrors the Islam preached in the homelands of Norway's Muslims. It's an Islam that has never given women a Golden Age or glory days. It's an Islam that, as we can see in Bernard Lewis's books and in UN reports on the culturally, socially, and economically underdeveloped Arab world, doesn't respect basic human rights – especially women's rights, free speech, and religious freedom. It's an Islam, in fact, that is the principal cause of the miserable condition of today's Muslim world. It's an Islam, furthermore, that has been imported into Europe and that is a big part of the reason why Norwegian citizens today are being subjected to involuntary marriages and genital mutilations. Similarly, it explains why the parents of tens of thousands of children and young people believe their progeny shouldn't have to grow up with our "defiled" world view – and why thet consequently send them to the Muslim world to be brought up.

The negative developments within Islam are the main reason for the high levels of emigration from the Muslim world. What's absurd is that the very aspects of Islam that are responsible for this emigration are taken along in the emigrants' backpacks and planted by them in Muslim communities in the West. And how do Muslim leaders in Europe respond to Muslims' integration problems? The answer they give is the same one given by conservatives throughout the Muslim world: *More Islam!* A return to true, pure Islam – *that's* the medicine. The tragic absurdity of it all is painfully obvious.

"Render unto Cæsar that which is Cæsar's…"

The Western world managed to secularize Christianity and establish democracies with popularly elected governments and man-made laws. Is there something in Christianity's nature that has made this possible – an element that Islam lacks?

First, some facts about the spread of democracy around the globe. The organization Freedom House annually measures the levels of democracy in the nations of the world. Today, according to Freedom House, more than three-quarters of the countries in the non-Muslim world – but only one-quarter of the countries in the Muslim world – are democratic. Freedom House classifies countries according to the degree to which they're democratic, labeling them as "free," "partly free," or "unfree." Its picture of the Muslim World is not comforting. In 2006, only three of forty-six countries with a Muslim majority were defined as "free": Indonesia, Mali, and Senegal. Twenty were "partly free"; twenty-three were "unfree."[157]

Experts such as Paul Berman and the Danish philosopher Kai Sørlander have pointed out that the Reformation, Renaissance, and Enlightenment, and thus the establishment of secular democracies, were made possible by certain basic aspects of Christianity. Some observers even believe that these aspects are essential to the formation of secular democracy. I will only mention a few key points here. One is that Christianity respects conscience. Another is that it recognizes a right to rebel. This began with rebellion against God Himself. In Genesis, Jehovah orders Abraham to sacrifice his son Isaac, and Abraham, far from obeying reflexively, questions the command. From the very beginning of the Western religious tradition, then, there has been room for scepticism and doubt – which, in turn, allow for the possibility of rebellion. Islam lacks these attributes. The Koran tells the same story, but places no emphasis on Abraham's questioning and resistance. In the Koran's version, Abraham hears God commands and prepares to obey; there's no hint of struggle or rebellion. As Paul Berman says, "In Islam, submission is all. Submission to God allows Islam to create a unified, moral, and satisfying society – at least potentially, even if the flesh-and-blood Muslims in any given era have forgotten their religious obligations. Submission is the road to social justice, to a contented soul, and to harmony with the world" (2003:44ff).

Another commentator observes that Christianity is not a law-giving religion, while Islam and sharia are one and the same. Sharia and jihad have always been pillars of Islam; Jesus's words about letting Cæsar be Cæsar and letting God be God have enabled Christians to distinguish between the worldly and the spiritual. Monotheism in Christianity is also weakened by the Trinity. As the Danish Islam expert Mehdi Mozaffari points out, the Christianity of the Trinity is "a kind of footnote monotheism: the text deals with only one God, but on the same page in the footnotes it still says three!...Such a state of affairs is unthinkable in Islam. Not only because Islam is a hard monotheistic religion, which is centred round Allah and Allah alone, but because it's also a religion in which rituals, ethics, and laws are intimately connected. It's very difficult to separate these intimately connected elements. It means that Islam, consisting of a holy, law-giving book and its proclaimed political ambitions, exhibits more opposition to democracy than many of the existing religions."

Islam is thus not particularly reform-friendly or good at adapting to modern democracy – as demonstrated by the powerful forces working to spread Islamocracy instead of democracy: "some of Islam's laws are utterly opposed to the Universal Declaration of Human Rights. It begins, according to sharia, with the fact that people are not born alike. Women are half of men...Nor can a Muslim leave Islam or convert to another religion, since Islam decrees the death penalty for apostasy, etc."[158]

The Danish philosopher Kai Sørlander notes some distinguishing differences between the central figures of Christianity and Islam, Jesus and Muhammed. While Jesus wasn't politically active and didn't preach about politics, Muhammed was a political, juridical, and military leader. While Jesus passively let himself to be led to the Cross and preached that his followers should turn the other cheek, Muhammed employed raw power

206

and physical violence. Muhammed also drew up clear guidelines as to how society should be organized politically. The fact that Muhammed, in his lifetime, also managed to establish a thoroughly Islamized society, which is still viewed today as the perfect society that Muslims should strive to emulate, makes the development of democracy and secularization difficult.[159]

8

Around Europe

You're sitting at the computer intensely seeking answers to the questions of daily life – both large and small. For example: Can I pluck out the hairs just above the top of my nose? I know it's not permitted to shape the eyebrows by plucking out hairs, but what about those hairs just above the top of the nose? Is it un-Islamic vanity to remove these hairs?

You send the question out into space. You might be sitting anywhere on earth. The computer from which this particular question was sent out happened to be in Denmark. The two young women who wrote the question, and who wear veils, received their reply from an authority who was reputed to know his Koran and be intimately acquainted with the details of Muhammed's life. His reply: yes, it's permitted to remove these particular hairs, but not the rest of the eyebrows.

The girls breathed a sigh of relief.

They had other questions. Such as: Is it really true that Muslim women don't have the right to drive a car? Saudi women, after all, aren't allowed to drive, and Saudi Arabia is the cradle of Islam. Is that law correct, then, according to the holy books – or not? And the answer comes back: It *is* okay to drive a car! Islam says so. It's the Saudis who have misunderstood.

Islamic youth awaken

For many young European Muslims, this kind of Q. & A. about Islam is an everyday situation. This particular example is borrowed from a report in the Danish weekly *Weekendavisen* about two young Danish-Turkish sisters.[160] I could just as easily have taken examples from websites in Norway, such as islam.no and koranen.no, at which young people pose similar questions to experts. These Danish girls are part of the new awakening among young European-born Muslims. They've thrown off their jeans and fully covered themselves in proper Muslim fashion, in jilbab, meaning that all their hair is hidden under a hijab, and the shapes of their bodies are concealed by a wide coat. After reading on the Internet that head covering is required, the girls tossed out their Western clothing. They've also studied a number of websites about Islam's relationship to music. It turned out that most of the experts on these sites believe that music is prohibited, or *haram*. The girls understand why music is haram – many song lyrics, after all, are about sex. So they've discarded music, too.

The girls' parents, born in a Turkish village, have never been as preoccupied with Islam on a daily basis as their daughters are now. For them, Islam has been a weekend activity. Or at least it was, until their daughters' awakening. The girls have now talked their mother into praying five times a day. They explain how they managed this: "We say to her that 'mother, you also have to think of your life in the hereafter. This life here is so short.' And so she prays with us." The girls have also had their way in regard to family social gatherings and weddings: men and women are now separated.

The girls' father gets a little tired of their fixation on religion and all the rules and details that the family now has to pay attention to. He feels that dancing and music are fine and that women and men should be allowed to eat together. And he'd rather go fishing on the weekend with his Danish friends than attend mosque, which his daughters say is in his best interests. At the same time, he's also a bit proud of them – proud that they've become so preoccupied with religion. So when they asked him to drop the family's annual summer vacation back home in Turkey, he let them have their way. This year, instead, the family is going to Cairo to visit the ideological centre of the Muslim world, Al-Azhar University.

The idea for the above-mentioned article in *Weekendavisen* originated in a study which showed that fully 6 percent of young Danish Muslims aged fifteen to twenty said Islam played an important role in their daily life. For young people aged twenty-one to thirty, 58 percent said the same, while only 25 percent of Muslims aged fifty-one to sixty did so. The pattern was similar when the interviewees were asked about Islam's importance to their view of Danish society and about various religion and political questions. Almost four times as many Muslims aged twenty-one to thirty than Muslims aged fifty-one to sixty said Islam was important to their political views.[161] The researchers concluded that integration has failed.

This study also demonstrated the importance of introducing some nuance into the conclusion of the previous chapter, where I pointed out that Muslims emigrated to Norway and Europe because their original societies suffered from social, cultural, political, and economic underdevelopment, thanks largely to Islam's influence. The Danish study indicates that young Muslims born in Denmark forge connections to Islam that are much closer than their parents' connections to it. My own observations suggest that the same is true of young Muslims in Norway. Their Islam isn't really the kind of demotic folk religion that most of their parents brought along with them when they left their homelands; it's much more a matter of being preoccupied with the literal word of the Koran.

The close relationship of young people to Islam is also well documented in the Netherlands, with a Muslim population of about one million. Han Entzinger, a sociology professor at Rotterdam University, has studied the sense of identity among third-generation Dutch Muslims, most of them the grand-children of Moroccan and Turkish immigrants and most aged between eighteen and thirty (2003). The majority of the young people in this study considered Islam their most important source of identity, followed by their grandparents' homelands.

These young people also admitted to having far more conservative values in regard to family and child-rearing than their Dutch agemates. Entzinger, who is the leading integration expert in the Netherlands, says the following about this finding: "It is striking that they don't identify at all with the Netherlands as a nation, even though they have lived here all their lives. This reveals itself clearly in their knowledge about (for example) Dutch politics. Many of the young people know more about what's going on in their homelands."[162]

The same patterns are found in Germany, which has a Muslim population of about 3.5 million. Well over two million of them are Turks, a group that began immigrating to Germany in significant numbers in the 1960s. A 1997 study by the German sociologist Wilhelm Heitmeyer showed that many young German-Turks express hostility toward Europe and the West. One in three of those interviewed by Heitmeyer wanted Islam to be the national religion in every country; over half said that Muslims shouldn't adapt to Western society, but live according to Islamic rules; more than a third were prepared to use violence against non-believers if they felt it would be a service to the Muslim community; almost 40 percent believed that Zionism, the EU, and the U.S. are threats to Islam.[163]

Britain has a Muslim population of over 1.5 million. A 2006 survey by the *Daily Telegraph* showed that 40 percent of these Muslims want sharia to be introduced in parts of Britain. They were especially eager to see divorce, child custody, and inheritance cases adjudicated according to sharia. Twenty percent felt sympathy for the suicide bombers who attacked London on 7 July 2005. One percent believed that this terrorist action was "correct."[164]

A similar survey in 2005, shortly after the July attack, showed that six percent of Muslims – that is, about 100,000 people – believed it was "completely justified," while 24 percent felt a degree of sympathy with the suicide bombers' motives. Eighteen percent said that they had little or no loyalty to the country they lived in. Thirty-two percent agreed that "Western society is decadent and immoral, and Muslims must try to put an end to it," and one percent of these people believed that violence is a legitimate means of attaining this goal. Young Muslims were considerably more hostile toward Western society than older Muslims.[165] Leading British Muslim organizations confirm that girls and young women embrace Islam far more strongly than do their parents – and the Islam they embrace is far stricter than their parents'. A visible sign of this in the public square, according to Muslims, is girls' increasing use of strict head coverings.[166]

In 2006, the first survey of Muslim attitudes in Norway was carried out. It showed that 14 percent wanted sharia to be introduced, as opposed to two percent of the population generally. Fourteen percent of Norwegian Muslims said they did not know whether sharia should be introduced in Norway, as opposed to four percent of the population generally. Which parts of sharia they had in mind was not specified. The groups that supported sharia most strongly were women, those with low levels of education, and those who were actively religious. Six percent of the Muslims surveyed believed that the terrorist bombs in London and Egypt could be justified, as opposed to one percent of the population generally. Young Muslims and those with low levels of education were least likely to oppose the terrorist bombings.[167]

I haven't noticed any similar studies related to identity and loyalty among other religious groups in Europe, such as Hindus, Jews, Buddhists, Sikhs, and Christians.

The surveys mentioned here show that many Muslims – and especially young Muslims – feel very little sense of belonging to the society they live in. Quite simply, integration seems to be going in the wrong direction. What brought this about? The answers can be found largely in the immigrant-packed neighbourhoods in major European countries – neighbourhoods of a type that that we're beginning to see take shape in Norway. I've chosen to look more closely at four countries (Sweden, Germany, France, and Denmark) which can give us an idea of what kinds of developments can be expected in Norway in the near future – provided, that is, that Norway doesn't become *the* European exception by successfully bringing off real, broad-based integration.

Sweden: goodbye to the "people's home"

Sweden's immigrant population is proportionally much higher than that of most European countries. According to Statistics Sweden, the total population is somewhat over 9 million. The Swedish Integrationsverket (which was dissolved in 2007) calculated that approximately every fifth citizen of Sweden is an "immigrant," which is to say either an immigrant or the child of an immigrant. Over 400,000 of these people are supposedly Muslims. Sweden hasn't been keeping records of the country's immigrants since 1985, and in 2005 researchers revealed a major discrepancy in the census. The official numbers may be off by as much as 100,000, meaning that the Swedish population may be under 9 million. Studies by public health officials and Statistics Sweden show that a number of immigrant groups have unusually low death rates and much higher life expectancies than native Swedes. Fertility and employment among immigrants seem be to be significantly underreported. This leads to unreliable demographics and employment statistics. It's also suspected that many people who have actually moved out of Sweden have not reported this to the authorities, so that they may continue to receive various forms of government support. Such support may continue to be paid out because Sweden lacks rules requiring that people who have left the country or settled in it report these facts to the authorities. Another factor leading to discrepancies in the census is the fact that older people who have died during stays in their homelands are not reported to the authorities as being dead so that their families may continue to receive their government payments.[168]

The development of ghettoes, also called enclaves, has exploded in Sweden.[169] Probably the most closed enclave in all of Scandinavia is Rosengård in Malmö. Almost half of those living in this southern Swedish city are immigrants; in the Malmö neighbourhood of Rosengård, over 90 percent of the residents are of non-Western origin, most of them Arabs.

I regard Rosengård as the antithesis of integration, and the neighbourhood stands as a monument to Sweden's misguided immigration and integration policies. In Rosengård one can live one's entire life without having any contact with mainstream Swedish society – the social-services departments excepted. Rosengård is thus a glaring example of what the Swedes call "outsiderhood," and has for this reason been widely discussed in international media, both in Europe and the U.S. It's especially the high crime rate, the almost lawless conditions, and the high level of Islamization that has caused laymen, writers, and professionals alike to sound the alarm. The specialist who has studied Rosengård most closely is the Swedish social anthropologist Aje Carlbom, who spent three years there doing field work. In his view, there are three factors in particular that explain why Rosengård has become a Muslim enclave. One is the deindustrialization that began in the 1970s and that caused immigrants to fall out of the labour market because of their low level of education. (Today about 10 percent of the women and under 20 percent of the men in Rosengård have jobs.) A second factor is the extremely high levels of immigration: relatively speaking, Sweden has received far more refugees than other European countries, and fetching marriages have been very common; since authorities have made little effort to regulate these marriages, large, culturally homogenous groups have been able to establish themselves. The third factor is Swedish ideology, which takes multiculturalism to another level, with "tolerance for foreign cultures" (in Carlbom's words) being viewed as "the highest of values."[170]

In Rosengård, the residents have access to cultural amenities of the sort available in their homelands and are able to communicate with the employees at government offices in their own language. They don't need to learn Swedish or acquire knowledge about mainstream Swedish society. Classes in public schools (as is true elsewhere in Malmö and, for that matter, elsewhere in Sweden) are taught in Arabic. Mosques have become the main meeting places: there, children can attend Koran school, get help with their homework, and are given clothing and food. Muslim day care and Muslim private schools are also available. Many Muslim children in this neighbourhood, including some who were born in Sweden, have grown up speaking only Arabic. Parents who fear that their children will be influenced by Western morals place them in religious institutions so that they may receive, as Carlbom puts it, "the ideological 'vaccine' that is necessary to keep them on the right path – the path of Islam."

In enclaves like Rosengård, Islamists have firm control over the residents and conditions are ripe for the spread of politicized Islam. One hardly ever sees a woman in Rosengård, for example, who is not carefully covered. As we've seen from the UN reports on the Arab world, the Arab residents of Rosengård come from countries with serious social, economic, and democratic problems; and they bring those problems with them when they migrate to Sweden and settle in an enclave like Rosengård. Their condition becomes one of "global marginalization"; they inhabit a "no man's land" where a meaningful existence is hard to come by. Such a marginal life leads many to make a life project of Islam. "The religion," writes Carlbom, "is used to organized their entire life."

Rosengård has turned its back on Sweden. The social problems have exploded, not only here but in Malmö generally. A series of articles in *Aftonbladet* in September 2004 contained an almost unbelievable tidbit: the police admitted openly that they didn't have control over Malmö. Brutal crime is ravaging the city. When the police are called to (for example) deal with a violent incident involving immigrants, they themselves require police protection. Ambulance personnel have orders to put off helping anybody until the police are in place to protect them from the mob. "We come to help and they spit on us," says one ambulance worker. "It's hard to work when you have to have eyes in the back of your head all the time." Similarly, firefighters are attacked when they try, for example, to save a burning mosque.[171] Public transport has been significantly reduced, since drivers don't dare to enter neighbourhoods like Rosengård. In 2006 it was decided to close down a middle school which had been set on fire several times. Teachers had been savagely attacked, in some cases by students wielding pistols, and the authorities saw no way of turning the situation around.[172]

Knives and other weapons are widely used, and passersby rarely dare to get involved when somebody is assaulted in the street, fearing that they, too, will become victims. One of the articles in *Aftonbladet*'s above-mentioned series quoted a woman who had fled war-torn Afghanistan in 2003: "For twenty years, while I lived in Afghanistan, there was war – and there's war here, too. I'm scared to go out, and I'm scared to let the children out." An employee of the Skåne police department puts it this way: "Everyone who works in the judicial system can see that it's getting worse and worse – more violence, worse violence."

On 7 September 2005, the newspaper *Expressen* focused on violent crime in Malmö, and outlined the incidents that had taken place in that city over a twenty-four-day period in August 2004. It was an endless litany of brutal assaults, knifings, robberies, and rapes. One telling statistic was that the number of rapes in Malmö had quadrupled during the previous decade.

The situation in Malmö is not unique in Sweden. In just fourteen years, the number of so-called "outsiderhood" areas in the country has risen from three to 136.[173] Certain neighbourhoods in Gothenburg and Stockholm could be described in essentially the same terms as Rosengård.

What's especially alarming is the drastic increase in the number of rapes reported in Sweden. Rapes of children almost doubled between 1995 and 2004, from 258 to 467 per year; in 2004, seven rapes were reported per day, for a total of approximately 2600 rapes a year.[174] A government study shows that among the perpetrators of serious acts of violence, rapes, and murders, men with backgrounds in the Middle East, North Africa, and Turkey are strongly overrepresented, while the victims of rape are mostly Swedish, about half of them being children or young girls.[175]

The increase in gang crime in immigrant-heavy neighbourhoods is also unsettling. In some areas, according to a 2005 report, residents consider the situation so threatening that they believe the only solution is to move. It's been revealed that gang recruiting is going on in Kurdish, Turkish, and Persian community organizations; among the reasons why people join gangs are a lack of belief in the future, family problems, group pressure, identity problems, and joblessness.[176] In Gothenburg, the authorities have warned people in immigrant-heavy areas not to go out after dark; in Stockholm, the chief of police has specifically warned women against venturing outdoors in the evening in unlit areas. Half of the women say that they no longer dare to walk alone in unlit places; among girls aged fifteen and sixteen, the fear of walking alone in unlit places is even stronger: eight of ten don't dare.[177]

Immigration has also cost Sweden dearly in economic terms. Several calculations show that government expenses are in the tens of billions. Economics professor Bo Södersten says that in 2003, immigration cost two to three percent of Sweden's GNP, or about forty to fifty billion kroner.[178] Another 2002 calculation shows expenses of 33 billion kroner per year.[179]

In the 2005 book *Exit folkhemssverige – en samhällsmodells sönderfall (Exit the People's Home of Sweden: The Downfall of a Social Model)*, sociology professor Jonathan Friedmann and others write that Sweden's situation won't improve, but will only get worse, thanks to a combination of high unemployment and high levels of immigration. The book's authors figure that the Swedes will be a minority in their own country by 2056.[180]

Sweden thus faces obvious economic challenges that point toward nothing less than a national breakdown. A 2002 report shows that the children of second-generation non-Western immigrants have four times as high a risk of unemployment as

Swedish children. At that time, the employment rate was 50 percent for non-Westerners aged sixteen to sixty-four years, and 80 percent for ethnic Swedes in the same age range. The report also shows that around 50 percent of the social-services outlays in Sweden are paid to families with non-Western backgrounds.[181]

It also appears that Islamists have gotten an especially strong foothold in Sweden. Sweden's Muslim Association, which with its 70,000-odd members is the country's largest Muslim congregation, demands special laws for Muslims in several areas. In a 2006 letter to the political parties represented in the Swedish parliament, the association demanded that Muslims have their own national holidays and time off for vacations and sundry Islam-related activities, such as Friday prayers.

The letter also demands that imams be permitted to teach in the public schools, that girls and boys have separate swimming classes, that Muslim congregations be granted interest-free loans for the construction of mosques, and, especially, that divorces between Muslims be contingent on the approval of an imam – the argument for this being that it's important for women to stay married and thereby keep families together.[182]

In 2003 it was reported that anti-Semitism is flourishing in Muslim communities.[183] In 2002 alone, the Swedish security police registered 131 anti-Semitic crimes; this is assumed to be the tip of the iceberg. Jew-hatred is especially widespread among Muslim and Arab schoolchildren.

In my view, Sweden is one of Europe's clearest examples of the fact that levels of immigration have been far too high in relation to countries' ability to ensure that the large new groups will become integrated into mainstream society both economically and (especially) in terms of values. There has been a lack of realism on the part of those whose job it is to oversee immigration. It has gone much faster than integration. The main reason for Sweden's naïve open-door policy, I believe, is its neutrality in World War II: consciously or subconsciously, Swedes are determined to make up for that failure by showing generosity to Muslims. One particular result of this generosity is that Sweden has been less and less able to guarantee fundamental security to its women and children.

Germany: An extension of Turkey

In other European cities, the general pattern is that immigrants' native cultures have become established in their new communities, and that the larger the groups grow and the longer they live in the country, the more poorly they're integrated.

A striking example of this is Turks in Germany. Life in the Turkish enclaves is lived almost entirely in accordance with Turkish norms and values. One socializes with one's own; community associations and political groups are organized according to ethnic origins. The lower one's income and educational level, the more likely one is to live as a "Turk." The members of the first generation identified mainly with their native regions in Turkey; immigrants from a given region would settle in the same part of town. The generations born in Germany, however, developed another identity, thinking of themselves as Turks in Germany or as Muslims in the Christian world.[184] As in Denmark, many second- and third-generation Turks have developed religious attitudes that are far more conservative than their parents'.

Islamist organizations work consciously to ensure that German-Turks retain their sense of attachment to Turkey and grow more attached to Islam. Living in enclaves, screened off from mainstream society, Turks in Germany are far less likely to find work. Islamist nationalists consciously play on Islam and ethnic isolation.[185] The largest Islamist organization in Germany, Milli Görüs, is a Turkish export; represented in most of the countries of Europe, it has a hand in running one-fifth of Germany's 2,500 mosques, from which its Islamist message is spread.[186]

The multicultural ideology that has characterized German immigration policy likewise helps impede integration. Many

German-Turks who aren't particularly religious identify strongly with their homeland; many, in other words, are physically present in Germany, but their identity and loyalty bind them to Turkey. Turkey has, in short, established itself in Germany. This means that the honour culture – especially the control of women's chastity – has put down deep roots in the enclaves.

The honour culture appears to have had a particularly unpleasant impact in Germany. In no other European country, it seems, does the estimated number of honour killings exceed that in Germany. Necla Kelek, born in Istanbul and trained as a sociologist in Germany, says that during every month between 1997 and 2004, on average, thirty women in Germany were the victims of honour killing; most of the victims are reportedly Turkish women.[187] This figure is so very high that I admittedly wonder whether it's correct. It's astonishing, in any event, that such an astronomical estimate hasn't caused a commotion in Germany and throughout Europe.

A murder that did arouse a considerable amount of consternation in Germany was that of twenty-three-year-old Hatun Sürücü, who in 2005 was shot down in a Berlin street by her youngest brother, then eighteen. In 2006, he was sentenced to ten years in prison; his two older brothers were prosecuted for conspiracy. The oldest brother was said to have obtained the weapon, and the middle brother was said to have lured Hatun to the scene of the crime; but the court did not manage to prove these facts. When the verdict was pronounced, the family celebrated and displayed the victory sign to spectators and the media. The youngest brother had most likely been chosen to execute his sister because under German law he would receive a far milder sentence because he was only eighteen.[188]

The execution of Hatun caused nationwide ire because she was, like Anooshe and Fadime, a young woman who'd managed to raise herself up against all odds and integrate in record time into European society. Hatun grew up in an enclave in Berlin, hidden from mainstream society. At the age of only fifteen she was taken to Turkey and married off to a Kurdish cousin.[189] At sixteen, pregnant, she left her husband. The next year she had a son. She finished grade school at an institution for young mothers and trained to be an electrician. Her friends and helpers describe a young, oppressed woman who raised herself up and flowered.

Hatun was about to take her final exam and begin work as an electrician when the shots were fired at her and her family's "honour" restored. The public consternation further intensified when it came to light that most of the Turkish students at a school near the scene of the execution – many of them the German-born grandchildren of immigrants – expressed support for Hatun's murder. Some openly praised it: Hatun, they said, had behaved like a German – i.e., she was a tramp – and therefore the murder was justified. On a radio program, a young Turkish woman said the same thing: Hatun deserved to be killed because she had taken off her veil. In Germany, little attention has been paid to the lives of girls and women in the enclaves. Hatun's murder, however, led to a political debate about immigration and the growing role of Islam in Muslim communities.[190]

The sociologist Necla Kelek has written books about the widespread oppression of Turkish women in Germany. She herself has lived in an enclave – she characterizes the enclaves in Berlin as "the new Berlin Wall" – and is well acquainted with the German-Turkish "honour culture." She believes that as many as fifteen thousand girls aged fourteen to eighteen are imported annually as the spouses of Turkish men in Germany. Many are poured right into the ghetto as slaves to their in-laws. They don't learn German; on the contrary, they live in anti-German isolation. The fact that these young, culturally isolated women are given the primary responsibility for child-rearing recalls the criticism made by the Namik Kemal back in 1867: that women are kept ignorant, and the first negative consequence of this is "a bad upbringing for their children." As the UN reports about the Arab world also indicate, the oppression of women is a crucial ingredient in the recipe for driving a society both culturally and economically into the gutter. Kelek characterizes the importation of Turkish brides as "suffocating" and calls for a new immigration policy that will put an end to the practice.[191]

As in Malmö, the poor integration of the generation that is now growing up has been manifested in violence and disorder at immigrant-dominated schools. The use of knives and other weapons is daily fare. Many teachers say that they don't dare to teach without having their mobile phones turned on, so that they're ready at a moment's notice to call for emergency help. From time to time, police have to physically protect teachers. Many students, for their part, say that owing to their concerns about ethnic conflicts among their classmates, they don't dare go to school unarmed.

Sexual assaults in France

France's Muslim population of between six and eight million constitutes about ten to twelve percent of the country's population.[192] As the French enclaves have grown, violence against women in them has not only increased but also become increasingly grotesque. Throughout the 1990s, this problem was wreathed in silence. The turning point came in 2002, when a young Tunisian-French woman, Samira Bellil, published *I gruppevoldtektenes helvete (In the Hell of Gang Rape).*[193] In the book she tells how she was repeatedly gang-raped, which first happened when she was only fourteen years old. Her own boyfriend offered her to his friends. According to Bellil, this is not at all an unusual practice. What was sensational was that Bellil's book marked the first time that anybody publicly acknowledged how vulnerable girls are to gang rape in Muslim enclaves. Samira Bellil made the rounds of radio and television studios, explaining that Muslim girls keep silent about being raped because they know that if they tell their families or friends, they'll be blamed for being raped. Bellil talked about how girls are forced to wear the veil and how they can't go out after dark without a male relative along to provide protection – since a girl or woman alone outside at night is defined as a non-Muslim and therefore deserving of rape. When they heard what the brave Samira had to say, the forgotten girls of France's Muslim enclaves were virtually struck dumb.[194]

That same year, France was shaken by a murder. On 4 October, seventeen-year-old Sohane Benziane, who was of Tunisian origins, was burned to death in a basement room outside Paris. The nineteen-year-old murderer, who also had a North African background, was her ex-boyfriend. It was said that he had lured Sohane into a garbage room in the basement, and that when she had refused to obey his orders he had tortured and raped her. Then he had doused her with gasoline and set fire to her.

The murderer was sentenced to twenty-five years in prison; a co-conspirator received seven years. At the trial, the prosecutor said that the very idea of a young women being burned alive had set France back "several centuries." He added: "Her death has become the symbol of the most extreme kind of violence against women."[195] Sohane's sister said: "They used to burn garbage heaps and cars – now they burn girls."[196]

Sohane's murder became more than a symbol. It led to a historic awakening in France. Inspired by both Samira Bellil and Sohane Benziane, six girls and two boys led a group of marchers who, starting out in Paris in February 2003, walked from city to city, insisting that politicians wake up and notice what was happening to the country's immigrant women and girls. They knocked on mayors' doors; they talked to journalists. And, almost to their own surprise, they were given a respectful hearing.

More and more people joined the pilgrimage; soon there were over a thousand participants. When it ended on International Women's Day, 8 March 2003, the six girls and two boys had grown into a throng of 30,000. This action resulted in the formation of the now internationally famous organization *Ni Putes ni Soumises* (Neither Whores nor Oppressed); Samira Bellil became its godmother.[197]

The next year, yet another murder set France back "several centuries." After Ghofrane Haddaoui, a twenty-three-year-old French-Tunisian woman in Marseilles, rejected a proposal from a French-Tunisian young man on the grounds that she was already engaged to be married, the young man flew into a rage and, with a friend, stoned her to death. *Ni Putes ni Soumises* held a march through the streets of Marseilles, protesting against (as one sign put it) "fundamentalism that imprisons women."[198]

In recent years, several multiple-rape trials in France have left strong marks on that nation's consciousness. One of the trials concerned the apparent rape of a thirteen-year-old girl by eighty-eight boys and young men over a period of four months; another related to the rape of a a girl of fifteen by eighteen neighbourhood boys. Sentences ranged from five to twelve years. In the latter case, what shocked the authorities most were the reactions of the boys' mothers. One of them said this about the sentence: "You call this justice. Seven years' prison for a little oral sex. It's the girl who should be behind bars."[199] A lawyer who has represented victims of gang rape characterizes the situation in this way: "We've allowed a subculture to develop with its own codes and references that have made sexual violence a banality."[200]

In France, Islamist organizations like the Muslim Brotherhood have formed extensive networks that receive considerable financial support from the extreme Wahabbists in Saudi Arabia. In many enclaves, Islamist groups have patrols that go from door to door and tell people that (for example) women must not be treated by male doctors, Muslims must not receive blood donated by Jews or Christians, and girls must not study science or take swimming lessons. Islamists' terrorization of ordinary people is clearly confirmed by a study from the enclave of Corneuve. Seventy-seven percent of Muslim women who wear the veil in that neighbourhood do it because they're scared of being harassed by Islamist patrols.[201]

During the violent riots in France in 2005, few in Europe noted the Muslim angle or the gender angle. The focus was on marginalization, unemployment, a lack of faith in the future, and racism. One honourable exception was the leading German feminist Alice Schwarzer. She pointed out that while the unemployment rate among young people in France with immigrant backgrounds is 40 percent, the gender breakdown is lopsided: among young immigrant-group men, the jobless rate is 25 percent; among young immigrant-group women, it is 60 percent. "In social terms, then," noted Schwarzer, "the women have twice as much reason to protest." But Muslim women didn't shout in the streets. Schwarzer put it this way: "They're whisked behind the curtains." When Muslim girls and women do go out and protest in the streets, it's rarely against the government: instead, they speak out against their own men's use of violence.

Schwarzer notes that in her country, young Turks are strongly overrepresented in crime statistics. No fewer than 25 percent of Turkish boys support the use of violence, as opposed to only six percent of German boys and four percent of Turkish girls. The level of violence in Turkish families is three times higher than in German families. The victims are women and children, including boys. Although the boys themselves are often the direct victims of violence, they identify with its perpetrators – that is, their own fathers. Schwarzer believes that so long as these facts are silenced with a "naïve reference to racism," we won't understand what's at the heart of the riots – namely, that boys are brought up in a highly patriarchal environment, where they learn that a "real man" is a violent man. And being brought up with violence (as many of them are), they learn to despise their sisters and mothers; in other words, they learn misogyny: "The use of violence is at the heart of male dominance in the enclaves. Violence is cool. Violence is the hallmark of 'male' identity – especially strongly called for when manliness is unstable and insecure." Schwarzer believes that Islamists exploit these young men's hopelessness. The young are offered a new and proud identity that will compel their own women – and infidels, too – to subordinate themselves to them. When these young men screamed at French police during the 2005 riots, they didn't shout political slogans, as young rioters did in 1968. What did they shout? "Sons of whores!"[202]

Another rarely mentioned factor in the riots is France's polygamy policy. Until 1993, French law permitted Muslim men to bring up to four wives with them from their homelands. The law essentially amounted to a friendly slap on the men's backs. Thanks to that law, polygamy was able to establish itself in France and has continued to thrive. It's been estimated that there are thirty thousand families in France today in which a husband lives with more than one wife. One of the consequences of this situation is housing problems, since it's difficult to find apartments – especially in the Muslim enclaves – that can house families with twenty to thirty members. Another consequence is that the children, and in this situation especially the boys, are often badly brought up. They grow up on the streets, where the gangs rule; neither their families nor their communities provide much in the way of discipline, and few of the boys are particularly close to their fathers. Their mothers, meanwhile, are often poorly integrated, and thus have very little in the way of social and intellectual resources to offer their children.[203]

The fact that Islamism's forward march is taking place at the expense of girls and women's quality of life has also been observed in French schools with large Muslim student populations. The major social change in the schools is an increase in the control and sexual harassment of female students and teachers and in openly expressed Jew-hatred. In an op-ed, the Danish writer Helle Merete Brix describes a book written by an anonymous French history teacher who demonstrates vividly that the schools in immigrant-heavy neighbourhoods are chockablock with anti-Semitism, racism, and sexism. For example, one teacher describes how a teenage Muslim girl who was active in school and thirsty for knowledge ended up being silenced by Muslim boys who called her a "filthy slut." The teacher understands that other Muslim girls refuse to open their mouths in class for fear of being treated the same way. The book also provides examples of classrooms that are controlled by budding Islamist boys who criticize Muslim girls if their clothes are "too tight" and who openly support polygamy without being contradicted by their classmates or teachers. Many Muslim students condemn the French republic's fundamental values, such as sexual equality and equal rights for all citizens. Jewish students are systematically harassed, both verbally and physically. At many schools, it's hard for teachers to cover the Holocaust because Muslim students quite seriously believe that the destruction of the Jews is a Jewish lie. (Where did they learn this? In the mosque.) More and more Jewish parents find it necessary to take their children out of public schools to protect them from bullying and physical violence.[204]

In some enclaves, religious leaders have been selected to be community and political leaders – and have openly declared their territories to be Muslim. When, for example, an imam met the mayor of Raiboux at the boundary of a Muslim-dominated area of that city, the imam declared the terrority under his control. The mayor didn't argue with him.[205]

Islamists' power over ordinary people's daily lives in Europe seems to have advanced further in France than anywhere else. It was precisely for this reason that France introduced the hijab ban in schools in 2004, and – in the name of equality – also forbade other obtrusive religious symbols. The ban on the hijab is an attempt to wrest power in the schools from the Islamists.

The question is whether Islamization has gone so far – and the Muslim population become so large – that it's already too late to reverse this development. Twenty to 30 percent of the French population under age twenty-five is Muslim. The Muslim birthrate is far higher than the French average. Add to this the high immigration rate, especially through fetching marriages, and it looks as if France will be the first country in Europe with a Muslim majority. This will likely happen within twenty-five years.[206] That the French government is engaged in dialogue with a national Muslim council (which has proven itself to be extreme) with the supposed goal of improving integration has drawn sharp criticism from secular Muslims – a class of people that has in recent years been betrayed by governments across Europe.[207]

Denmark: best in class

No country in Europe has had as broad and open a debate on immigration and the challenges of integration than Denmark. It was kicked off in 1999 by Poul C. Matthiessen, a professor of demography, and it strongly influenced the fact that Denmark, three years later, became the first European nation to radically alter its immigration policy. Limits were put on the stream of new spouses through fetching marriage, in order to give Denmark the breathing room to focus on serious integration efforts. I'll discuss the new Danish immigration policy more extensively in the next chapter.

Matthiessen got top billing in *Jyllands-Posten* on 29 August 1999 when he issued a powerful warning about the scale of immigration to Denmark and its probable future consequences. Immigration, he said, would change Denmark: it would bring results that nobody seemed to want to discuss, but that would affect the country's culture, religion, and way of life. Denmark would undergo a comprehensive transformation – and the crucial factor would be the Muslim population. Would Muslims be secularized, Matthiessen wondered aloud, or would they cling to their religious traditions and perhaps take their faith in a more conservative direction? Whatever the case, he predicted that as Danish Muslims increased in numbers, they would likely intensify demands for respect for their religion, traditions, and customs. Matthiessen warned against a cultural clash, and took note of population-growth prognoses: in 2020, 13.7 percent of the people in Denmark would be first- or second-generation immigrants, most of them from non-Western countries.

Matthiessen soon received an answer to his charges: leading politicians and opinion-makers accused him of arrogance and inaccuracy and of painting a dark picture of things – and, yes, of being something of a racist. Few paid attention to the facts. The Social Democratic prime minister, Poul Nyrup Rasmussen, responded to Matthiessen with a blunt dismissal: "The comments are not relevant," he insisted. But some listened to Matthiessen, among them the social minister in Nyrup Rasmussen's government, Karen Jespersen. She clipped out his *Jyllands-Posten* article and when, six months later, she was named interior minister – a position that put her in charge of immigration policy – she made copies of the article and handed them out to key members of the government bureaucracy. Jespersen wanted to appoint a commission to evaluate immigration and its consequences; she also wanted to limit the fetching of new spouses. But her colleagues in the government rejected her proposals. In their view, the problems should be killed with silence.

But at least the debate had begun – if on a small scale – and several statistics and prognoses were put on the table. They showed that Matthiessen's research was of the utmost relevance: the continued high levels of immigration could hardly be called sustainable as far as the possibility of real integration was concerned.[208] The Social Democrats nonetheless refused to change course. As a result, they were compelled to cede power in 2001.[209] Danish voters were concerned about divisions within their society: they feared that the strong sense of solidarity among the Danish people would dissipate over time unless an entirely new immigration policy was put into place. The Social Democrats' years of cowardly inaction on immigration had a great deal to do with their loss in the next parliamentary election, in 2005.

Almost six years to the day after Matthiessen's 1999 article, he issued another warning in *Jyllands-Posten*.[210] This time his focus was on values, the role of women, and parallel societies, or so-called enclaves. The empirical foundation of Matthiessen's article was the fact that fewer than half of the non-Western immigrants in Denmark had jobs. Non-Western immigrants accounted for about five percent of Denmark's population, but received just under 40 percent of its social budget. Young immigrants from non-Western countries and their children committed crimes twice as often as young Danes did. The enclaves were growing, and the children and grandchildren of immigrants were (in general) doing poorly at school. Many never attended school at all; others never completed it. More and more immigrants and their children, Matthiessen warned, viewed themselves as living outside Danish society and as isolated in their own culture, tradition, and religion. Everyone, he pointed out, agreed that the situation needed to be changed. But where should the changes begin? "I think the key lies in a rebellion by Muslim women....If you cling to your old view of the relationship between man and woman, you can't believe that you'll be integrated into the labour market in Denmark. The men have to give the housewives and the daughters their freedom. If they don't do that, the women must rebel – if only for the children's sake. For if the children just see their mother go home without being able to speak Danish, without a job, the sex-role pattern will be passed down to the next generation."

Matthiessen further pointed out that, historically, this is the first time that Denmark has experienced a wave of immigration by people who are explicitly antagonistic to Danish values and norms. He pointed out that all earlier immigrant groups, right up to the mid 1970s, had adjusted quickly to Danish norms and values. This included Dutch farmers in the 1500s, French Huguenots in the 1600s, Swedish and Polish workers in the 1800s, Jewish refugees from Russia around the year 1900, and Chileans in the 1970s. Today's arrivals huddle together in enclaves, said Matthiessen, who warned against the current immigration project: "In reality we have done something terribly bold. The question is whether we can and should do something about it."

Once again, Matthiessen offered not only comments but prognoses. He had just concluded a study of population growth in the Middle East, which showed that in twenty-five years the population there would increase from 377 million to 571 million. He noted the high level of immigrant pressure this would place on Europe, and referred to UN reports about the lack of economic and societal development in the Arab world, especially owing to a lack of sexual equality: "It is not far from the Middle East to Denmark in this context. If a woman is kept in a sex-role pattern that prevents her from contributing in any real way to social development outside the home, it places great limitations on social and economic development. It can be a problem for the countries of the Middle East. It is unquestionably a problem in relation to the immigrants' situation in Denmark." Was Matthiessen totally against immigration? "I'm not. It should just be an immigration that serves both the immigrant and the countries that take them in. Otherwise we risk affecting the ability of people in Denmark's welfare society to work together. It's happening now."

These comments in the late summer of 2005 did not cause any alarm in Denmark. Too many Danish politicians had already declared integration a failure. I'll mention only a few key details that confirm the failure: in Denmark there are 463,000 immigrants with children. Of these, 136,000 are from Western countries and 328,000 from non-Western countries. Immigrants from Western countries constitute two and a half percent of the population, non-Western immigrants six percent. It is estimated that over 200,000 immigrants, about 3.5 percent of the total population, is Muslim. A 2005 report showed that about 100,000 non-Western immigrant women of working age and that 50,000 of these are outside the labour market.[211] Those worst off in this regard are Somali, Lebanese, Iraqi, and Afghani women, 85 to 90 percent of whom are outside the labour market. Of the 100,000 immigrant women, fully 13,000 essentially exist outside of Danish society. They receive no government benefits, since their husbands, who brought them to Denmark, are supposed to support them. The women are thus entirely beyond the authorities' purview. And nearly all of them live completely isolated from Danish society, often on their husbands' orders.

The head of the social-services office in the immigrant-heavy neighbourhood of Nørrebro in Copenhagen, Bodil Vendel, puts it this way: "We know from experience that if the women become too well-informed, they will, in many cases, be literally beaten back into place by their husbands."[212]

Among those who speak out about immigrants' increasing isolation – a situation that especially affects women – is the Copenhagen integration consultant Manu Sareen, who is of Indian extraction. Sareen describes the development of a powerfully growing underclass in which, he says, "the women are particularly isolated." Sareen has observed an increasing radicalization, one aspect of which is that men increasingly keep their wives at home. But there are several explanations for women's isolation. One reason is that women themselves feel that their role is in the home; others are tied down because they're having one baby after another; still others fear taking part in mainstream society because they neither know nor understand it.[213]

The 2005 report also showed that government officials who are supposed to help immigrant women enter the work force have instead formed an "unholy alliance" with those women's husbands.[214] The husbands want the women to stay home, keep house, and raise children; and the employment counselors don't want to harass the women by trying to push them into jobs, since their chances of finding employment are poor anyway. So instead they arrange for the women to take hobby-like courses in subjects like food preparation and needlework. Far from bringing them closer to the work force, these courses ensure that they won't neglect their domestic duties. The government, in short, has made a compromise: it keeps Muslim women busy within their husbands' strict boundaries, and ignores their need to develop into skilled workers – and active citizens.

The report further reveals how women themselves seek to avoid employment by such actions as turning down work in day care if it involves having to change the diapers of non-Muslim children, or refusing to take jobs that involve contact with pork or alcohol. Some Muslim women, when they show up for meetings to discuss possible employment, veil themselves more fully than usual, deliberately speak worse Danish than they're capable of, and/or invent medical and practical problems to avoid being hired. In some cases, women have played these games on orders from their husbands so that they wouldn't be put to work.[215]

Another problem is that the children of non-Western immigrants in Denmark do poorly at school. Half of the non-Western children in Copenhagen are functional illiterates when they finish grade school. Sixty percent of the immigrant and second-generation students who begin an education in a technical or commercial school drop out, and only a few of them go on to some other kind of education. In upper secondary school, the dropout rate among non-Western students is twice as high as among ethnic Danes.[216]

In 2005, however, another report came out that inspired optimism with the news that young immigrant women who educate themselves have almost as high an employment rate as young Danish women.[217] Yet another report shows that when a woman is in the work force it has an integration-positive effect on her whole family, but when a man has a job it has virtually no effect on his family's integration.[218]

Denmark has rolled up its sleeves and shone a searchlight into pretty much every single nook and cranny in an effect to confront and resolve its integration crisis. And the more searchlights are turned on, the more problems are revealed. Many people are concerned about the future. Today, the expenses caused by immigration and its consequences are believed to amount to approximately 36 billion kroner a year. Denmark's finance minister Thor Pedersen calls Denmark's integration policy its "greatest welfare reform."[219] This is confirmed by statistics showing, for example, that in Copenhagen schools 45 percent of all first-grade children have immigrant backgrounds. (Most are Muslims.) In ten years, then, 45 percent of all seventeen-year-olds will be immigrant youth.

Ten years later, 45 percent of all twenty-seven-year-olds in Copenhagen will be immigrants.[220] These figures should actually be higher, because they don't include people who will immigrate to Denmark between now and then. One population forecast says that within ten years, the number of young people with foreign backgrounds between ages sixteen and nineteen will triple.[221] Such prognoses, combined with poor education and employment conditions, and the already substantial government outlays for social services for non-Western immigrants, explain why alarms are going off in Denmark over immigration policy. But the debate and the initiatives are about a great deal more than finances; they're now just as much about values.

One of Denmark's most popular politicians is not a member of any of the governing parties. Nor is he a Dane by birth. He was born in Syria and immigrated to Denmark as a child. He represents the Danish Social Liberal Party, which ideologically is more or less comparable to Norway's Liberal Party. His name is Naser Khader and he's such a hero to the people of Denmark that his popularity is more like a pop star's than a politician's.[222] Why? Because he's left no doubt whatsoever about which side he's on in Denmark's culture wars. He's for secular democracy – 100%. It's for this reason that he enjoys the public's confidence. Seen through Norwegian eyes, this can seem amazing, since many Norwegians seem to take it for granted that leading Muslims support secular democracy – even when they plainly don't. It's not that way in Denmark. Thanks to Denmark's spirit of open debate, in which native Danes don't feel obliged to walk on eggshells with members of other ethnic or religious groups, one Islamist after another has been exposed. This open debate is possible because Denmark's media, generally speaking, are not hypnotized by myths and partisan prejudices regarding immigration. In my experience, there are far more journalists and editors in Denmark than in Norway who have competence in the field and who don't refuse to cover immigrant-community conditions that deserve critical attention. It was no surprise, then, that it was in Denmark that a certain event in world history took place: the 2005 publication of the Muhammed cartoons in the newspaper *Jyllands-Posten.*

The cartoon controversy began with an act of self-censorship. Was it true that in Denmark curbs had been put on the freedom to express opinions about religion – that self-censorship was taking place owing to fear of extremist reprisals?[223] And it was in the wake of the Muhammed cartoons that what had long been suspected was confirmed once and for all – namely, that top imams in Denmark weren't devoted to Danish democracy's fundamental values. The press revealed that the imams, on the contrary, not only were playing a double role, but were busy using lies and deception to weaken Denmark's international reputation and to strengthen their own national and international power.[224] It was also revealed how broad a network the imams had among Islamists in the Muslim world – for example, they collaborated with the Islamist ideologue Yusuf al-Qaradawi. It was in the midst of this international crisis that Khader, already a well-known politician and member of Parliament, stepped forward with an unambiguous message to the undemocratic forces: "If the imams don't like the smell in the bakery, they can find another place to live. I'm so tired of hearing them complain about the conditions in this country that has given them protection, freedom of speech, freedom of religion, and immense opportunities for their children."[225] Khader founded the organization Democratic Muslims, which soon acquired several thousand members and which has been praised by business people and politicians alike.

The revelations about Islamist leaders in Denmark surprised the secular Muslim Khader, who was unsettled to know about their cozy, well-developed international network. "We are facing a mind-blowing internal enemy," he told *Berlingske Tidende* on 2 April 2006. "We have to wake up. We have to deal with an internal enemy that is more dangerous than you can imagine. I've realized this only recently." His life project is now to battle this internal enemy, the Islamists: "I'm about to throw up from them and their full beards (...) Many of the refugees who have fled from Iran have fled from precisely these things – and then they run into them here! Their goal is to impose sharia upon Muslims who live in the West." Khader says he'll fight the Islamists "to the last" on behalf of democracy and will do everything to ensure that the "marginalized Muslims are drawn away from the Islamists and incorporated into Danish society."

Khader, who has received death threats for his views and his public activities, must be accompanied everywhere by bodyguards. His "crime," he says, is that he believes Islam and democracy can be reconciled. On Internet discussion boards, Muslims rage against him. A survey shows that only 13 percent of Danish Muslims view Khader as their spokesman, and that only one in five Muslims in Denmark supports Democratic Muslims. [226] This is, alas, not surprising. Precisely the same situation obtains in Norway: open democrats with Muslim backgrounds – such as the comic Shabana Rehman, her brother Shakil Rehman (who entered the debate with a newspaper op-ed in 2006), and the author Walid al-Kubaisi – are unpopular among Muslims generally; in the press and on popular debate websites, young Muslims condemn them almost unanimously, regarding them as traitors for embracing Norwegian freedom.[227]

The image that Norwegians have been given both of the new Danish immigrant policy and of the climate in Danish society that's resulted from the integration debate is dispiriting. Many Norwegians now thunk that Denmark is a virtually racist state. This misconception is firmly disproven by recent surveys of Danes' racial views. These surveys show that Danes are very positive about having immigrants as colleagues.[228] In fact, the Danish are more open to and tolerant of immigrants today than they were before the new immigration and integration policy was introduced in 2002, and the percentage of immigrants who consider themselves the victims of discrimination has dropped significantly in the last few years.[229] Even after the publication of the Muhammed cartoons, which created such a hullabaloo, this positive development has continued.[230]

Danes have also been described as the happiest people in Europe, with an extremely high level of trust for their fellow citizens and their politicians. Compared to other countries, in short, Denmark has a very strong sense of social solidarity.[231] But like other countries, it's having a tough time integrating Muslims. A 2006 survey showed that 11 percent of the Muslims in Denmark sympathized completely with those who had attacked Danish embassies and Danish goods in the Mideast in reaction to the Muhammed cartoons. Thirty-six percent had some sympathy, while barely half of Danish Muslims were directly opposed to the actions. Fifty-three percent of Danish Muslims derived their sense of identity overwhelmingly from Islam; 37 percent identified themselves, in roughly equal measure, as both Muslim and Danish; only two percent felt more Danish than Muslim.[232] Like other surveys, this one confirmed that social solidarity can be damaged by poor integration of immigrants.

Multiculturalism and human rights

This tour of several European countries shows that more and more minority-group citizens of those countries link their identity to their religion and to the countries in which they have their cultural roots. Many openly reject the countries of which they are citizens. They don't have a sense of community or of shared values with the members of mainstream society, but have instead retained their homelands' values and norms. They view their new countries' basic values and norms as a threat to their identities, and live wholly or partly on the outside of mainstream society. Indeed they inhabit a parallel society, a sort of satellite society, in which their bonds and loyalty to their countries of origin are strong. Europe is their economic base. Physically, they commute between two continents.

No doubt about it, Europe has become multicultural. Multiculturalism is embraced by politicians on the left, in the centre, and on parts of the right. The ideology is also deeply rooted in the mainstream media. Multiculturalism is about groupthink: the group's interests matter more than the individual's. Individuals with non-Western roots are regarded as being intimately bound to groups whose values and traditions, anchored in their homelands, are untouched by any concept of fundamental human rights. Within these subcultures, the reigning power structures thrive at the cost of the individual. Mainstream society's social and legal systems, which can help protect the individual, are, to a large extent, rendered unavailable to him or her through the efforts of the subculture's governing authorities, who almost invariably are highly patriarchal, hierarchical, and authoritarian.

The multiculturalist argues that cultures are equal in terms of values and that all cultures should thus be treated with the same respect. Different cultures should thrive side by side, even if their values are essentially different. People are encouraged to cultivate a so-called diversity, and are warned against criticizing and disapproving the distinctive traits of cultures other than their own – even if they're plainly at odds with human rights. Multiculturalism is thus also highly static; it's about the preservation of cultural traits, no matter how harmful or inhuman those traits might be.

Norwegian culture, of course, has never been static. Nor is our democracy linear: it develops and changes continuously, for example through the introduction of new laws that are meant to secure and protect individual rights and thereby limit bastions of power and strengthen the hand of the weak. For me, multicultural ideology seems absolutely antagonistic to the goal of improving society and the individual's status. Multiculturalism protects the power structures – the reigning collective – and the individual disappears. Meanwhile multicultural ideology rocks the pillars supporting the edifice of democratic solidarity in countries with equal rights for all. It contributes to discord between groups and intensifies a counterproductive focus on ethnicity which says: "Show me your skin colour, and I will tell you who you are and what needs you have."

In a country like Norway, society is based on shared history, language, values, and culture, including political culture. Does this mean that you has to have particular ethnic origins to be a part of this society? No, not at all. You can be an equally good citizen of Norway if you were born in the jungles of Gambia; by the same token, you can be Norwegian-born and reject your Norwegian identity. You may be loyal to other countries, as is true of many people in Europe's enclaves. And you may be loyal to ideologies other than secular democracy, as is the case with political extremists on both the left and right, and now also certain religio-political activists – namely, Islamists.

In Norway, there's still a strong sense of solidarity. Power inheres in a community based on a shared way of life and a feeling of interdependence and mutual trust. The community is founded on the experience of a "we" – a "we" that supports the rights and obligations that the community takes for granted. Democracy, as we know it today, is dependent on the fact that members of a society trust one another and think of themselves as belonging together. They're willing to take responsibility for society as a whole, and hence for one another's rights and obligations – for example, for the welfare state. If that trust and feeling of interdependence crumbles, society itself will be weakened, and people will begin to accept conditions for others that they wouldn't accept for themselves. In such a society, an individual's human worth will be increasingly dependent upon his or her cultural roots – a state of affairs that we've observed in places such as France and Germany.

Not all of Norway's citizens, to be sure, were active participants in a democratic community before the recent immigration wave. Evangelical Christian groups, for example, have typically lived in more or less isolated communities and had fundamental values that differed from those of the majority population. But this hasn't usually represented a challenge to the nation-state, since these groups haven't been large enough to cause significant social and political divisions. It's true, however, that society at large, in the name of diversity, has stood idly by while members of these religious groups have been denied their human rights by family and community leaders.

Not all new citizens of Norway will be integrated into our democratic society and embrace its basic values. We can't expect this or make it our goal. But it must be our goal to ensure that most immigrants will become full members of society. This is especially important if we want to prevent the growth of tyrannical, subculture-based power structures and the intensification of social and political divisions between different segments of the population.

In other words, it's a matter of scale. The larger the number of people living outside mainstream society, the more imperiled will be the survival of a national state that ensures all citizens' rights. The larger the number of people who fail to come together as part of a more or less common culture – especially insofar as its basic values are concerned – the more seriously Norway's solidarity will be weakened, and the more people will fall outside its protective structures. Yes, the concept of human rights can include the idea of rights for specific cultural groups – such as the Sami people in northern Norway, who have been given certain rights as a people – but in a democratic context, cultural rights must always be predicated on the understanding that individual rights come first.[233]

The poor integration that can be observed across Europe is not simply the result of a lack of awareness of how crucial it is for new groups to experience a sense of belonging to a democratic community and to be integrated into its rights and obligations. It is also the result of years of denial, rationalization, and wishful thinking. For a long time, both politicians and intellectuals fervently refused to admit that there were problems with integration; they claimed that immigrants constituted such a small portion of the population that integration problems didn't represent a challenge to society as such; and they insisted that integration would occur naturally over time, for of course immigrants themselves *wanted* to be full participants in democracy. *Naturally* they would embrace freedom.

Another means of denying or minimalizing the problems has been to lower the bar in regard to what is meant by integration. This, I believe, is what the last Norwegian government did in its white paper "Diversity through Inclusion and Participation" (2003-2004). This paper includes the following statement about common values: "One view is that we should seek the broadest possible agreement – that we should try to come closer to one another in culture and values. Another view is that we should define a minimum set of human and political rules that everyone must respect. The maximum solution – the broad community of values – has as its goal to strengthen the feeling of oneness among the citizens. The minimum solution protects, to a larger extent, the right to be different, even if the human rights and political rules set limits on that difference. This report comes closer to the latter understanding." It's difficult to interpret this in any other way than by reading it either as a retreat – politicians have recognized that full integration of new groups isn't possible, and have thus lowered the bar in regard to what's considered an acceptable degree of integration – or as an expression of a desire to charge full speed ahead into a multicultural society. Given today's level of immigration, both solutions will lead to the development of parallel societies, the relativization of human values in accordance with ethnicity, and the splitting up of the democratic community. In the long term, such developments can lead to the collapse of a peaceful state like Norway.[234]

Another crucial reason why integration has gone awry is that we've denied our own values. We haven't dared to make it clear that we're proud of the values upon which our democracy is based. Many people consider it inappropriate to express pride in Norway and enthusiasm for its virtues. Such talk is viewed as chauvinistic, and such chauvinism is acceptable only at football games and outside the Royal Palace on Constitution Day. To wave the flag for our own fundamental values is even more problematic. When it comes to values, we've gone a long way toward pure self-effacement in public conversations and debates

241

– even if most of us, deep within, and in private conversations, probably do believe that other parts of the world could profit by emulating our values. When I first argued in 2003 that immigrants must *be assimilated into democracy's basic values* – equal rights, freedom of speech, and freedom of religion – I knew well that I had shoved my hand into a wasp's nest. To this day, that statement is used against me in newspaper columns by cultural relativists, who use my remark as evidence of my supposed chauvinism and cultural imperialism. On the contrary, isn't it oppressive and discriminating to claim that immigrants shouldn't be able to enjoy these freedoms?

It also seems clear that we've underestimated the meaning of cultural difference and the degree of Muslim opposition to integration. We've essentially taken it for granted that other people want to live by our values, customs, and social conventions. Fetching marriage, which in most cases means family-arranged marriage, is one of many phenomena that underscore the intensity of our delusion that these new groups wish "to become like us." We've also dangerously misjudged the importance of those who wield power within these communities – from family patriarchs to community leaders – who strive to thwart the integration of individuals who wish to become full members of Norwegian society.

The dream of democracy

It seems as if neither Norway nor Europe at large has acknowledged the conditions that are necessary to maintain a secular democracy and a well-functioning welfare state. So far, immigration levels have been much too high in relation to our ability to integrate the greatest possible number of new citizens into mainstream democratic society. Family-arranged fetching marriages play a particularly strong role in destroying the possibility of integration, because these marriages cause the problems raised by first-generation immigrants to be reproduced over and over in subsequent generations. The marriages, in other

242

words, keep larger and larger groups of people locked into the values of their ancestral homeland.

Similarly, we've tolerated intolerance at the cost of new citizens' liberation. From a political perspective, immigration has become both headless and planless. Slowly but surely, multicultural ideology, combined with low levels of integration and high levels of immigration, is creating *de facto* states within the state. The young people who are born here – especially those who grow up in enclaves – have no sense of belonging to the country of which they are citizens. Their mothers are often isolated from mainstream democratic society, and are thus unable to help their children become a part of it. Instead, young Muslims link their identity to Islam – and are helped to do so by national and international Muslim networks whose missionary work has as its long-term goal the establishment of a caliphate in Europe.

It's precisely for this reason that so many isolated European girls and boys sit at their computers with religious questions both large and small – questions about practical daily challenges and about what they have to do to win a life in the hereafter. So it is that they come to see their marginalized life here on earth as nothing more than a passage to the hereafter. Don't they deserve much better than this?

9

Sustainable Immigration

Statistics Norway's population forecast (SSB 2006) shows that by 2060 Norway's non-Western immigrant population will have risen to somewhere between 600,000 and 1.2 million. For Statistics Norway, the immigrant population consists of immigrants and their children, the assumption being that later generations will be "Norwegian." The question is this: when can a member of an immigrant group no longer legitimately be considered a member of that group? Statistics Norway, for its part, has decided that so-called "third-generation immigrants" – that is, the children of the children of immigrants – and children born to one Norwegian and one foreign parent don't belong to the immigrant population. The current state of affairs in Europe underscores the limitations of Statistics Norway's definition. Its calculation methods may well be in line with the standard practice of professional statisticians, but they may also involve the concealment of potential sociopolitical problems related to the growth of ethnic minorities.

One of Statistics Norway's alternative prognoses assumes that immigration will flatten out after 2010. In another alternative prognosis, immigration drops. Meanwhile an obvious third prognosis – namely, that immigration will increase in proportion to the increasing immigrant population, owing to the continuing practice of fetching new spouses – isn't mentioned in Statistics Norway's report. Statistics Norway's assumption, once again, is that integration will occur naturally over time and that the minority will become more and more like the majority – and that this will apply to marriage, too. This assumption is a bold one – and is unsupported by the facts.[235]

The flimsiness of Statistics Norway's prognoses can be illustrated with a glance at only one group: children and young people with non-Western backgrounds in Norway today. In 1980, the number of people in this group was 8,120. By 1990, it had risen to 28,500. In 2000, the group consisted of 62,300 people. By 2004, it had increased by another 20,000 to a total of 82,700. Once again, the "third generation" isn't included in these figures.

We're now facing an explosion of children and young people with roots in non-Western countries who are either of marriageable age or who will be ready to marry within a few years. Another calculation shows that in Norway today there are around 80,000 first- and second-generation children and young people under nineteen years old with roots in countries where family-arranged marriage is the norm.[236] An exceedingly optimistic estimate is that only half of these people will fetch spouses in their ancestral homelands, which means 40,000 new immigrants. A more realistic estimate is that three out of four will fetch spouses in their ancestral homelands, which means 60,000 new immigrants yielded by this group alone. If this current group of 80,000 continues to expand at the same rate that it has during recent years, by 2015 it will already number around 150,000 persons.

Economically sustainable?

Even if Statistics Norway's predictions turn out to be correct, we still face a dramatic transformation of Norway's population in the coming decades. As in Sweden and Denmark, this rapid change will have negative economic effects – unless a miracle occurs. Unless, that is, that Norway, unlike all other European countries, manages to achieve real educational integration and thus also real labour integration. There are no official cost estimates of the expenses that will result from immigration and integration (or the lack thereof). But there are figures on the table that suggest that immigration today is already costing Norway dearly.

The first non-Western labour immigrants who came to Norway in the early 1970s were, naturally enough, all employed. Opportunities for work were their only reason for coming here. For this reason they had somewhat higher employment levels than the majority population and during their first years in Norway were thus an asset to the economy. But by 1997 only half of those who'd come from India, Morocco, Pakistan, and Turkey between 1971 and 1975 had jobs.[237] The fetching of spouses that followed the initial labour immigration has been an especially important factor in the resulting low employment rates and high levels of welfare consumption. Indeed, welfare dependency among these groups has increased over time. Today, among Moroccans, Pakistanis, and Turks aged 55 to 59, respectively 67, 45, and 55 percent are on disability. One would expect, to be sure, that refugees, owing in part to the lingering psychological effect of the traumatic experiences that led them to seek asylum in the first place, would, as a rule, have trouble entering the labour market; yet a study shows that after a certain period of residence in Norway, non-Western immigrants – most of whom have come here through marriage – actually have higher levels of welfare dependency than refugees. After five years in Norway, 36 percent of non-Western immigrants are receiving one or another form of welfare. For Western immigrants, the figure is 18 percent.[238]

Professor Kjetil Storesletten of the Economic Institute at the University of Oslo has studied the costs of immigration in the U.S. and in a typical welfare state such as Sweden. Storesletten estimates a net loss in Sweden of about 170,000 kroner per non-Western immigrant for the entire period that the immigrant has lived in the country. Storesletten considers this estimate a conservative one, and notes that there's little reason to believe that the situation is significantly different in Norway. Storesletten believes that the study undercuts the claim the welfare state's need for a labour force can be satisfied with the help of today's brand of immigration.[239] On the contrary, the current form of immigration – that is, the fetching of spouses, mostly from pre-modern villages, who are unlikely ever to enter the labour market – only intensifies the welfare state's difficulties in obtaining a qualified work force.

The above-mentioned studies of the expenses occasioned by today's immigrants, combined with population forecasts showing that the demographic clock is ticking steadily toward an ever larger non-Western immigrant population, point in only one direction: toward the ultimate collapse of the Norwegian economy. Statistics showing that fully 40 percent of immigrant students drop out of higher secondary school only darken the prognosis for Norway's economic and social health in the near future.[240]

The Confederation of Norwegian Enterprise (NHO) has acknowledged this problem as well. In June 2006 it issued the following warning: within a few years, the national petroleum fund will be depleted. This will happen as a result of immigration by people who aren't qualified to work and who haven't completed their educations, and who consequently have low unemployment rates and high levels of welfare consumption. If today's immigration policy continues, the immigrant population will quadruple by the year 2015. At the same time, the elderly population will skyrocket as the baby boom reaches old age. A reduction of the workforce by seven percent, the NHO warned, will be equivalent to the loss of the entire petroleum fund.[241]

Only a few days after the NHO issued this warning, the government revealed for the first time how much it was spending on welfare payments to non-Western persons in Oslo. Just over 46 percent of welfare recipients in the city are non-Western, and fully 55 percent of the city's welfare budget goes to this group.[242]

Norway isn't in a unique position, then, when it comes to having pursued a "bold project" (to borrow a term used by Matthiessen to describe today's immigration). For many people, the immigrant project is still about humanism – about helping others to make a better life for themselves in Norway or elsewhere in Europe. The myth is that the higher the levels of immigration one advocates for, the greater one's moral purity. The hollowness of this myth can be illustrated with the following depressing facts: the world's population is increasing dramatically every year. In the last seven years, Pakistan's population has increased by an amount equal to seven times the population of Norway – that is, by 30 million, for a present total of 162 million. By 2050, Pakistan's population will have increased by an additional 100 million, to 260 million. In Turkey, the population in 2000 was 65 million; by 2050, it's expected to reach 103 million. The picture is nearly identical in the Arab world and in the other countries that are major sources of immigration for Norway.[243]

You don't have to have a remarkable imagination to be able to look at these figures and recognize that in years to come, formidable pressure will be exerted on Europe's borders. When other countries are pursuing such irresponsible population policies, it's simply not possible for Europe to make everything all right by taking in millions upon millions of new immigrants. In the long term, a Europe that's falling to pieces can't do any good for anybody. It can hardly be an act of humanism to drive Norway and other European countries into the gutter, since humanism is, after all, also about safeguarding established societies that provide welfare, freedom, and human rights.

No, it's not unproblematic to be a freedom-loving human being and at the same time propose laws and rules that may limit individual freedom. But in the real world, new laws and rules must be instituted precisely in order to preserve freedom – including the freedom of immigrant-group members who are denied human rights by their subculture's imported tyrannies. Now, and in the past, we've been able to use the law to deny power to the abusers of power and to empower the vulnerable. What we're also talking about here, then, is empathy and the willingness to sacrifice our own privileges. This was the main reason why I took the position that the fetching of new spouses should be radically restricted. And the more documentation I've obtained from other European countries, the more convinced I've been that Europe should follow the example of Denmark, the first country on the continent to radically alter its immigration policy. Denmark's approach is the most humanistic for today's – and tomorrow's – Europe; and it's thus also the most humanistic for the immigrants who live here today and for their children's and grandchildren's future.

"What is happening in the immigration debate is that the problems are being allowed to grow to major proportions before there is sufficient will to do anything about them," says Karen Jespersen. "And when the problems are not major, people say that there's not a major problem. But there will be."[244] This is almost exactly where we stand in Norway: we're in the early phase, in which many leading politicians are trying to decide whether or not we have problems with immigration generally, and what, if anything, should perhaps be regulated.

But the most important politician in the present Norwegian government, integration minister Bjarne Håkon Hanssen, seems to have completed the first evaluation phase. He believes we have a problem. In January 2006, he sent up a test balloon: he called for a debate about whether Norway should copy Denmark's new policy, including a higher age limit for bringing spouses to Norway and a so-called connection requirement. In most quarters, Hanssen was quite simply cut down. I say "cut down," because the arguments served up by his opponents made it clear that most of those participating in the debate – politicians as well as journalists and editors – weren't really acquainted with the Danish rules. Nor were they willing to lift the debate up into a conversation about the sustainability of immigration for the survival of democracy and the welfare state. Lacking any documentation, one after another of Hanssen's critics went on a disingenuous frontal attack against the "xenophobic" Danish policy. Few seemed to want to have a fact-based, realistic debate. What's encouraging, however, is that Hanssen has shown repeatedly that he sees no challenge as more important to Norway's future than that of immigration and integration.[245]

There's a significant gulf between the exchanges underway in the arenas controlled by the intellectual establishment and the debates taking place online. The intellectuals'continuous steamrollering of public opinion in the established media has driven many of those with concerns about immigration to Internet blogs, where there's vigorous discussion of these issues. Immigration also seems to be increasingly at the centre of conversations in private get-togethers and at workplaces. I choose to interpret this to mean that Norwegians in general are ready for a change in immigration policy.

So what do the Danish rules say about the fetching of new spouses? I'm almost entirely certain that debates in Norway about the Danish rules will intensify in the years to come. It can be useful, then, to be aware of the rules' real-life consequences before you decide whether or not you support them. It's also worth noting that the principal rules were formulated under the Social Democratic government that held power in Denmark before the turn of the century, but that they were not put into effect on a large scale until after Fogh Rasmussen's government took over.[246]

First a clarification: this is not about *family reunification* – that is, about a person being granted residency in Norway and then bringing to the country from his or her homeland a previously established family – a spouse, and perhaps one or more children. On the contrary, the rules that are being discussed here concern new marriages – that is, so-called fetching marriages.

To try to protect very young immigrants from being married off in their homeland, Denmark raised from eighteen to twenty-four the age at which an individual is permitted to bring a new spouse to the country from outside the EU. The rule applies to everyone who lives in Denmark. The foreign party must also be twenty-four years old (cf. Necla Kelek's concern about the massive import of young Turkish brides to Germany). The 24-year rule exists mainly to protect the young from forced marriage

– the idea being that if they're more mature and independent when their families try to marry them off, they'll be better equipped to resist the pressure.

It's unreasonable to imagine that the rule will put a stop to all forced marriages. But it does put the brakes on the practice. As Denmark's new integration minister, Rikke Hvilsøj, says: "If parents, family, and relatives in Denmark or their homeland are jolly well determined to force their will regarding a forced marriage upon a young person, then no law will help, including a 24-year rule."[247]

The point of the rule is also to ensure, as fully as possible, that young people are able to complete their higher educations in Denmark and thus prepare themselves adequately for the Danish labour market. The government also hopes that the rule will help more young immigrant-group members to find partners in Denmark or in nearby countries, and thus limit the demonstrably problematic immigration from these people's non-Western homelands. Denmark has realized that the constant reproduction of the first generation of immigrants through fetching marriages makes integration extremely difficult, if not impossible.

The EU has ruled that member countries may introduce an age limit of twenty-one, and the Netherlands did so in 2004. An age limit of twenty-one has also been proposed by the Norwegian government's Aliens Law Committee.[248] Such a law, though, would have limited effect. Most fetching marriages among young immigrants take place when the spouses are between twenty-one and twenty-three;[249] also, most students don't complete their higher education by age twenty-one.

The connection requirement has to do with the question of where newly established married couples may settle. A person born and raised in Denmark may bring a new spouse to Denmark from his or her ancestral homeland; but if the Danish-born party has lived for a time in his or her ancestral homeland and wants to bring a new spouse to Denmark from that country, the Danish government's position is that the couple's connection to the ancestral homeland is greater than its connection to

Denmark, and that the reunification and the couple's life together should therefore take place in the country to which their joint connection is strongest. The parties' ages don't enter into the calculations at all. Many people, including leading politicians, claim that if a woman in Denmark wants to import a husband from outside the EU, Danish law demands that the husband be younger than her. But this isn't the case. The connection requirement involves an accounting of the parties' connection to Denmark, and has nothing to do with the age of the person who applies to live in Denmark.

When these rules were introduced in 2002 – along with other rules, including income and residency requirements – the government didn't make a detailed study of the rules' possible unintended effects. The thinking was that it's easier to introduce restrictive rules at first and then perhaps relax them in certain respects, rather than to do the opposite.[250] One unfortunate and unintended consequence of the rules soon came to light: people who, for example, had studied for a period in a country outside the EU, such as Australia, and who'd found Australian partners, lost their connection to Denmark as a result of the new law. In the autumn of 2003, accordingly, the government introduced the so-called 28-year rule. It says that if you've been a Danish citizen for twenty-eight years or have resided legally in Denmark for twenty-eight years and grew up in Denmark, the connection requirement will be waived.[251]

Thanks to the new rules, the fetching of spouses by non-Western immigrants to Denmark has been dramatically reduced. Over 70 percent of the population of Denmark supports the new rules: people can see that immigration is under greater control, and that there's more room now to achieve real integration of those immigrants already living in Denmark. Immigrant parents, meanwhile, find that the rules give them a winning hand in their dealings with relatives in their homelands who want to marry off their children in order to secure them Danish visas. When facing pressure from those relatives, these immigrant parents can now point to the 24-year rule, a rule that is absolute. It's also been reported that young people with immigrant backgrounds find that the rules allow them time to complete their education before they marry.[252] The widely reported protests against the rules, which took place mostly in 2002 and 2003, came mostly from Danes who'd lost their connections to Denmark as a result of residence abroad. The introduction of the 28-year rule has virtually silenced the protests.

It's also very interesting to note that Denmark now takes in many more students and workers than it did before the rules were changed. No fewer than 25,000 visas for students and workers were issued in 2005, as opposed to 12,500 in 2001 – which rather bursts the balloons of those who are still trying to keep alive the shameful myth that Denmark is xenophobic.[253] Another piece of good news from Denmark is that more young people are now completing their educations. During the 2000-2001 school year, only 10 percent of young people with immigrant backgrounds between twenty and twenty-four were in higher education; in 2003-2004, the figure had risen to 17 percent. The age at which marriages take place has also risen. In 2001, the most common age of marriage for non-Westerners when they married abroad was twenty; over a period of just two years it rose to twenty-five.[254]

With the above-mentioned rules in mind, it's especially interesting to look back at Ahmed's family in Chapter Two. If the Danish rules had been in effect when Ahmed was first living in Norway, the fetching of spouses would probably have stopped with his wife. Mina and her siblings had strong ties to Pakistan, where they had spent their first years, and would therefore have had to spend twenty-eight years in Norway before being permitted to bring over a spouse. A family like Mina's would never have put off a child's marriage until she was well into her thirties; thus a spouse would have been found for her – perhaps she would even have found him herself – in Norway. And as a result Mina's tragedy, along with all the other tragedies that have been brought about by fetching, would have been averted. Mina would also have received the education she wanted so desperately but never got.

Conflict with human rights?

Opponents of the Danish rules often argue that they conflict with human rights. They point to the "right to family life" enshrined in Article Eight of the European Convention on Human Rights Convention (ECHR). The article, however, says nothing about which of the parties' countries that family life should take place in. Nor has the European Court of Human Rights ever ruled a state's rejection of an application for spousal reunification to be an infringement of Article Eight. On the contrary, there have been rulings which deny that a couple has the right to decide which country it settles in.[255]

The ECHR's Article Eight further says that the state can intervene when it is "necessary in a democratic society in the interests of national security, public safety or the economic well-being of the country, for the prevention of disorder or crime, for the protection of health or morals, or for the protection of the rights and freedoms of others." I interpret this to mean that a government is completely within its rights when it regulates immigration through marriage, both on human-rights and economic grounds.

Many people also say that raising the age limit for fetching new spouses is a violation of human rights. Their argument is that it amounts to differential treatment, favouring those who marry here at age eighteen and who are allowed to live together, and mistreating those who marry outside the EU at eighteen and can't live here together. That the EU itself recommends an age limit of twenty-one renders this argument pretty weak.

I consider the connection requirement a highly ingenious measure. It would keep the great majority of immigrants' children in Norway. If the rule went into effect in Norway, the thousands upon thousands of children here who would otherwise be sent to their parents' homelands for long stays in the next few years would instead likely be kept here. This would have a decisive impact on their integration.

If the connection requirement had been in place in Norway in 2002, there is good reason to believe that Awa and her sisters wouldn't be living in Gambia today. It seems clear to me that Awa's father's plan is to marry his daughters off in Gambia and then bring their husbands to Norway. So far, the girls have lost three years' worth of connection to Norway. Under a Danish-style rule, then, they wouldn't be able to import husbands from Gambia until after they turned twenty-four years old.

A full integration package must be put in place

If we truly want to integrate people who are already living here, it's critical that we put rules into effect restricting the fetching of spouses. But there's a lot more than this that has to be done. We need a comprehensive policy for genuine integration. I'll itemize only a few key points here:

- To keep young people in school, Denmark has converted government child benefits into educational support for everyone between sixteen and eighteen years old. This is an ingenous measure, considering that 40 percent of young Norwegian immigrant-group members drop out of upper secondary school.

- Parents must be held responsible for the fact that children who were born in Norway, or who came here at age two or three, must be able to speak Norwegian when they start school. It must also be obligatory under the Education Law to learn Norwegian.

- A national register of children in grade school must be set up, so that the state knows who's actually in school in Norway. This is crucial for the implementation of the connection requirement.

- If parents want to send children to school outside the EU, the school must have prior approval from the government. So must the child's residential situation. The "free flight" of unprotected children is unworthy of a free country that stands for human rights.

- The founding of new private religious schools must be stopped. So far there are no Muslim schools in Norway, while there are several dozen in both Sweden and Denmark.[256] The conditions in many of these schools have been shown to be reprehensible.[257] They thwart integration, too. No setting plays a more important role in the integration of children than public schools.

- In public schools, zero tolerance must be practiced toward the special requirements that segregate the sexes. Zero tolerance must also be practiced in regard to every kind of harassment, with a special focus on protecting girls and Jews.

- Medical check-ups of children must be put in place in order to prevent and uncover cases of genital mutilation. As in France, parents shouldn't be able to collect child benefits unless their children have valid health cards.

- To combat the rising influence of political Islam, Norway must, like France, introduce a ban on the wearing of conspicuous religious symbols by students and school employees. This ban should also apply to government employees.

- The automatic granting of Norwegian citizenship to the foreign-born children of Norwegian citizens encourages polygamy and should be put an end to. The policy is especially harmful to women, for it renders mothers abroad virtually powerless in the face of demands from their husbands in Norway. Children should only be separated from their mothers in cases of deficient parenting.

- When a marriage is the basis for immigration, it must be required that the Muslim marriage contract ensures the wife a real right to divorce – regardless of whether she is the immigrating party or the party who lived in Norway prior to the marriage.

- The fetching of new spouses who are first or second cousins must be forbidden.

- To counteract pro forma marriage, and for other reasons, immigrants must be required to live in Norway for ten years before they can receive Norwegian citizenship.

- The Netherlands and Denmark require foreigners to pass tests in language and sociocultural knowledge before they can apply for marriage immigration. Norway should do the same. This is especially important in gauging new immigrants' potential success on the labour market.

- One of the government's main areas of concentration is employment. It's crucial for the integration of families that women enter the labour force, and this consideration must guide the formulation of labour-market measures.

- We must be careful about giving in to special demands generally. The more we give in to them, the more we strengthen community and religious leaders in immigrant enclaves, and the more we aid the growth of parallel societies that impede integration and threaten democracy.

- The various Muslim congregations' ideologies and political agendas should be examined with an eye to re-evaluating their qualifications for government support.

- The falsification of documents and the purchasing of other people's identity documents are widespread in major non-Western countries. Today we have no control over who is actually moving to Norway. Everyone who comes here through family reunification or family establishment should be identified – for example, through fingerprints or a DNA test.[258]

- We need a new population prognosis that takes into account the role of fetching marriages in population growth – and we also have to include in the tabulations the third and fourth generations of "immigrants."

The ethics of consistency

One very serious dilemma that must be resolved is how Norwegian authorities should deal in practical terms with assaults on children and young people – such as Samira, who was tricked into going to Somalia and denied her freedom, and such as Awa and her sisters, who were kept under lock and key in Gambia. So far, our political leaders have simply turned their backs on these unprotected children. The question is: how should government officials address the fact that some new citizens' relationship to their Norwegian citizenship does not seem to be any more genuine than a pro forma marriage?

I think that some kind of radical preventive action needs to be taken in regard to parents and other adults who aren't really interested in full participation in Norwegian democracy and who view their Norwegian citizenship as an expediency and nothing else – as the father of little Awa obviously does. It may be expedient for him, but it's a quandary for the Norwegian state and a torment for his children. Do we need to introduce a law that makes it possible to withdraw citizenship when a Norwegian citizen exhibits total indifference toward Norwegian democracy, justice, and the welfare state – and when that indifference is so powerful that it affects the human dignity of innocent children? And, moreover, when that citizen doesn't need Norwegian citizenship to be protected from persecution in another country?

The messages that are spread throughout Muslim communities, and that led Awa's father to keep his children in Gambia and to live very comfortably on his wife's welfare payments, are obviously very negative: acquaint yourself with Norwegian law and the Norwegian system – in order to exploit them to your own advantage. Abuse of the country's social system is a means of showing contempt; if we in Norway accept this abuse, it's nothing more than an expression of our own self-contempt.

If Norwegian officials really want to prosecute a test case against this man and others like him in Norway, it could be attempted. It would doubtless have a distinct preventive effect. We could also raise the consciousness of the population generally about the fact that basic legal protections and human rights apply to *everyone* in Norway – no matter what an individual's ethnic background may be.

10

"Take care of the future"

Undoubtedly, it's at the fortress of values that the great integration battle is taking place. So we shouldn't let ourselves be fooled into believing that being educated and having a job, for example, are necessarily the same thing as being integrated into Norwegian society. For an illustration of this fact, we need look no further than the men behind the 2005 London bombings: four young men, born and raised in England and all of them seemingly well-integrated. The leader of this little group, Mohammed Sidique Khan, even studied at the University of Leeds. Could integration go any worse? Another vivid example is the fact – established by a secret 2006 British report – that British police officers with so-called "Asian" backgrounds are ten times more corrupt than their non-"Asian" colleagues; Pakistani-British police officers are especially corrupt. The reason for this high level of corruption is supposedly pressure from the officers' families and communities. The report says that officers with Pakistani backgrounds live in a money culture in which it's considered one's duty to help one's family and where relatives and friends make sizable loans to one another.[259]

A comparable example in Norway is that of Zahid Mukhtar, now a doctor, who as a medical student publicly supported the death fatwa against Salman Rushdie for *The Satanic Verses*.[260] A more quotidian example is the statement, frequently made by young Norwegian Muslim men and women, that they can't imagine marrying a non-Muslim. Case in point: in May 2006, young Muslim women who were born in Norway, who attend college, and who speak fluent Norwegian said without hesitation on NRK radio that Norwegian men are entirely unthinkable as spouses.[261] In the same year, young Muslims in Kristiansand looked into a television camera and proclaimed that they didn't want to marry Norwegian girls – they wanted to "be clean."[262]

The ugliest and most beautiful images

At the heart of the Norwegian struggle for integration are four fundamental values. The first is equality among all people, no matter what their social, religious, or ethnic background, and (in today's Norway) also without regard to clan, tribe, or caste. The second value is sexual equality. The third and fourth are religious freedom and freedom of expression. For me, these values summon three unforgettable images from recent Norwegian history. Two of the images are the strongest and most beautiful manifestations of equality in Norwegian public life that I know of. One of the images is of an event that took place on Christmas 2000 at the royal palace of Skaugum. Spontaneously and playfully, Queen Sonja got down on her knees on a polar-bear rug that had been allowed to keep its frightening head. Playing at the head of the polar bear was a fascinated, slightly scared little boy – the new member of the royal family, Marius, whose father, a convicted felon, had been the boyfriend of the Crown Princess, Mette Marit, before she married Sonja's son, Crown Prince Haakon. The Queen's open embrace of Marius as a full and beloved member of the family was a formidable blow for equality – a blow whose importance as a symbolic statement of values I think she herself well understood. At an earlier time in Norway, children like Marius would have been considered bastards. Today, many of Norway's new citizens don't consider such children the equal of children born in wedlock.

The next image also involves the royal family. When Haakon married Mette-Marit, they broke the last barrier in the

Norwegian population regarding who can marry whom. Mette-Marit, not just an ordinary girl but a single mother, was found worthy of becoming the kingdom's next queen. Only a few decades earlier, this would have been unthinkable. Even though some people still criticize the marriage, Mette-Marit appears to enjoy broad acceptance among the Norwegian people. For me, the royal marriage is the single most important manifestation of equality in today's Norway. I've asked Muslim acquaintances in Oslo what their coreligionists, generally speaking, think about the fact that Mette-Marit, a single mother, was permitted to marry Crown Prince Haakon Magnus. The answers are unprintable. (I'll simply refer readers back to Chapter Eight, where I recorded some of the adjectives that Turkish students in Berlin used to describe Hatun Sürücü.)

In terms of values, the ugliest image in contemporary Norwegian politics is of an encounter that took place in the government offices in Oslo. In August 2004, Qazi Hussein Ahmad, the aforementioned leader of the extremist Pakistani party Jamaat-i-Islami, was given permission to travel to Norway. He received this permission even though he, an Islamist, had been denied entry into several other countries, such as the Netherlands, on security grounds. That wasn't all: Ahmad was also granted an official meeting with the then integration minister, Erna Solberg. When the decision was made to have conversations with him – a man who stands for an international Islamic revolution and a caliphate in which Muslims would rule over other people, where criticism of religion would be considered blasphemy and be punished with death, and where the view of women would be of a sort that we've never experienced at any point in Norwegian history – one might expect that Solberg would have waved the banner of Norwegian values high. Or that she would, at the very least, have reached out to him her fully equal Norwegian hand. But no: Solberg put one hand on her chest and bowed – greeting him in precisely the way that an Islamist would expect a woman to greet him. A more illustrative picture of a value-related prostration on

Norwegian soil I have never witnessed. I'm inclined to interpret Solberg's action as indicative of a lack of knowledge about the man she was meeting; either that or she was sending out, in the name of democracy, a misguided gesture to Ahmad's Norwegian-Pakistani followers. The gesture, in any case, amounted to an expression of disdain for the housewives of all the Pakistani men who cheered Ahmad during his Norway visit, and a betrayal of all freedom-loving Norwegian-Pakistanis in Norway. The gesture may also have been the expression of a misguided humility. When we visit other cultures, we follow the unwritten rule: "When in Rome, do as the Romans do." Solberg acted as if "Rome is also Norway," and thereby enacted an absolute cultural self-subordination on her own country's soil.

Things we don't want to see with our own eyes

If we hope to keep Norway's secular democracy, welfare state, and sense of interdependent community from breaking down, it's utterly obligatory that we have a popular awakening in regard to values. In this connection, there are three points that I consider especially important. The first point has to do with Islamism's comprehensiveness. The second has to do with veils on Muslim girls and women. And the third concerns family-arranged marriage. At the heart of all three points is the struggle for the souls of girls and women.

First, let's look at family-arranged marriage – a topic about which Norwegian society has exhibited a sensational forgetfulness in regard to our own history and a tendency to deny our own values. Family-arranged marriage is incompatible with basic democratic values: equal rights, sexual equality, religious freedom, and freedom of expression. Family-arranged marriage doesn't establish equality between the sexes; on the contrary, it helps to maintain the oppression of women and encourages the tyranny of beauty. On the "marriage market," the ideal future bride is the certified virgin. It is precisely for this reason that the youngest available girls are the ones that are most valuable in the marketplace, since they're the ones least likely to have been "defiled." There must be no suspicion that she's willful and thus potentially insubordinate. There should not be doubt that she understands and accepts her subordinate wifely role.

Nor must there be any question as to whether she's fertile. As the first young woman I met who had been forced to marry said to me: "I was considered a good prospect because I'm wide in the hips." There must also be a guarantee that she's learned her housewifely duties down to her fingertips. And the chastity of her sisters, aunts, mother, and other female relatives must be beyond question. If their honour is "soiled," then it will be said that "she has it in her genes." The prospective groom encounters virtually no comparable demand for sexual purity on the marriage market. This can be illustrated by a Pakistani saying: "A man is like a horse. No matter how dirty he becomes, he can always be washed clean. But a dirty woman can never be washed clean."

On the subcontinent, the prospective bride is evaluated with regard to her hair, her facial skin, her teeth, the shape of her nose, her eyes, her waist, her breasts, her hands, and her feet. The ideal hair is long and thick. The skin must be free of blemishes, and the paler it is, the better. The teeth should be unstained, normal in size and not crooked. The nose must not be big, and it should have a gentle curve. Large almond eyes with long eyelashes are regarded as most beautiful. The bride should have a womanly figure: a small waist and breasts that can contain plenty of milk are preferable. She must not be too slim, since this can be interpreted as a sign of low fertility; nor must she be overweight, since slimness is the ideal.[263] Her hands and feet should be small and narrow.

The requirements for the groom have less to do with his looks than his social status and finances. Possibly the most important thing about his appearance is his skin colour – the paler he is, the more attractive he's considered to be. (Recall that Mina was married off to "the ugliest" – i.e., the darkest – of the candidates for her hand.)[264] What's crucial is the future husband's potential as provider and protector.

On this marriage market, equality is conspicuous by its absence. One marries one's own. Marriage within the family is often preferred because such marriages guarantee "clean merchandise." Even those who venture outside their families still marry within their own ethnic group, clan, caste, or tribe. Others – outsiders – are unworthy of being considered as potential mates. At bottom, then, this custom is extremely discriminatory and, in practice, explicitly racist.

The inequality also leads to a lack of religious freedom. It's just as unthinkable to seek a prospective spouse outside one's own religion as outside one's own ethnicity, clan, caste, or tribe. The marriage market is thus religiously homogeneous.

And what about freedom of speech? A glance at the Norwegian media provides the answer: how many articles have been published in which people whose native cultures embrace family-arranged marriage say that they reject the custom, that they want to marry out of love, and that a prospective spouse's ethnicity or religious background doesn't matter? Answer: extremely few. And those few, most likely, are themselves married to people whom they chose out of love and live outside the Muslim communities as integrated members of Norwegian society. But how often, by contrast, do you read interviews in which young and middle-aged people alike laud family-arranged marriage? Very often – which is hardly surprising, given that those who live in Muslim communities know what will happen to them if they criticize arranged marriage. Such a critic is seen as a dissident, a traitor to his or her own culture. He or she has become "Norwegian" (or, as they say, a "cocoanut" – "brown outside and white inside"). Muslim girls and women who criticize the institution are condemned with particular intensity. To support an open marriage market on which young people are allowed to seek out love and romance is almost synonymous with speaking up for sexuality outside of marriage; it represents total rebellion against the entire extended-family power system –

indeed, rebellion against Islam itself. In such a way is free speech about family-arranged marriage silenced.

Obedience is also a key factor. Respect for one's parents' wishes is a hard and fast law in Islam. The Cairo Declaration reflects this reality when it says that "parents are entitled to certain rights from their children…in accordance with the tenets of the Shari'ah." What I think the Declaration is referring to here, above all, is parents'right to be obeyed, to marry off their children, and to be taken care of in their old age.[265]

Family-arranged marriages create the optimal conditions for the violation of the right to marry in accordance with one's own wishes. They also violate the human-rights principle of equality between men and women, and the principle of religious equality and freedom. This kind of marriage is a blast from the past – from a time when human rights was a non-concept.

It's as if we've forgotten our great historical figures from the nineteenth century – authors like Amalie Skram, Jonas Lie, Alexander Kielland, Bjørnstjerne Bjørnson, Henrik Ibsen, and Camilla Collett, to mention the most important. All of them rebelled against the oppressiveness of the system of arranged marriage in their own day, especially as it was practiced among the well-to-do. In *Kommandørens døtre* (*The Commodore's Daughters*) by Jonas Lie (1886), we meet the distinguished, strong-willed commodore, who wants to marry his daughters off without regard for their feelings. In *Amtmannens døtre* (*The District Governor's Daughters*) by Camilla Collett (1854-55), a young woman named Sofie is ruined because she dares to express her feelings. After publishing this book, which caused widespread offense, Collett was expelled from polite society for over thirty years.[266] The reviewers were merciless. They felt that Collett had exaggerated – had cherry-picked a few accounts and generalized them into a social problem. Collett answered the complaints twenty years later in her preface to the novel's third edition, writing that her book's title could just as well have been *A Country's Daughters*: "It gives, considerably softened, a description of the kind of life that awaited the daughter in the more well-bred classes....In my long life, spent under these conditions, I hadn't experienced anything other than tragedies in families, nor, as far as the tradition goes back, heard any report of anything else." To those who thought she was generalizing from a handful of unhappy stories about love-hungry souls (an accusation often leveled at critics of arranged marriage in Norway today), Collett said this: "Keep quiet about the truth: our society's rules are organized and adopted in such a way that the women's happiness depends only on a possibility, a mere chance, that is approximately as calculable as outcome of a state lottery drawing in which one has a ticket." She also emphasizes that her description is considerably toned down because "it would be all too alarmingly sudden to tear the veil away from conditions that we've all agreed not to see with our own eyes."

The way in which contemporary Norway has betrayed its own Sofies (and its own versions of Bjørnson's Øivind Plassen, the poor boy who couldn't marry the farm girl Marit) is, to put it mildly, scandalous. It's also scandalous that intellectuals, then as now, claim that romantic feelings are something Western, that "we" must respect the fact that "others" marry for practical reasons.[267] As if romance had anything to do with genetics! Such thinking on the part of Norwegians reflects condescension both in terms of culture and values. What's striking about this condescension is that Norwegian policy effectively rewards a custom that's contrary to basic democratic values: family-arranged fetching marriage between strangers or relatives – whose first encounter usually takes place on another continent and on their wedding night – is rewarded with immigration and a Norwegian passport.

Are undemocratic Muslims good for Norway?

One of those who have warned of the danger of Islamism in Europe is a man whose experience makes him worth listening to. Mehdi Mozaffari, a profesor at Aarhus University, is the first professor of Islam in Denmark. Mozaffari fled Iran in the late

267

1970s, when the Islamists began to march – a march that ended in 1979 with the world's first Islamic revolution. In the strongest possible terms, Mozaffari calls Islamism *the* totalitarian ideology of our times, on a par with Nazism, fascism, and Communism. The shared attributes of these ideologies are Jew-hatred and a belief in supermen: "Nazism, fascism, and Bolshevism are now no longer powerful ideologies; Islamism is the totalitarian ideology and movement of our time. And it has a dimension that the three others didn't have: the religious. This makes it even more dangerous. Stalin, Hitler, and Mussolini tried to justify their decisions using ordinary human reason: people would be mobilized to make war for worldly motives. But Islamism doesn't need reason; it's based on a religious obligation. One is loyal not to a state or a leader, but to Allah."[268]

The parallels between Islam and, for example, Nazism and fascism are far from strained. One of Germany's leading intellectuals, Hans Magnus Enzenberger, also points out this fact in his book *Men of Fear: The Radical Loser* (2006). Enzenberger shows, for example, how the Communists' revolutionary project, the world proletariat, has been replaced by the umma, and Mao, Marx, and Lenin by the Koran: "The party is no longer the masses' self-appointed representative; that role has been taken over by the Islamist warriors' widely ramified conspiratorial network." It's also a historical fact that there were intimate ties between Hitler and Mussolini and leaders of the Arab world.[269] Hitler and Mussolini had deep respect and admiration for the aggressive and violent elements of Islam, especially in armed warfare. The Nazis' positive view of Islamism can also be observed in Norway today: the neo-Nazi Norwegian group Vigrid admires Hamas for the same reasons that Hitler did – namely, its violent and militant aspects.[270] Similarly, the Arab leaders' affection for Germany was grounded in the hope that Hitler would succeed in wiping out the Jews.[271]

Mozaffari believes that European politicians have yet to realize that Islamism threatens the continent's free secular democracies. He notes that democracy is founded on the principle that all people have the same human worth: "In Islam they don't. Infidels don't have the same rights as believers." Mozzafari notes another crucial difference: that in democratic states laws are formulated and passed by elected officials, while Islamic sharia law "is God-given" and therefore can't be changed by mere human beings. According to Mozzafari, our task is to "annihilate a number of taboos in order to get Muslims to fully accept equality and the understanding of democracy that we regard as natural in Denmark."[272]

When he uses the word "taboos," Mozaffari is alluding to the Muhammed cartoons, which he believes Islamists exploited in order to attack the basic pillars of democracy. It was for this reason that Mozaffari, during the cartoon riots, joined eleven other intellectuals – including Salman Rushdie and Ayaan Hirsi Ali – in issuing an international manifesto against Islamism.[273] The manifesto, which eulogized democracy and condemned Islamism, chided Western politicians, media, and opinion-makers who directly or indirectly supported "a certain form of self-censorship and censorship in order to oblige the Islamists." Mozaffari notes that Islamists are using globalization as an argument for censorship and self-censorship: "They say that the West, in a globalized world, should respect other cultures: for example, the press should not be able to print drawings of the prophet Muhammed. But what this amounts to is *them* forcing their own culture on *us*....If we gradually give in to those who don't want a democratic society, there's a danger of succumbing, step by step, to a spirit of resignation, because they shout loudly, burn embassies, and beat people to death." Mozzafari says explicitly that European democracy is already in a struggle against Islamism: "It's a struggle that can't end in compromise. You can't take a little democracy and a little dictatorship and make a synthesis out of it. It's either/or."

The Satanic Verses was far more blasphemous than the Muhammed cartoons. Rushdie portrayed Muhammed as both devil and gigolo, and depicted the holy city of Mecca as a bordello where Muhammed's favourite wife, Aisha, was the most expensive whore. But after the Rushdie fatwa, the author was fervently defended in Norway and throughout Europe. Few Europeans cautioned against offending religion. Several European countries even responded to the death threats against Rushdie by calling home their ambassadors. Why did so many people react so differently to the cartoon controversy? Mozaffari believes that the reason is that we've come to take freedom of speech for granted: "Until now we've had the privilege of believing that freedom of speech is free. Now we're discovering that freedom of speech can also cost something. It will cost income, jobs, freedom, security. Are people ready to pay only a fraction of the price that so many other fighters for free speech – in the Arab world, in the Soviet Union, in China – have had to pay?"[274]

Ten years from now, Europe will be home to about twenty-five million young Muslims. If these young people aren't brought up to support secular democracy, we'll face a dangerous scenario: "An undemocratic population of young Muslims will constitute a significant power bloc in Europe and perhaps Denmark," says Mozaffari. "It's the worst scenario." He warns in the strongest terms against making concessions to anti-democratic, intolerant forces in the name of tolerance. On the contrary, Islam's entry into Europe requires that we revive the same methods that were employed during the Enlightenment. "If people criticize Muslims, they're perceived as intolerant and discriminatory – in other words, reality is turned on its head. Muslims are people like all others and should not be judged by any other measure." Mozzafari believes that we must learn from our own Enlightenment and the criticism of Christianity that was an integral part of it: "When you criticize something holy, it's suddenly not so holy anymore. It is normalized."[275]

"Norway has acquired a people of faith"

After the Muhammed cartoons appeared and the Islamist storm broke – both at home and in the Muslim world – the

Danish government made no concessions. Prime Minister Anders Fogh Rasmussen was crystal clear in his statements about democracy and religion. He pointed out that European countries owed their enormous progress over the past few centuries to the fact "that there had been people who had the courage to provoke. Some were even called heretics, and it cost other people's lives. But it is liberating that there were some who dared to take on the heretical task of insisting that the world was not flat, but round. In a totally fundamental sense, this has to do with the fact that enlightened and free societies advance further than unenlightened and unfree societies, precisely because some people dare to provoke and criticize authority, whether it is political or religious authority."[276] Fogh Rasmussen noted that there had also been controversy about the boundaries of free speech in relation to Christianity, and that criticism of religion always gets people worked up. He nonetheless warned firmly against letting a fear of extremists' reactions silence necessary criticism: "If that fear is allowed to paralyze our freedom of expression, then it will paralyze our democratic government, and then the radical circles will have achieved just what they want. We'll limit our freedom of expression and live another way. We'll be so scared by the threats that we'll suddenly curb ourselves and no longer dare to lead our lives and live up to those principles that we would like our society to be founded on."

Just over half a year later, in May 2006, when both the riots and the debate about the Muhammed cartoons had calmed down, Fogh Rasmussen wrote an op-ed for the Danish newspaper *Politiken*. In it, he argued that religion should occupy a smaller part of the public space, and pointed out how important it is to distinguish clearly between politics and religion. If this distinction isn't maintained, he warned, society will fall behind, and the nation's sense of solidarity will also be weakened: "There is a reason to issue a warning about fundamentalists and fundamentalism in every camp. Religion can take freedom and personal responsibility away from people....It becomes totally grotesque when it is demanded that people today uncritically and literally obey ingenious interpretations of rules set forth in thousand-year-old holy scriptures. It is pure darkening. Finally, there is a risk that fundamentalist religion will, quite simply, put the brakes on development and progress. This is true especially if the religion places itself above science and education and forbids research and education in certain scientific areas or theories that might clash with religious dogmas. Such societies are doomed to fall behind in renewal and development, growth and prosperity....we should be more aware of those principles and attitudes that have made Denmark a society with a strong feeling of community. We will do this by insisting that religion is, above all, a private matter."[277]

Fogh Rasmussen's tone in this op-ed could hardly have been more different from the tone taken by the Norwegian government during the cartoon crisis. At that time, Norway's leaders went a long way towards fulfilling Islamist demands for censorship and self-censorship. The mantra was "yes, we have full freedom of expression, but not all expression is wise," and the clear insinuation was that the first Norwegian newspaper to print a fascimile of the *Jyllands-Posten* cartoons, a small evangelical publication called *Magazinet,* had acted indefensibly and unethically.

It was widely asserted that "freedom of speech" is not the same as "the obligation to speak." In the heat of the controversy, we heard these words from Norwegian Foreign Minister Jonas Gahr Støre: "Norway has acquired a people of faith." Støre's statement was an unambiguous reference to the desire for respect for (many) Muslims' religious sensitivity. But doesn't such a statement generalize about, and thus stigmatize and discriminate against, people in Norway whose roots are in Muslim cultures? Isn't it also an indirect expression of disdain for all other groups' beliefs, whether they're Jews, Hindus, Catholics, Buddhists, Sikhs, Protestants, or atheists? And doesn't it betray a lack of awareness of what can drive a society into the gutter – in regard to solidarity as well as development, growth, and prosperity? And finally, doesn't it invalidate our ancestors'

272

struggle for freedom, which is the entire foundation for immigration from non-Western countries?

My enthusiasm for Christian conservative thinking is extremely limited; I am not myself a personal believer. But in early 2006, in the heat of Norway's own national crisis over the Danish cartoons, it was hard not to feel sympathy for the editor of the Christian newspaper *Magazinet,* Vebjørn Selbekk. To be sure, he played his part in encouraging the government's open mixture of politics and religion – a cause which is perhaps close to his heart – but the treatment he received at the hands of both politicians and the media was way out of bounds. He was essentially labeled an extremist on a par with the violent radicals of the Muslim world. It was unsettling to see a person who represents no threat whatsoever to peace or to secular democracy being linked with such people. And as far as the ill-timed mixture of politics and religion was concerned, the Norwegian government outdid itself when it called a press conference at which the "enemies" – the Islamic Council of Norway and Selbekk – were reconciled. Selbekk apologized for the dramatic consequences that his publication of the cartoons had had for Norway's international position. He apologized for the murders that had been committed in the Muslim world by violent Islamists, and for having offended Muslims' religious feelings; it should be noted that he *didn't* apologize for his freedom of speech. The Islamic Council accepted his apology, and Selbekk, who had been threatened with death, was given the council's "protection" – that is, the council would see to it that he would not be assassinated. The council turned itself, that is, into a judicial authority of the Kingdom of Norway – and the government didn't object. On the contrary, every TV viewer in Norway could see that the cabinet members were thoroughly satisfied with the reconciliation. The fear of reprisal was abating. The government submitted to Islam – Islam, which of course literally means submission.

The Islamic Council praised the government for its exemplary handling of the case – it had, after all, taken the side of the so-called offended party. Next thing we knew, two of the council's members and a leading official of the Norwegian Church – Olav Dag Hauge, Dean of the Oslo Cathedral – were in Qatar, at the expense of the Foreign Ministry, for friendly conversations with the Islamists' "pope," Yusuf al-Qaradawi. On 14 February 2006, Hauge told *Aftenposten* that he had met "a person who was open, who wanted dialogue, and who was not extreme, as far as I can see. He was very clear about the fact that he wanted dialogue and peace."

Hauge also said that al-Qaradawi was satisfied with the Norway's handling of the matter: "Al-Qaradawi clearly stated that further measures on the part of Norway are not necessary, now that the apology has been made. He is satisfied with the Norwegian reaction....He has now dropped all the demands he made of Norway." Thus did the world's leading Islamist ideologue – a man who, with a fatwa, can mobilize millions of Muslims – gain entry into the Norwegian political arena. It's precisely for this reason that Walid al-Kubaisi considers al-Qaradawi more dangerous than Osama bin Laden.[278]

The Norwegian government's handling of the crisis created by Islamists in Denmark and in parts of the Muslim world was, in my opinion, a setback for serious critical reflection. At the finish line of its ideological slalom run, the government trampled the spirit of the Enlightenment, thereby betraying secular Muslims who want to live free lives and think for themselves. The government granted Islamists in Norway a larger role in the public arena. "It was a pure darkening," to borrow Fogh Rasmussen's words.

You could call the Norwegian government's action a preventive capitulation, motivated by a fear of (perhaps) losing billions in future oil revenues, combined with a fear that extremists' threats of violence would be carried out on Norwegian soil. If the government's "respect" for its Islamist interlocutors was founded on fear, it's a despicable respect, for it's really not about genuine respect at all but about giving in to tyranny. Also dropped down the memory hole was the simple history lesson is that it's individuals – not gods or prophets – whose freedom needs to be safeguarded.

What we also witnessed, in all probability, was a forewarning of more inflamed religio-political issues that may find their way onto the Islamists' agenda. A particularly obvious example is the demand that sharia law should decide whether Muslim women can get a divorce.

The new vocabulary of power that manifested itself in the assault on freedom of expression included the term "to offend": to offend religious feelings, or (more correctly) to offend religious dogmas. Few noted the obvious offense given to the foundations of democracy. Nobody remembered that Collett, in *The District Governor's Daughters,* had also given offense. Nor did anyone point out that Ibsen, in his time, had insulted myths, dogmas, and the abusers of power, or that Bjørnson, too, had rebelled against inequality. There was also silence about the historic speech given by the author Arnulf Øverland to a students' organization in 1931: "Christianity, The Tenth Plague." Early in his speech, Øverland had said the following words, which today are once again relevant:

> This is probably blasphemy. Then again, I'm not so sure exactly what it is. I only know that even though I'm right, the priests will start to scream and carry on, because somebody has offended them – or has scoffed at God, which amounts to more or less the same thing.
>
> If, for example, they aren't given the right to determine the National Theater's repertoire – if, for example, we heathens, those of us who go to the theater, want to see a drama that isn't particularly religious, they become sensitive and sore, and then there's screaming and complaining beyond compare.
>
> But what should one do now? I'm seriously afraid that anyone who tries to give a clear and honest account of the Christian faith will inevitably be found guilty of blasphemy.

Øverland was indeed prosecuted for blasphemy, but was freed after defending himself. He was never threatened with death by religious or political extremists; nor were there violent riots. Many a Christian leader was offended by him, but this didn't result in people beginning to put limits on their speech. On the contrary – Øverland kicked in the doors that have remained open ever since.

When it really counted, then, all of our offended foremothers and forefathers were forgotten. Nor did anybody in Norway take note of the most macabre action of our time, as far as religious offense is concerned.

I'm referring to the two thousand-year-old Buddha statues in Afghanistan – treasures of world culture – that the Islamist Taliban government blew up in March 2001. In response, no Buddhists held violent street riots, burned flags, or set fire to embassies. Nor did any Islamist movements or governments in the Muslim world loudly protest the offense given by the Taliban to the Buddhist religion and culture. Nor did we see massive Muslim demonstrations. As Hans Magnus Enzenberger says, "To wound the infidels' feelings is everyday fare....There are loud demands for respect, but they show no respect for others." Indeed, offending people who think differently belongs "to the Islamic media's standard repertoire" and the detonation of the Buddha statues "is understood in Afghanistan as an action welcomed by God" (2006:40ff).

For the purposes of integration, it's hard not to conclude that Norway's handling of the Muhammed cartoon crisis was a setback. The Islamists' power was manifested in their view of the world as consisting of two antagonistic spheres: the world-embracing ummah – the community of believers that crosses lines of race and nationality – and "the rest of us." And now almost all of us have become more sensitive and scared to carry on the Enlightenment heritage – a heritage that must be preserved if we're to survive as a free secular democracy. What we need now, in the wake of the Muhammed cartoons, are more people who follow in Øverland's footsteps and dare to be heretics and give offense by formulating an "Islam, the Eleventh Plague." As Ayaan Hirsi Ali puts it: "Let us [Muslims] have a Voltaire" (*The Caged Virgin,* p. 41).

In the months surrounding the controversy, I received several highly revealing communications from uneasy writers and journalists. One of them, who'd written a book that was in the process of being printed, read aloud to me some excerpts that touched on Islam, then asked: "Do you think I can be killed for these sentences?" Another author had the same concern, and asked me whether certain passages about Muhammed in a manuscript that hadn't yet been submitted for publication would make the author's son fatherless. Yes, Europe has definitely acquired an "incomprehensible enemy within," as Naser Khader noted in *Berlingske Tidende* on 2 April 2006. Islamists are using benevolent multicultural ideology as a cover to introduce sharia bit by bit. The European democracies will be forced to wear fetters – and sell out democracy. The Islamists were not seeking an apology for the fact that centuries-old Arabic images of Muhammed, the armed warlord, were modernized in *Jyllands-Posten* into a Muhammed with a bomb. What they were after was to subordinate our society, step by step, to their ideology and culture.

The veil, the Star of David, and the swastika

Which brings us to the most powerful symbol of the way in which Norwegian politicians on both sides of the political fence are working hand in hand with Islamists to help advance Islam's interests in Norway. These are Norwegians who, in their blind friendliness and naivete, behave the same way that the Western "friends of the Soviet people" did toward Communism – the ones whom Lenin called "useful idiots." The symbol in question – which I think of as the Islamists' "engine of war" – is the veil. It's placed on Muslim girls and women to consolidate their subordinate position, and to ensure their continued non-integration into a free mainstream society. It guarantees that they won't have the same rights as other women. It is, make no mistake, an ideological weapon – a means of taking power in the public space: the more females who wear the veil, the greater the influence political Islam will have on people's daily life, and the closer the Islamists will come to "paradise on earth."

An article on the Islamic Cultural Centre's website illustrates clearly the apartheid nature of the veil:

> As a Muslim, the woman should make herself beautiful with a veil of honour, dignity, virtue, purity, and integrity. She should avoid all actions and gestures that might excite the passions of people other than her husband or trigger evil suspicions about her morality. She is warned against exposing her charms or showing off her physical attractions to people she does not know. The veil she must put on is a veil that can save her soul from weakness, her mind from wandering, her eyes from lecherous glances, and her personality from demoralization. Islam is highly preoccupied with the woman's integrity, with the protection of her morals and sexual morality, and with concern for her character and personality.[279]

The veil, then, strengthens social subordination. It also represents enormous political power. One of the few who have understood this is Mehdi Mozaffari. Mozaffari has been at the centre of Islamists' struggle for the souls of women: he taught at the University of Teheran in the late 1970s, when the Islamic Revolution was brewing. It's worth attending to Mozaffari's account of what happened when Islamist students turned up with veils: "The other girls didn't dare not to do the same. They were afraid that they would be regarded as indecent. I remember that when the girls from the well-educated classes put on the headscarf in order to be left in peace, they chose the stylish Parisian headscarf. But then the headscarf turned into the fully covering veil. It ended with an Islamic revolution."[280] Of course Mozaffari doesn't mean that the Iranian Revolution itself can be explained by the veil. What he's pointing to is the veil as political symbol – the power that lies within it and the political shifts that it reflects and portends.

Another Iranian refugee in Europe has had the same experience as Mozaffari. Her name is Chadortt Djavann, she lives in France, and she's an anthropologist and author. Djavann has dissected the veil's role in the Islamist struggle against European values.[281] Her conclusion, as discussed in an article by the Danish writer Helle Merete Brix, is that the veil is "the Islamists' foremost engine of war" in the public space. For Djavann, Europe is "the Islamists' ideal laboratory." In democratic Europe, the Islamists, largely without government interference, are able to establish Islamist norms and rules in the public square and at educational institutions on various levels, especially where sexuality and marriage are concerned. The veil is the paramount symbol of the Islamists' ongoing ideological struggle, which is a struggle against the integration of Muslims, against Western values, and against women's liberation. Women must be covered so that men won't be tempted. Covering women advances the Muslim order. Djavann explodes the myth of the "innocent veil." As she makes clear, there has never been a Muslim veil whose purpose was not to indicate the subordinate status of women. The veil identifies the woman as an object and reduces her to a sex organ. In Djavann's view, then, the veil is – quite simply – pornographic.

Precisely how the veil contributes to the sexualization of women became clear to me in 1994 when I was visited by a woman from Pakistan. She'd never been in the West before. The experience unsettled her – in a positive sense. She was astonished that she could walk freely in the street without any covering, meet men's eyes, respond to smiles, sit alone at a café – all without being sexually harassed! She'd never experienced this in her homeland, even though she'd always been veiled in public. "For the first time in my life," she said one day, "I know what it's like to be treated like a human being and not a sex object."

279

For me, the veil is also the most effective expression of a refusal to take part in democratic society. Djavann is on to exactly the same thing when she says that the primary reason for veiling women is to underscore women's commercial value: the covered woman is a commodity – one that only Muslim men can deal in. She's the property of the Muslim men in her family, and can only be purchased by another Muslim man. The veil is an indication that the woman wearing it belongs only to Muslim men and to men who want to convert to Islam.

A key question is this: can Islam exist without the veil? Djavann says that Islam can, but not Islamism. For Islamism, the veil is "the emblem, the flag, and the key to the Islamic system."

The West's "useful idiots," however, regard the veil as a matter of individual choice. They smoothly overlook the fact that many girls and woman are forced to wear the veil (cf. the above-mentioned study by Courneuvre, which revealed considerable fear of diverging from the veiled masses). In such countries as Iran, Saudi Arabia, and Afghanistan, the choice for women is simple: either choose subordination or be punished. Djavann urges European supporters of the veil to open their eyes to the Islamists' strategy. Islamism's imperialistic ideology is reflected, she believes, in the mobs' shouts of "Allah akhbar!" (Allah is the greatest) as well as in the use of the veil. To cover women is a means of humbling and winning over Muslim women who might be tempted to liberate themselves from Islamism's system and ideology. This is why the veil is an "engine of war."

For me the veil also brings to mind two very different symbols: the Star of David and the swastika. The Star of David, because the veil symbolizes women's subordinated position and limited rights; she's an underling, both morally and intellectually. The swastika, because Islamists regard Muslims as supermen who are intended to reign over others. To quote the Koran, sura 3, verse 110: "You are the best community ever raised among the people." And "the best community" is supposed to rule over the other people, who under sharia law are accorded the subordinate role of so-called dhimmis – that is, non-Muslims who are given protection by Muslim authorities if they willingly submit to those authorities. They are accorded limited rights and must pay a special tax to the Muslim state. As the Koran says (sura 9, verse 29): "You shall fight back against those who do not (…) abide by the religion of truth – among those who received the scripture – until they pay the due tax, willingly or unwillingly."

In the debate about the veil, the "useful idiots" and spokespeople for Muslim organizations cite the right to be different, invoke religious and individual freedom, and argue that the veil gives women a secure identity. By wearing the veil and wide coat, they claim, women escape the tyranny of beauty. Isn't it about time that the veil's supporters recognize what it is they're protecting and promoting? Isn't it about time they realize who they're collaborating with – namely, the Muslim Brotherhood, Yusuf al-Qaradawi, the Islamist communities in Norway and an ideology that is "pure darkening"?

And what about Muslim women themselves? Of course not all those who wear the veil are forced to do so; nor are they all Islamists in their hearts and minds. Some wear it out of habit, having first learned to do so in earliest childhood. Others do it because of group pressure or family pressure. For still others, it's a way of communicating their rejection of mainstream society and its fundamental values. Some believe their religion demands it. And some are motivated by Islamist ideology. Perhaps what's most striking is how unaware veiled women are of the values they're communicating. Few, moreover, take responsibility for the fact that by wearing the veil they're promoting apartheid-like values, and helping to pressure other women into wearing it. It can't be, can it, that Muslim women are born victims?

Is Norway worth defending?

Norway today is different from the Norway of twenty years ago. And in twenty years it will be different from the Norway of today. But there are certain fundamental elements of Norwegian society about which we clearly need a broad debate. We need a debate, for example, about why intolerance is tolerated in the name of tolerance. We need a debate about which values and social structures in Norway are worth defending. We need a debate about the reasons why we've become one of the world's best countries to live in – which of course has to do with a lot more than our oil billions. In this debate it has to be permissible to raise high the banner of values – without being self-effacing or (on the other hand) overvaluing ourselves. Our focus must be on democracy – and on how we can maintain citizens' feeling of belonging to Norwegian society. Our focus must be on preserving solidarity through common language, fundamental values, and knowledge about our history and culture – the glue that holds us together as a people.

We must also be on guard against contracting the "Swedish disease." In Sweden, which can perhaps be characterized as the most politically authoritarian country in Western Europe, the political and intellectual elite, with plenty of help from a generally servile national media, has laboured tenaciously, and with increasing intensity, to keep factual documentation out of the public eye and to avert public debate. Things have gone so far that any problem caused by Sweden's massive immigration is deemed a result of structural racism – that is to say, it's the Swedish state, Swedish culture, and ethnic Swedes who are the root of all evil. It can hardly be believed, but the Swedish state even renounces its own culture and history. This was perhaps most vividly encapsulated by comments made by the Social Democratic minister of integration, Mona Sahlin, in a 2004 address to a Kurdish audience. Sahlin, wearing a veil, said that immigrants living in Sweden are fortunate because they have such a rich culture and history, whereas Sweden only has such corny, silly things as Midsummer Night.[282] I had this anecdote in mind when I stood up in the audience at a 2005 conference in Stavanger and asked a representative of the Swedish government, parliamentary secretary Lise Bergh: "Is Swedish culture worth defending?" The answer came promptly: "Well, what is Swedish culture? And with that I guess I've answered the question." Bergh made no attempt, by either word or gesture, to hide her cultural self-loathing.

In no other European country, it seems, do the leaders exhibit as much self-loathing as in Sweden. As Bergh herself made clear in her Stavanger lecture, this self-loathing was essentially made official policy in 1997. In that year, as she explained, the Swedish government outlined a new immigration and integration policy, "a new way of thinking," whereby Swedes were to view their country not as distinctively Swedish in its culture and fundamental values but as a "culture of diversity," and were enjoined to respect and develop this diversity. In short, Swedish culture as such was declared undesirable; it was history. Henceforth, the principal focus would be on making so-called structural adaptations to accommodate immigrants, and on systematically combating the bigotry of native Swedes against new groups of citizens. Bergh explained that since so-called "everyday racism" was rooted in a distinctly Swedish notion of what is and isn't Swedish, it was decided that Sweden must turn away from those things that are viewed as Swedish.

Europeanized Islam or Islamized Europe?

The British historian Arnold J. Toynbee wrote that Greco-Roman civilization had died by suicide, not murder.[283] Swedish civilization and culture seem to be well on the way to suicide. If so, this may have dramatic consequences for those of us in Norway, Denmark, and Finland. Pessimists in Denmark think it's only a question of time before that country will have to stop allowing people from Sweden to cross the bridge over the Kattegat without visas – mainly because it's expected that the Swedish welfare state will collapse in the foreseeable future, which could lead to mass migration.[284]

As for Europe's future, the Syrian-born German professor Bassam Tibi says that the question of the preservation of

European culture and values comes down, quite simply, to this: either Islam will be Europeanized, or Europe will be Islamized. By a "Europeanized" Islam, Tibi means an Islam that's thoroughly secularized – and thus privatized. He warns explicitly against the wolf in sheep's clothing – namely, Euro-Islam as preached by Tariq Ramadan.[285] Bernard Lewis, the world-class historian of Islam, goes a step further. Lewis, who is known as a friend of Islam and an admirer of its golden age, believes that Europe will have a Muslim majority within a hundred years. Europe will then be an extension of the Arab world. It will become "the Arabic West."[286]

And at the heart of the struggle to capture Europe's soul, now and in the future, will be the Muslim girls and women, symbolized by the veil, the Islamists' "engine of war."

"Take care of the future"

A few days after Theo van Gogh was murdered on an Amsterdam street on 2 November 2004, I was in that city for a meeting with Ayaan Hirsi Ali that had been arranged several months earlier. Because of the assassination, Hirsi Ali had immediately gone underground, and Dutch security services had whisked her out of the country and to safety on a Marine base in the U.S.; the Netherlands could not afford to risk yet another political assassination.[287] But since I had a ticket that couldn't be refunded, I went anyway – to talk to people, to get a sense of the atmosphere in the country, and to place flowers at the site of the murder.

I also wanted to see the mosque to which the murderer belonged: I wanted to see who went in and out of it, what kind of people they were. And I wanted to take a picture of it.

The experience turned out to be quite special – indeed, frightening. From the moment I pointed my camera at the building, it took just under ten seconds before seven Arab, Pakistani, and Afghani men stormed out of the front door and physically attacked me and my camera. They were between

284

twenty-five and thirty-five years old, and were all wearing wide pants and coats in accordance with the standard Islamist dress code. Some also had full beards and typical Islamist head coverings. They exhibited an aggression and self-confidence that were out of another world. It was plain that none of the Dutch passersby who witnessed this incident so much as considered intervening. After the men had yanked me around a bit, slightly scratching up my arms and causing me some neck pain, they got their way: the pictures were erased. And they said farewell in this way: "You go back home. This is our country."

At the funeral of Theo van Gogh on 9 November 2004, his mother spoke over her son's casket. She said: "Freedom is not for frightened people." She concluded with these words: "Take care of the future."

Afterword

Do We Have Intelligence and Courage?

When I began writing this book, I didn't know exactly which topics I would cover.

I thought I would illuminate the problems of fetching marriage, the shipping off of unprotected children to their ancestral homelands to be schooled in the Koran, and the mutilation of girls – the issues closest to my heart for many years. I also realized that problematic aspects of Islam would have to be covered, and that it would be necessary to discuss immigration's growing threat to democracy and a national sense of community.

I was, however, surprised to realize how central the theme of women is to the ideological struggle for Europe's future. I was also fascinated that one expert after another considers Islam's view of women a crucial factor in the religion's decline, the Muslim world's stagnation, and the development of European Muslim enclaves plagued by social problems.

And I realized how fragile Europe's democracies are – precisely because of their openness, trust, and freedom.

I've undergone a thorough process of consciousness-raising in regard to the foundations of European democracy. I'm also profoundly convinced that critical reflection and free thought are essential to the preservation of secular democracy. No matter which dogmas and myths one takes on, the right to free thought must be protected. Our Enlightenment legacy – the ideas and values we have inherited from such Norwegian "heretics" as Camilla Collette, Henrik Ibsen, and Arnulf Øverland, to name only some of those who helped give rise to today's society – is an inheritance we cannot afford to lose.

It's also become clear to me that Islamism is, without question, the greatest political and ideological challenge of our time. It is discouraging to see the influence that Islamism has already managed to acquire in European democracies, whose openness it has exploited in order to establish networks and attain a political influence that reaches from the topmost political circles down to the street. It's frightening to see how well-organized these networks are, how closely the different movements collaborate, and how successful they've been at allying themselves with Europe's "useful idiots," who have eagerly come together with them in a struggle against capitalism, the U.S., and Israel. For the "useful idiots," it's all very clear: the West is the white oppressor, Islam the black victim.

It's also unsettling to see Christian church leaders, politicians, and political parties here in Norway carrying on dialogue with people who stand for turning back the clock. The will to resist what these individuals represent is conspicuous by its absence. The so-called "dialogue" shrouds reality and shelves discussion of anything sensitive. The hard questions are swept into dark corners – a true sign of a lack of honesty and of mutual respect.

One of the cardinal sins is that political leaders have made freedom of speech negotiable. Yes, some speech acts can be immoral – but not freedom of speech itself. The fact that freedom of speech is a principle, and not a moral question, has been forgotten. Muslim immigrants, and also Norwegian converts, have become sacred victims who are not to be offended. The result is political paralysis – a chronic political migraine.

This blindness and misguided tolerance of intolerance can be our curse. It is clear to me that in a diverse society such as Norway's, it's impossible for us not to offend one another from time to time. To offend is necessary – yes, even praiseworthy – because offending is a prerequisite for social change and progress. This is a historic fact. If freedom means anything at all – to borrow a formulation from George Orwell – it has to mean the right to tell people what they don't want to hear.

In any event, I think that the time for serving up examples of the problem has passed. We don't need to be presented with any more stories about the victims of our misguided approach to integration and immigration. We don't need to dissect any more personal tragedies that have been caused by current policies before we start looking for a diagnosis. At this point, it should be obvious to anyone what kind of conditions these policies have engendered.

Where are the feminists?

To me, it's infuriating to be a citizen of a country that won't safeguard its citizens' fundamental rights and needs. And as a member of a society with a proud history of women's rights, I've often felt a sickening feeling of shame.

In the 14 December 2003 issue of *Aftneposten*, Samira Bellil asked these three timely questions: "Why does no one see the enormous pressure to which girls in the suburbs are subjected? Where are the feminists? Don't they see what's happening to us?" At that time, no feminists responded to Samira Bellil. She died of cancer the following year, only thirty-one years of age. Out of respect for her efforts on behalf of women's freedom, I'll try to answer her question: Why *does* silence reign among feminists?

The answer is that the feminists are obsessed with their own ethnic Norwegian causes: longer maternity leave, shorter work days for the same pay – in short, everything that can give them a better life, materially and socially. They're also deeply preoccupied with a renewed struggle for the right to sexual pleasure, the right to "be on top." At the same time, many of the classical feminists appear to be old socialists blinded by the multicultural dream – a dream, alas, that has led them to accept the oppression of women in sizable segments of the population.

288

In their self-centred little world, the feminists don't see all the women who are having one baby after another against their own will and who, not daring to consider using protection, are on maternity leave year round. The feminists don't see all the women who yearn for the right to work. (As socialists, they have a tradition of not recognizing extreme and dogmatic forces when they encounter them in public.) Nor, though known for their struggle against the stiff-necked reactionaries in the Norwegian church, do they recognize Islam's stiff-necked reactionaries as such – mainly because these new reactionaries are dark-skinned. These feminists are unable to treat people equally: they're blinded by colour, by the twisted idea that a woman with roots in a place like North Africa has, by definition, basic needs and dreams different from their own. This kind of thinking is extremely discriminatory – and deeply offensive. And the betrayal embodied in such thinking is immensely repulsive – because we're talking here about little girls, young women, and older women some of whom live next door to some of those feminists and who are treated in their own communities as pariahs. Many of them don't even want to "be on the bottom," because their sexual organs have been destroyed, or because the man who's on top isn't the one they want to share their lives with; he may have purchased access to her body from her father and brother, and (with the Koran in hand) may be demanding sexual subjugation from her. All this is simply too much for "good" Norwegian feminists to deal with; they'd rather close their eyes to it, deny the reality of their new "sisters'" lives, and apply their empathy to other situations that deserve it far less.

The classic feminists, however, are quick to speak up about the "right" to wear the veil. In the good name of "freedom of choice," they're also the first to throw a veil over reality when a Muslim woman is murdered by her family, saying that such murders are not essentially different from a murder committed by a Norwegian man in a jealous rage.

In June 2006, nine people stood trial in Denmark. One was charged with having shot his sister, Ghazala, an eighteen-year-old Danish-Pakistani, in the street. The eight other defendants, members and friends of the family, were his collaborators in what turned out to be an out-and-out hunt for Ghazala. The family set up sentries and patrols, communicating closely with one another in the effort to circle in on the girl, and trapped her by exploiting her weakest point: her hope for forgiveness from the people she loved in spite of everything – her own family.

Forgiveness for what? For having married the man she loved. This small, unassuming hope ended in a carefully plotted murder in which nine people conspired. All were found guilty. Ghazala's father received life in prison for having ordered her death. Her brother, who was selected by the family to carry out the murder, got sixteen years in prison and deportation. The aunt who lured Ghazala into the trap by exploiting her longing for her family's love was sentenced to fourteen years in prison and deportation, since she was not a Danish citizen. The mildest punishment was for the person who drove the taxi in the hunt for the girl – eight years in prison. These sentences were a milestone in the history of European jurisprudence. They're entirely different from the kind of sentence given to someone who murders in passion – a murder in which no one close to the victim is involved in planning the crime and hunting down the prey, and where no one applauds the murderer when the deed is done. The feminists have yet to grasp this sea of difference.

Norwegian feminists have forfeited their credibility. How they'll win it back is a mystery to me. They might consider devoting their next celebration of International Women's Day to the struggle for decent living conditions for Muslim girls and women in Norway.

I'm sorry to say that when it comes to the willingness to make an effort on behalf of Muslim females, I have much more faith in Norway's men than in its women. Of all the mail I've received from members of the public who are concerned about these issues, the great majority comes from Norwegian men in their forties and fifties. They're deeply troubled about assaults on wives, mothers, and daughters in immigrant communities.

They're appalled; they look at their own wives, daughters, and mothers, and shudder at the thought of such things happening to them. Perhaps it's men's role as protectors that makes the difference here? I don't know; but I do notice with interest and wonder that it's men who seem to be the most deeply touched by these matters, and who – with both their heads and their hearts – seek out practical means of lifting immigrant girls and women into a worthy life as full members of a democratic society. The feminists chose long ago to sacrifice these girls and women on the altar of multicultural ideology; they've accepted conditions for other people that they never would accept for themselves, their friends, or their daughters. This is racism, pure and simple, and in our time racism has rarely had such dire consequences. I continue to undergo a deep inner conflict over the question of whether I should continue to define myself as a feminist. One thing is certain: I absolutely refuse to associate myself with this form of feminism.

Where are the intellectuals?

Another unavoidable question is this: Where are the Norwegian intellectuals? Don't they see the kind of pressure to which Norway and its secular democracy are being subjected? Don't they understand that freedom is on the line?

My confidence in the reigning intelligentsia in the Norwegian academy is more than tattered. Yes, there are a few honourable exceptions, such as Nina Witoszek, Inger-Lise Lien, Unni Wikan, Ottar Brox, and the brothers Gunnar and Sigurd Skirbekk. But most of our academics, and intellectuals generally, not only seem to refuse to take on our time's most burning political questions; they also all but deny the legitimacy of these questions. At times, indeed, they openly mock and ridicule those who try to bring these questions into the political arena.

I've seen intellectuals deny the crucial social significance of religious traditions and cultural values. This denial – combined with a blind belief that everyone, deep down, wants to live in a modern society that respects human rights – is, in my view, the intellectuals' Achilles heel. They're waiting for the "God-given awakening" – the magical moment when everyone will suddenly embrace democracy. While they await this miracle, they tolerate customs and traditions that involve treating women and children abominably. The intellectual laziness and cowardice of all this is unbelievable. As the American writer Paul Berman puts it, one of the factors that aid totalitarian movements is "the treason of the intellectuals."[288]

It's also very interesting to note how Norwegian intellectuals explain their decision to stay out of the debate. Political scientists and philosophers say that they don't know enough about Islam to discuss it; some fear that if they participate in the debate they'll be labeled unflatteringly; others feel that the public clamor will be too much of a distraction from their daily work.[289] But perhaps they should think about the noise that will be made in a few years because of the problems that are being suppressed now. That noise will take up all their time.

I think that in the relatively near future those intellectuals and politicians who have been evasive and passive will not be shown a great deal of sympathy. Like other major figures in society, they'll one day be asked: Which side were you on when it really mattered? Were you one of those who stood on the side of freedom and democracy, or did you stand for dialogue with totalitarians and step aside in misguided respect?

The low level of debate

It's understandable, of course, that many people don't dare to risk taking on the personal burden that can present itself when one criticizes immigration generally and Islam in particular. Criticism of today's immigration policy is often equated with criticism of immigrants themselves. In many quarters, such critics are quickly branded as "controversial" – a popular label. Once this label is in place, the pieces start falling like dominoes:

"controversial" is identical with "xenophobic"; and "xeno-phobic" is simply a nicer word for "racist." And at the end of this train of associations is "closet Nazi."

It's all thoroughly base and dishonest. To oppose today's immigration policy is not inconsistent with liking and feeling concern for people who immigrated to Norway, or who have been born here of parents with roots in non-Western countries. On the contrary: it's easy to love immigrants and refugees who do well in Norway and who are proud and happy to be Norwegian citizens. It gives one an especially good feeling about social concord to know that people with different ethnic and religious backgrounds can come together in gratitude for, and pride in, the good society that Norway continues to be.

A timely question is this: What should we call, say, a North African or Norwegian-Pakistani who thinks that Norwegian immigration policy has become irresponsible and unethical? Yes, racism can be found among all groups of people, so one could call *them* racists, too. But I doubt that many Norwegians would choose to label a non-Western person in this fashion, thus excluding that person from debate. The idea that a Westerner is a racist until proven otherwise has created an Orwellian world and has paralyzed any possibility of debate. The word "racist" has definitely become *the word that marks the Devil* – to borrow the title of anthropologist Inger-Lise Lien's book about the widely abused term "racist." As Lien writes: "The word racist has attained almost the same moral status as the word devil in Christianity. The problem is that when you conceive of racism as something widespread, the devil becomes omnipresent and normal, while the demonic is by definition extreme and abnormal. There is, however, a tendency to expand negative words so powerfully that an inflation occurs and they lose their force. This is what has happened, in my view, with the concept of racism" (1997:41).

Yes, the concept has indeed undergone inflation; the general paralysis that has resulted from the use of the word has especially damaged politicians' ability to act reasonably. It's for this reason that they treat fetching marriage as inviolate, close their eyes to the shipping of helpless children out of the country, and defend the veil.

In recent years, two clever new concepts have been formulated. Both represent an attempt by the left-wing intelligentsia and so-called "anti-racists" to reinforce the paralysis that stymies action and stifles free debate. One of these concepts is *Islamophobia*. The readiness to accuse others of Islamophobia is an ailment that has spread itself across Europe. As far as I can see, our society is not suffering from an abnormal anxiety about Islam. The respected humanist Levi Fragell was not abnormally afraid of Islam when he publicly warned against Islamism in 2003.[290] Nor are other Islam critics – such as the author Walid al-Kubaisi from Baghdad, Professor Mehdi Mozaffari from Teheran, and Ayaan Hirsi Ali from Mogadisu – Islamophobes. On the contrary, they maintain the right to promote free, critical reflection, especially when there are high-profile extremists in the public square. To use words like "phobia" is to copy methods used by Stalin, who defined dissidents as sick and therefore interned them. In our enlightened society, we should be able to rise above this level. If our society is suffering from a weakness, it must be that large segments of the elite are Islamo*philes*.

The other clever new concept is *neoracism*. The neoracist is also someone who criticizes aspects of Islam. The cleverest thing about this concept is that it turns Muslims into a race. This loathsome concept is plainly designed to inhibit free debate.

Those who use this term also tend to claim that Muslims have become Europe's new Jews – that they're treated the same way Jews were treated in Hitler's Germany before World War II. The comparison is cruel and ugly – not least because one report after another shows that in fact Jews are being increasingly persecuted in Europe today, especially by Muslims.[291] Are today's European governments treating Muslims the way the Nazis did Jews? Hardly. In prewar Germany, the Nazi government persecuted Jews; today, European governments not only hand out billions upon billions in taxpayer-funded welfare payments to Muslims every year; they also protect Muslims against discrimination, take care of Muslim women who are abused by their own families, and give financial support to mosques and other Muslim organizations – among much else. It's unfathomable to me that intellectuals and media people don't put an immediate stop to this indecent, insidious rhetoric about "Europe's new Jews."

I'm often asked whether I receive threats because of my work, and whether I fear reprisals. Yes, I've been threatened a few times for having pointed out negative aspects of Islam and Muhammed. This is, alas, not surprising given the murder of Theo van Gogh, the death threats against Ayaan Hirsi Ali, and all the threats that followed the publication of the Muhammed cartoons. An atmosphere has been created in which threatening and harassing critics of Islam is almost seen as legitimate. On the contrary, I view the media's intellectual compliancy and relentless politicization as a greater threat – because the media have the power to demonize those they ideologically differ with, and such demonization can lead indirectly to politically motivated violence. This has been my greatest fear in writing this book. And this fear has driven me, too, to self-censorship.

I believe that one of the major problems we face in our attempt to address the greatest challenge of our time is this: we're so sated with our prosperity, our freedom from care, and our hunt for even greater prosperity and even more pleasures that we're incapable of waking up and facing the problems until they've grown so immense that it's impossible to do anything at all about them. The good news behind these grim words, however, is that in Norway, at least, I don't think the problems have yet become insurmountable. But if radical and comprehensive action isn't taken now, they *will* be insurmountable – within, at most, one or two decades.

And even if meaningful action *is* taken in the near future, I suspect that a number of worrisome new problems will be uncovered.

I'll just list a few here.

295

- First, we can expect a rise in the number of honour killings, because the communities in question will grow and close themselves in even more, as has occurred elsewhere in Europe. Girls and women who violate the demands for conformity will be met with powerful reactions as a warning to others who might be thinking about breaking out. Sources in Pakistani communities in Oslo say that the death of Rahila Iqbal, who died under unusual circumstances in Pakistan in 2005, has had such an effect. In Oslo's Pakistani communities, her death is viewed as an honour killing, especially because she married a man against her family's will. As one young woman said to me: "What Pakistani girl will now dare to marry against her family's wishes? They see what they're risking."

- It will be revealed that gender-selective abortions of female fetuses – already a familiar phenomenon on the subcontinent – are taking place in Norway. Abortion is legal in Norway, and immigrants wanting late-term abortions need only go to private clinics in their homelands.

- We'll also see more and more converts to Islam – mainly women, but also men. It's especially common to see men migrate from left-wing totalitarianism to religio-political totalitarianism. As for the women, they convert mainly out of a desire to liberate themselves from the complex demands of a woman's role in a democratic society with sexual equality. These women are drawn to the fixed rules of Islam, which govern everyday life in extraordinary detail, and which they think will rescue them from the so-called tyranny of beauty.

- We'll see a radicalization of female Muslims, especially Norwegian converts. This phenomenon can already be observed in Belgium, the Netherlands, and Germany. At its most extreme, this radicalization can turn ethnic Norwegian women into suicide bombers.

- There will be increasing pressure to introduce a sharia court that would be empowered to decide family-related disputes involving marriage, divorce, child custody, and inheritance. The pressure to establish such a court will increase proportionally as the Muslim population grows, especially in Oslo.

- The strict covering of women with niqab and burka will spread significantly. This will lead to debates about security in a Europe increasingly imperiled by terrorism.

- It's already been revealed that a number of enclaves in Europe are run by unofficial local governments and that the official municipal governments have no real power in these places. This has happened partly because criminal gangs have taken control and partly because local Islamists have used both pressure and violence to ensure that at least some parts of Islamic law – especially those pertaining to the control of women – are enforced within their "territory." Such a development will also soon be observed in parts of Oslo.

- Sexual harassment and rape, especially of ethnic Norwegian women and girls, will only continue to increase (as we saw in the summer of 2006). The government will come under pressure to release statistics indicating which groups the perpetrators and victims come from. Those statistics will show the same pattern as in Sweden: the great majority of victims will be native girls and women, the assailants mostly non-Western men.

- Members of mosques and political parties that have close ties to the Muslim Brotherhood and other worldwide Islamist movements will be publicly identified. It will also be established that such religio-political movements have strong footholds in Norway.

- Studies will reveal that many second- and third-generation Muslims connect their identity most strongly to Islam and that their sense of identity as Norwegians is very weak.

- We'll see a radicalization of young Muslims, some of whom will form militant cells.

- Radical imams who spread hate and encourage violence will be deported.

- We'll witness radicalization, especially among Somalis, and the men behind this development will mainly be members of Saudi Arabia's Salafist movements. The already well known integration problems involving Pakistanis in Norway will receive competition for attention from heretofore less well known integration problems involving Somalis and Iraqis in Norway.

- It will be revealed that major Norwegian prisons are Islamist hatcheries.

- It will be revealed that Norwegian authorities don't know the real identities of many of the people who have settled in Norway, because they don't fingerprint immigrants who come here under the family-reunification policy. Terrorists with false identities, for example, can acquire citizenship after four years by entering into pro forma marriages. This national vulnerability will lead to demands for policy changes.

- Statistics will show that immigration and integration are costing Norway a great deal of money.

- Population projections will estimate that by the year 2100 a majority of people in Norway will have non-Western backgrounds.

Without a doubt, the social democrats in Norway and elsewhere in Europe bear most of the responsibility for the continent's exceedingly bold multicultural immigration project. In countries such as Norway, Sweden, Denmark, Germany, the Netherlands, and Britain, it's the social democrats who have held power for the longest periods during the last forty years.

Torbjørn Bernten, a former Labour Party member of Parliament, said on 4 March 2006 on a Norwegian news program that a few decades ago it was impossible to foresee that immigration and integration would be so difficult. He said explicitly that he "had no idea" how great the differences were between "our Christian cultural heritage" and the culture that Muslims bring with them. Berntsen thought that most politicians at that time didn't understand what had been set in motion; he claimed that the whole thing came as a surprise.

This is only a partial truth. In the summer of 1971, when the non-Western "tourists," as previously mentioned, were starving in Oslo's streets, cabinet member Oddvar Nordli was responsible for immigration policy. That year Nordli commented on immigration in the 3 June issue of *Arbeiderbladet,* and the government appointed a commission to examine the challenges of the new immigration.

"As long as we receive a supply of labour from the Nordic countries and other European states," Nordli wrote, "this will not lead to major social problems. It is easier for these workers to slip into the Norwegian social system. But groups that come from Pakistan, for example, encounter a society here that is totally different from what they're used to. And the new committee must devote great attention to this." Nordli understood, then, that the new immigration was problematical – but he didn't convert this understanding into practical policy.

Politicians have clung to the illusion that "things will work themselves out over time." Ayaan Hirsi Ali, too, reacted to the weakness of social democrats. She began her political career as a member of the Dutch Labour Party, but jumped over to the liberal conservatives when Labour made clear its unwillingness to take on immigration and integration problems, especially those afflicting women and children. In Denmark, social democrat and former cabinet member Karen Jespersen quit Parliament in protest out of love for that country's secular democracy. Her conscience would no longer permit her to represent a party that she didn't trust to retain the new Danish immigration policies if it was returned to power. And in Germany, the social-democratic ex-chancellor Helmut Schmidt has also acknowledged that the idea of the multicultural society – an idea that dominated his entire term as chancellor of the Bundesrepublik – was a failure.

I must add that these brief critical comments about the social democrats are unfair – for conservatives are generally no better. For example, Norway's two conservative governments under Kjell Magne Bondevik didn't show a trace of willingness or ability to change course. On the contrary, the multicultural dream has been popular both in the Norwegian centre and in the Conservative Party. The picture isn't black and white.

The alarm goes off

There's no time to lose.
It can go wrong again.
What is it we want?

So writes Inger Hagerup in her poem "Be Impatient!" We must want to defend our fundamental values. We must want to create a society based on these values. This is what we must want.

All the parties in the Norwegian Parliament are founded on human rights, on sexual equality, and on a preservation of secular democracy. On that fundamental level, the similarities are greater than the differences. All the parties should therefore be able to understand the seriousness of the arguments and the proposals I've put forward in this book.

The current Norwegian government, a majority coalition consisting of the Labour, Centre, and Socialist Left parties, has power in a country that increasingly resembles the *Titanic*. The orchestra is playing more and more loudly, and on the dance floor the politicians are swinging more and more fervently to the multicultural dance, while the vessel heads toward a shipwreck in the dark, foggy Arctic night.

In the spring of 2006 there was much talk behind closed doors to the effect that key Labour Party politicians wanted to follow a new course, closer to Denmark's, but that the Centre and Socialist Left parties were sitting on their feet. If Labour doesn't manage to convince its colleagues in the government that a new policy is needed fast in order to keep things from going wrong, Labour must take responsibility. It certainly must do this if the party, in the years to come, is going to have credibility with the public. For it was Labour that initiated this bold project. Labour must put an end to the project, and must work to repair the damage. If the Centre and Socialist Left parties will not take responsibility for our common future, I can't see any alternative other than Labour dissolving the coalition and trying to make a minority government work. In the Parliament, they could easily win a majority for a new, sustainable immigrant policy. If Labour doesn't take responsibility for this change, other parties will do so. This can cause political polarization in Norway to intensify – a development by which no one will profit. Great national tasks should be solved by the major parties acting in concert.

Afterword

to the English-Language Edition

Since the publication of the Norwegian edition of this book, there have been many interesting developments on a variety of fronts. Herewith, some updates:

Anooshe

In November of 2007, Kripos, the division of the Norwegian police charged with investigating organized crime and other serious infractions, invited me to come to their annual meeting to give a talk about honour-related attacks. When the talk was over, a female police officer came up to the lectern and said: "I know where Anooshe's boys were taken away to in secrecy right after the funeral. They were immediately gotten out of continental Norway."

She mentioned an island, which I choose not to identify here out of concern that others may wind up in an equally precarious security situation and be transported to the same place. She added this: "The fact that they were taken of continental Norway says everything about the kind of threat we felt the boys were facing."

Shortly after the Norwegian publication of *But the Greatest of These Is Freedom* in the autumn of 2006, Anooshe's closest Norwegian supporters and friends, a married couple, contacted me after I held a talk about the book in Kristiansund, the city in which Anooshe was executed. They thanked me for my involvement in the case, and they confirmed the account of

Anooshe's fate presented in this book. I asked delicately how Baborsha and Sharokh were doing. The couple, still deeply grieving, told me that they didn't know where the boys lived now, but that it was possible to send letters and gifts to them via the local authorities in Eide, which they did. They also said that when the boys were old enough to tackle emotionally their mother's painful life, they would also be sent Anooshe's diary.

Anooshe's friends, then, were not sure exactly how the boys were doing. But as the wife put it: "Given the circumstances, they're doing okay, we're told, but they have a very heavy burden to bear all their lives."

Triple murder

The Anooshe case is historic, in that the victim herself had warned of an imminent honour killing. Another horrible new Norwegian story, however, would be written in the autumn of 2006 – a story so horrible that one can hardly take it in. I woke up early on the morning of Monday, October 2, in a hotel room in Copenhagen, to find a message on my mobile that had been sent to me at 3:45 AM: "Three sisters dead in an honour killing in Kaldbakken. Damn Pakistanis!" The message was from a Norwegian-born friend of mine whose parents are Pakistanis and who lives in Oslo, in a neighbourhood bordering on Kaldbakken.

Three sisters killed in their own home, the principal weapon being an axe, the secondary weapon a pistol: Sobia Khan (27) was chopped up with the axe in such a way that she died quickly. The youngest sister, Nafisa Shaheen Khan (13), was also killed with the axe and died of head wounds. The last sister, Saadia Shaheen (24), was attacked with the axe and also shot several times. The murderer was their own brother, Shahzad Khan, 31.

The sight that greeted the policemen at the scene of the crime was so unbelievably grotesque that even very experienced police officers had serious psychiatric problems with doing their jobs afterwards and required emergency psychiatric treatment.

How could a brother kill all of his sisters? Khan himself said during the court proceedings that he couldn't remember anything because he was intoxicated, and that an inner voice had exhorted him to perform the crime. The prosecutor didn't manage to establish a firm motive, but Khan was convicted of premeditated triple murder under especially aggravated circumstances to the most stringent punishment allowed by the law, 21 years in prison.

Among the Norwegian Pakistanis whom I know, however, the honour motive was obvious. Khan was losing control over the two older sisters. Their "crime," in all probability was a sum of the following. At 19, Sobia had been forced to marry a cousin in Pakistan. The marriage had ended in divorce in 2000 after the cousin-husband went after her with a knife.

During the investigation of the triple murder, a 28-year-old friend of Sobia's told police that Sobia had feared another forced marriage, and that her sister Saadia had, too. Both, the friend said, were afraid of being murdered if they opposed their family's marriage plans for them. At the trial, however, the friend remembered nothing of what she had told police. A similar loss of memory afflicted another witness, who had heard rumors that the sisters feared they might be killed.

Investigators also discovered that Sobia had bought an apartment in Oslo only a few hours before the sisters' murder. The plan was that all three sisters would move out of the extended family's home: the sisters could no longer stand the control and lack of freedom that characterized their daily lives. The police believed that this act of breaking away provoked the killings.

The Norwegian Pakistani woman from whom I received the cell-phone message in Copenhagen told me that her then boyfriend, also Norwegian Pakistani and an acquaintance of Khan and the sisters, had already predicted a year before the triple murder that this would be the sisters' fate. I urged her and the boyfriend to go to the police with all the information they had. But they didn't dare. I asked the same woman why little

Nafisa, only 13 years old, was also murdered. She replied: "Preventive work." When the two older sisters are disobedient rebels, he took it for granted that Nafisa was, too."

For the police and prosecutors, it was very frustrating not to be able to establish a motive. The police ran into a wall in the Muslim community. The honour culture, that merciless culture of fear, has indisputably sunk deep roots in Norway. It is the fear of reprisals that holds sway. As another Norwegian-born woman, aged 20, also with Pakistani parents, told me: "Our parents use the Kaldbakken killings against us. They make threats: 'You see what happens if you reject our plans for your marriages?'" 292

Marriage immigration

The immigrant population of Norway has risen more quickly in the last few years than ever. Records are set almost annually, mainly due to increases in labour immigration. In 2006, immigrants made up 8.3 percent of Norway's population; as of 1 January 2010, immigrants account for 11.4 percent of the population. The first generation of immigrants includes 460,000 persons and the second generation, 93,000, making for a total population group of around 550,000 people. All together, 510,000 individuals were granted Norwegian residency permits during the period of 2000 – 2009, which led to the following conclusion by Statistics Norway: "...without comparison the largest level of migration we have experienced."293

The increase in Oslo is especially dramatic. Of the capital's 587,000 inhabitants, 160,000, or 27 percent, have immigrant backgrounds, while 20 percent have non-Western backgrounds – a figure that has climbed four points since 2006.294

The population growth is very pronounced in Oslo's schools. In March 2010, figures were released which stirred debate: at the beginning of 2000, 31 percent of the pupils in primary and secondary schools had minority backgrounds. In the next ten years, the percentage climbed to 40 percent. Ten years from now, in 2020, ethnic Norwegians will be a minority in Oslo schools. This is already the case in 58 of Oslo's 136 primary and secondary schools.[295]

Two years earlier, in 2008, Human Rights Service (HRS) drew up a demographic analysis for Norway and Oslo, because Statistics Norway has never wanted to provide a forecast of Oslo's future population growth, and because we suspected that Statistics Norway's earlier calculations for Norway have been too low. Statistics Norway uses three alternatives in its demographic prognoses for Norway: a low alternative, a middle alternative, and a high alternative, in which the high alternative is expected to be a nearly unrealistic future scenario. We used the same demographic methods in our analysis that Statistics Norway has employed in its previous studies of Norway's population growth, and we were quickly able to state that for several years Statistics Norway's "unrealistic high alternative" was lower than the actual immigration figure. Our 2009 calculation showed that in Oslo, ethnic Norwegians could be a minority in 2029, and in Norway immigrants could be a majority by the end of this century. And this includes only first- and second-generation immigrants.[296]

Only a year later, the actual immigration figures for 2008, which set yet another new record, showed that our estimate for Oslo was too low. Norwegians may be a minority in Oslo in 2026.

If it's essential to get these facts on the table, that's because our political leaders are given tools to be able to carry out a immigration policy that is sustainable, both financially and in terms of values. It is about something as obvious as the fact that the politicians must know the facts to be able to plan resources for schools, medical services, the welfare system, and so on.

In 2009 we were able to report that the immigration now underway is expensive in kroner, and in time can reduce the amount of social benefits that citizens can expect to receive from the welfare state. Once again, HRS was taking on a task that Statistics Norway should have performed long ago – namely, calculating the costs and benefits of current immigration.

Statistics Norway has, in other words, chosen *not* to publicize the costs and benefits of immigration. In our 2009 report, "Don't Count Me: Immigration's Costs and the Welfare State," in which we intentionally made conservative calculations, we reported that immigration's annual costs come to at least 23 billion kroner, but more likely at least 50 billion kroner. This includes the actual expenses on refugees and welfare payments, and lower tax revenues on account of immigrants' lower employment and tax rates. We did not include the additional amounts paid by the national and local government for health care, schools, the justice system, and so forth. And we confined ourselves to the economy of continental Norway (meaning that the nation's oil economy was omitted from the study).

Our conclusion was unambiguous: if today's immigration policy is continued, it will mean that the Norwegian government, in time, will have to make dramatic welfare cuts and move toward an Americanizing of (for example) the health-care sector.

Another interesting prediction was made public in 2010: the government ascertained that Norway will have a million immigrants by 2025 or 2030 – that is to say, a doubling of the current level. Foreign Minister Jonas Gahr Støre (Labour) came out and said the following: "we have to live with this." As if it were a law of nature. As if the politicians didn't have the means to influence the composition of Norway's future population. Just as interesting were the challenges he took up in his statement: marriages between cousins. As he put it: "Where I come from, it's not okay to marry your cousin. This is a topic that I think touches on the freedom of second- and third-generation immigrants, if they have to systematically marry relatives." And he said: "The fact that women choose to go home is something we obviously cannot prevent ourselves from regulating, but this may lie on the borderland between freedom and force." And he concluded as follows: "Women's position will be totally central in our work on the Integration Committee. We must have a set of regulations that makes it illegal to keep women down. But norms and values count, too."[297]

Mina – a deep disappointment

The Foreign Minister did not wish to address the economic challenges, but he revealed that he and the government have understood that the sustainability, in terms of values, will encounter powerful challenges in times to come. Hardly any example in this connection confirms the Foreign Minister's observation more clearly than what happened with Mina and her children during the last few years. In the summer of 2007, my phone rang. The voice at the other end told me that Mina's oldest daughter, then 16 ½ years old, would be traveling to Pakistan the next day. The person told me that the girl was either to be engaged or married to a cousin – the same cousin for whom Mina's niece Nadia had, with a cry for help, managed to avoid being a living visa. What had happened? Why would Mina allow her daughter to relive her own fate? The person on the phone believed it was about coming in from the cold and back into the extended family's embrace: by using her daughter as a visa for this cousin, Mina would be able to receive forgiveness from her extended family for having divorced.

The administrative director of Human Rights Service phoned Mina at once and asked if it was true that her daughter was going to Pakistan the next day. It was not a gracious Mina who, for the first time since we had met her in 2002, quite simply hissed: we had "no business interfering in private family matters." Period.

Our next phone call, which we made immediately, was to the police at Oslo Airport. We explained our concern for the 16-year-old girl, and the next day the police took her aside and talked to her for over an hour. The girl, however, remained loyal to her mother and extended family: she was going to Pakistan on vacation, nothing more. The police were therefore unable to help her and had to let her walk through passport control and board a delayed flight to Islamabad.

In Mina's village, the engagement between the girl and her cousin was celebrated in the summer of 2007, and the next year, just before Christmas, when the girl turned 18, she was married off to this close relative who is 12 years her elder. At the same time, the 18-year-old's sister, two years her junior, was engaged in the same village to this cousin's younger brother.

I have hardly ever been so disappointed as I was by this experience with Mina. All the help she had received, not least from Barnevernet, lawyers, and the social-security department, to enable her and her children to live a free and dignified life, as full citizens of Norway! And it all ended with her turning her daughters into living visas. My conclusion is that Mina is not capable of being, nor does she want to be, a part of Norwegian society. She was too caught up in the spider web – in honour culture.

Family-arranged marriage

The debate about marriage between close relatives flares up every so often. Key questions in the debate are whether the practice should be prohibited and what the consequences are for children whose parents (and perhaps grandparents, too) are closely related. This happened in 2007 after the Deputy Director-General of the Norwegian Institute of Public Health, Camilla Stoltenberg, released statistics about the prevalence of marriage between close relatives.[298] The report showed (again) that marriage between close relatives is especially high among Pakistanis. Between 1977 and mid 2005, 44 percent of first-generation Pakistanis were married to cousins, 5.5 percent to other close relatives, and 5 percent to relatives whose relationship to them was unspecified [299] The total percentage of marriages to close relatives, then, was 54.5 percent. For the second generation, the figures were respectively 35, 4.7, and 6.7 percent, for a total of 46.5 percent. Between 2002 and mid 2005, the incidence of cousin marriage in the second generation was 29 percent, and the overall rate of marriage between close relatives was 40 percent.

It turns out, however, that 6.7 percent of those in the second generation did not specify anything other than that they were related to their spouses and 5.7 percent did not respond. This means that we do not have date for possible marriages between close relatives on the part of 12.4 percent of marrying members of the second generation. Among this 12.4 percent there may, in other words, be cousin marriages whic the Norwegian-born Pakistanis wish to hide from the authorities and others, perhaps to avoid stigma (given that such marriages are not looked upon with admiration in Norwegian society) or perhaps because they are themselves in despair over the fact that they have been married off to cousins or other relatives and are in denial about the situation. It is impossible to attribute the lack of reporting to language problems, since only one percent of first-generation Pakistanis have failed to identify the nature of their family relationship to their spouses.

I especially took note of a statement in the ongoing news coverage of the medical aspects of the issue. Rolf Lindemann of Ullevål University Hospital said that health personnel see a wide and varied spectrum of birth defects: "Everything possible, from coronary, urinary tract, and skeletal problems to diseases of the brain. Many of the children die from the defects they are born with." Lindemann maintained that many parents who are related know about the risk of having a sick child, but prefer not to consider the consequences: "They say that their fate is in Allah's hands, and that this is the point."[300] The statement did not surprise me, as I have personally heard such views expressed by Pakistanis in Norway and Pakistan, but the statement was valuable because it came from a leading medical figure, and it makes it clear to our politicians how insignificant an impact efforts to spread information about cousin marriage and birth defects will have on the incidence of marriages between close relatives.

A study released in 2010 showed that seven times as many Norwegian Pakistani children have progressive diseases of the brain than ethnic Norwegian children. Among Norwegian Pakistani children with parents who are cousins, the figures are even higher: such illnesses are 11 times more common among such children than among ethnic Norwegian children.[301] According to the doctors who performed the study, this is "one of the most serious consequences of cousin marriage," and no fewer than "15 to 30 professionals can be involved in the care and treatment of one person."[302]

In 2007 the debate raged in the newspaper opinion pages, on TV, and on radio. Spokespeople, medical students, and doctors with Norwegian Pakistani backgrounds defended the practice of marriage between close relatives tooth and claw, and claimed that the major solution to the problem is still that of providing information to the affect groups – as has been done for several decades. One could sense a desperation on the part of Norwegian Pakistani "leaders" when the then Minister of Children, Equality, and Social Inclusion, Karita Bekkemellem, proposed banning marriage between close relatives, out of concern both for possible birth defects and for the possible use of force in arranging such marriages.

But the debate petered out. The Minister did not persuade the government to forbid the practice. When the new information about the diseases of the brain was released three years later, when it also emerged that about 40 percent of the children died at less than eight years old, I took up my pen (again), writing in *Aftenposten*:

> The sufferings at the individual level, based in a pre-modern and inhuman practice, are enormous. When it comes to integration, it has led Pakistanis in Britain to the bottom of the socioeconomic ladder. Pretty much all of the leading Pakistani spokespeople in Norway have intimate experience with compulsion in such marriages. Nonetheless, the practice should not be banned – and the second generation (doctors included) agrees. How one can be so unconcerned with the well-being of one's own is in itself sensational. Sensational, too, is the lack of consequential ethics: what if all groups in Norway followed the same practice? Our society would collapse within a

generation or two. What about the health-care resources, for instance?

(...)

Norwegian Pakistani "leaders" and politicians should call themselves seriously to account and should especially challenge their own view of humanity. The politicians must use their common sense and make use of the most important tool – the law – and the Minister of Health should obtain the statistics relating to the expenditure of health-care resources on children who are cruelly affected by a lack of enlightenment.[303]

There was no response. The debate never took place – probably because no politician called for action on any level.

Polygamy and fraud

The debate took off quickly, however, in August 2010 when a Norwegian Somali woman publicly pointed out the odd fact that one in three Somali women in Norway are registered in this country as divorced, She noted earlier figures from Statistics Norway which show that the number of single breadwinners among Somalis is two and half times as high as among the rest of the population. You would have to look long and hard to find a more obvious case of abuse of our welfare system, for the fact that many of these women are still married under sharia law to their "ex-husbands" is as clear as day.[304] Key Somali spokespeople completely denied that this had anything to do with fraud and charged that they were being "stigmatized."

This example also clearly shows the incidence of polygamy, and according to what I am told by Somalis, but which I cannot document, is that in the largest Somali mosque in Oslo, with about 4,000 members, the Tawfiq Islamic Centre, there is a special marriage register, and also a special divorce register, some are kept hidden from the government. Here, one marries and divorces according to sharia law, and it is of course important to know whether a women is divorced before she (for example) becomes a man's second, third, or fourth wife. If this is true, one can really talk about a completely sequestered society within Norwegian society, a society whose workings are virtually inaccessible to the authorities.

I assume that the head of NAV Collections and Control, Magne Fladby, had good reason to claim in 2007, in connection with this kind of welfare abuse, that "At present it is this kind of fraud that is increasingly the most common in the new welfare state." [305]

Stripped of freedom

In 2009, when the new Norwegian government presented its political platform for the governing period ending in 2013, those of us at Human Rights Service were overjoyed. Finally politicians would be doing something about immigrants who "dump" their children, sending them back to their home countries. The platform stated that the government would "improve the coordination of efforts to follow up Norwegian children abroad."

Which specific measures has this led to? The answer is still unclear. That the issue was so high up on the political agenda can be attributed to the important work we have done in the field. For in 2009, too, we presented an unsettling report to Norwegian officials. This time, in addition, we had a good many more hard figures showing how many children and young people might have been sent to their parents' lands of origin, not only an estimate, as in 2004. We took two sets of documents: the school directory, which shows the percentage of pupils in Norwegian primary and secondary schoolss (including private schools), and government statistics about the number of children and young people in the country. On September 1, 2009, we issued our report, "De glemte barna – om barn og unge som ikke er i den norske grunnskolen" (The Forgotten Children: On Children and Young People who Are Not in Norwegian Primary and Secondary School"), and in a press release on the same day we wrote the following:

Norwegian authorities have no control over where school-aged children are. Human Rights Service has checked the number of children aged 6 – 15 who are registered as pupils in Norwegian schools against the population statistics for the same age group. The disparity between the children registered as residents and the children registered in primary and secondary schools is dramatic:

- In Oslo, 1,852 pupils are missing.

- In the entire country, 3,877 pupils are missing.

We can say this: Norwegian authorities do not know what percentage of Norwegian children have "disappeared," who these children are, where they are, or what their national background is. Our assumption is that the great majority of the children have immigrant backgrounds and have been sent to their families' countries of origin.

The police, statisticians, and academics could not explain away the figures. For us, it was striking that our 2004 estimate that, at any given time, as many as 4-5,000 children and young people may be staying abroad (typically in their parents' country of origin), could not possibly have been exaggerated. On the contrary. For the new statistics do not count children under five, or between 16 and 18. The report made it impossible for the government to ignore the so far "forgotten children."

A baby can't tell tales

On 22 June 2007, Norway awoke to a shock: after going on a reporting assignment to Somaliland, where many Norwegian Somalis have their roots and build properties, Tormod Strand of NRK reported that 10 circumcisers he had interviewed said that they had genitally mutilated 185 Norwegian Somali girls over the last three years. In the following days, one appalling report after another was broadcast on radio and television in which Norwegians heard, among other things, the heartbreaking cries of an 8-year-old Somali girl, Anisa, during her mutilation. Between her cries, the little girl begged the circumciser several times to stop, to "finish up."

Anisa's sweet and innocent face when she was interviewed, before she was led unsuspectingly in to her encounter with the circumciser, where she would emit her cries of pain, combined with the things the 10 circumcisers said, resulted in a pressure on the government that was so intense that it simply had to be dealt with. Emergency measures were quickly drawn up which were especially concerned with attempting to prevent the transportation of girls that summer for the purpose of genital mutilation. The most interesting measure was the government's decision to map the incidence of genital mutilation among Norwegian girls.

But, and this is a major but: the mapping project would not be clinical in nature. In other words, there would be no physical examinations of actual girls. Therefore the results did not tell us more about the incidence of mutilation. The researchers collected information from the police, Barnevernet, health stations for children and young people, schools, maternity wards, and so forth, in order to learn about specific cases of genital mutilation that had already been uncovered during the preceding two years (2006 and 2007). The result was 15 cases of already uncovered genital mutilation. The researchers, in collaboration with the cabinet minister responsible for this area, Minister of Health Sylvia Brustad, made used of this information to go out into the media and claim a "decline" in the incidence of genital mutilation and to maintain that the soft measures of information and dialogue were working. The Minister of Health was already an outspoken opponent of medical examinations of girls' private parts, and the researchers belong to the political wing that warmly supports soft, not "hard," measures. How these findings could be interpreted as indicating a *decline* in the incidence of

316

genital mutilation, when we in Norway have never known just how widespread mutilation was, nobody could explain.

The mapping study was simply misused in the crassest way – to uphold the status quo and probably avoid the discomfort of facing the truth. I was so despondent over this falsification that I wrote an entire chapter about it in my 2009 book *Rundlurt*.[306]

The four sisters in Gambia

What has happened with little Awa and her three sisters who were dumped in Gambia in 2003 and genitally mutilated? They're still there. But something important has happened: in June 2008, the case took a new turn. The second youngest girl, the fifth oldest of the children, who lives in Norway, was a few months old in 2003. The authorities took it upon themselves to examine the girl because they were concerned that she, too, could have been mutilated. The girl, who in 2008 was five years old, *was* mutilated, and with this solid evidence, the authorities were able, for the first time in Norwegian history, to prosecute parents and place them in protective custody on account of a genital mutilation. More specifically, the father was imprisoned, while the mother was spared this fate because of complications with her seventh pregnancy. I was present at the sentencing at the Oslo courthouse. The father promised that the girls would come back to Norway after completing another half year's schooling in Gambia, for which he had already paid. He also told the judge that he was unaware that his daughters were genitally mutilated. This was a man from rural Gambia on the dock. The term *integration* has no meaning to him or his kind. Mentally, he and his wife live in Gambia.

Christmas came. The girls didn't. The sisters, now aged 10 to 16, have still not come. Seven years have passed, and yet the girls are still officially registered as living in Norway.

There is nothing the police and government can do now about these Norwegian-born girls. The police could only hold the parents' passports for a limited period, and in the autumn of

317

2009 the parents were able once again to travel freely out of Norway – that is, able to return to Gambia to visit their family and manage their properties and daughters.

Just before the parents were given their passports back, I received a message from Gambia that the girl who was then 15 years old was going to be married off to a cousin.

In all probability, these girls' case is lost. Perhaps they will be able to come to Norway as adults – with Gambian spouses – and with a rewritten story in their baggage about what was done to them.

These girls' fate, and how simple it has been for the parents to thumb their noses at Norwegian authorities, led me to write an op-ed which appeared in Norway's largest newspaper, *Verdens Gang*, on 19 June 2010. I concluded the op-ed by pointing out a measure that I think demands to be taken in a case as serious as this one:

> The parents have broken the social contract that is implicit in citizenship. They remain loyal to Gambian law and the Gambian mentality. They completely refuse to recognize their Norwegian-born children's human rights – and worse, they do not have to suffer any consequences as a result, which, moreover, sends a particularly unfortunate signal to those who think like them and live around them.
>
> Therefore: rescind their Norwegian citizenship and assume custody of those of their children who are still living here.
>
> Such dramatic measures are essential in the so-called New Norway, if we are going to take human rights seriously. After all, if such measures had been in place in 2003, the four sisters would have had a far better life – in Norway.

I continue to maintain that it would not be an overreaction to mete out such harsh treatment to parents who have so brutally failed in their role as caregivers. I have deliberately tested out reactions to these measures, first and foremost in talks given to police officers, in political settings, and to general audiences. So far I have not heard any protests. What about the fact that it has been documented that the 5-year-old here in Norway was also genitally mutilated, probably in 2003 when she was only a few months old, along with her four sisters? Her parents have yet to be prosecuted for this – despite hard evidence.

What has to happen before Norwegian authorities make use of the existing legislation to prevent such gross and irreversible assaults? A police officer said the following to me on the telephone earlier this year: "I think we'll have to catch a circumciser here in Norway in the middle of the act in order to be able to get a trial and conviction." This statement confirms my assertion that the struggle against genital mutilation in Norway is barely at the starting line.

Sweden loses its innocence

The situation in Sweden is becoming more critical with every year. Two things particularly disgust me: the dizzyingly high rape statistics and the fact that parts of the country may be emptied of Jews.

When it comes to rape statistics, Sweden beats out the rest of Europe. An EU project covering the years 2004-2008 showed that the country has twice as many rapes per 100,000 inhabitants as Britain, which comes in second in Europe, and four times as many rapes as countries like Germany and France [307] Each year, the number of reported rapes rises dramatically. When you look at the statistics, you get a feeling that there is a kind of low-intensity war underway.

In only one country on earth are there more reported rapes than in Sweden – namely, in the African country of Lesotho.

Here are the figures for 2009: almost 6,000 reported rapes, which comes to about 16 rapes a day. The Swedish National Council for Crime Prevention (BRÅ) believes this is only the tip of the iceberg. BRÅ estimates that only 10 to 20 percent of the rapes are reported.[308]

Of the nearly 6,000 reported rapes, the percentage of raped children was record high. Just under 2,000 of the rapes were of children under 15 years old, which means that over five child rapes are reported daily.

In the summer of 2010 yet more records were broken. The number of reported rapes, including violent rapes, went up by 25 percent from the summer of 2009 to the summer of 2010 (the months of June and July). The reported rapes of children under 15 rose by a full 53 percent (!) in the same period.[309]

To my knowledge, no leading Swedish politician has grasped this reality. Nor have the major media done investigative work in the field. Thousands of children are being raped. For me, it is incomprehensible that these children, especially, haven't set off the nation's alarms. Rape seems, quite simply, to have become accepted as a normal state of affairs in Sweden.

Who, then, are the major perpetrators? Swedish authorities don't have the statistics to answer that question. But in 2002 Dr. Jur. Ann-Christine Hjelm studied one of the provincial court jurisdictions, Svea Hovrätt, which includes the districts of Stockholm and Uppsala, and found that 85 percent of the violence criminals were of foreign origin.[310]

A crisis for Swedish Jews

Of Malmö's 260,000 residents, 60,000 are Muslims. The city's Jews are increasingly subjected to harassment and threats, especially from extreme Muslims. During the last two years, more than 30 Jews have found it necessary to leave Malmö, most of them toward Israel, and most of them young people who see no future for their children in Sweden.

In 2010, Jews in Malmö told NRK that they don't dare to wear a yarmulke. The police have to guard the synagogue, and the chapel has been set on fire. Hate crime against Jews has doubled in the last year.[311]

A very thought-provoking event took place when Sweden and Israel were supposed to take each other on in the Davis Cup match in Malmö in 2009. Because of threats of demonstrations, the match had to take place in front of empty stands and the players were flown into the sports arena in helicopters for reasons of security. Only selected schoolchildren, members of the press, and sponsors got to see the teams clash in person.

For anti-fascist, Islamist, and neo-Nazi groups threatened a real clash outside the stadium. About 10,000 demonstrators were expected, and there was an imminent danger of rioting. The police therefore mobilized 1,000 officers from their own ranks. But that wasn't enough: in addition to bringing in tanks from other parts of Sweden, the Swedish police – for the first time in history – found it necessary to ask for help from Denmark. Danish polish supported their Swedish colleagues with 12 tanks.

Six thousand demonstrators filled Malmö's streets on 7 March 2009. Extreme elements attacked police with bombs and fireworks. One can hardly wonder that the tiny Jewish minority in Malmö felt unsafe. The Swedish history professor Kristian Gerner went so far as to call the situation "the worst crisis for Jews in Sweden since World War II."[312]

There is no sign that the situation will turn around. On the contrary. The city to which the Jews fled from the Nazis during World War II may thus, in a few years, be emptied of Jews. That would represent an ideological defeat – indeed, a veritable ideological breakdown that Sweden can hardly live with.

The riots by the boys and young men who have immigrant backgrounds and live in immigrant enclaves also seem to get worse year by year. Raging immigrant youth who go amok and attack police and ambulance personnel, set fire to police stations, schools, and cars, have become so commonplace that you can hardly avoid the stories in the newspaper.

For example, the situation in June 2010 in Rinkeby, near Stockholm, got so bad that the police had to bring in reinforcements from other parts of the country to help them quell a disturbance by 50 to 100 youths who were throwing bricks and setting fire to buildings. Eyewitnesses described the area as a "war zone."[313]

The political shock

Sweden's innocence was partially destroyed by the national election in 2010. For the first time in history, a party that speaks out for immigration sceptics, love of country, and Swedish culture and tradition got voted into Parliament. The Sweden Democrats (SD) received over 300,000 votes and won 22 seats in the highly politically correct Riksdagen – even though they had been frozen out of media debates during the election campaign, had had to break off campaign events again and again because of violent demonstrations, and also saw some of their own party members assaulted.

There are several reasons for the violent reactions to SD: back in the 1970s it had Nazi views (which the party today officially rejects, and which are not reflected in the current party platform).[314] Then there's the ruling political establishment, which sees the very existence of SD as a challenge to the glaring weakness of its immigration and integration policy. It has now become almost impossible to continue to try to conceal the dramatic problems that have been created by uncontrolled mass immigration.

The strong reactions by the political establishment – members of which, for example, have refused to shake the hands of SD members of the Riksdag, have asked for a new arrangement in the Riksdag cafeteria so that they will not have to stand in line with SD members, and have refused to sit in the same makeup room as them before a TV debate – bear witness not only to a lack of decent manners, but also to a kind of desperation: the established parties do not know, quite simply, how to deal with the *political* challenge that SD represents. Instead of holding a poltiical debate about the obviously real immigration and integration problems, they turn the whole thing into a question about *morality:* those who subscribe to the politically correct consensus are the good people, and the members of SD are the evil ones. I fear that this attitude will only intensify the conflicts in Sweden in the years ahead.[315] I believe especially that the level of political violence will increase, something Prime Minister Fredrik Reinfeldt himself helped prepared the ground for during the election campaign. A member of SD was violently attacked, and the Prime Minister condemned the act. But he added this sentence: "I would like to point out that those who make a career out of promoting an us-and-them way of thinking and, at bottom, a hateful way of viewing relations between people, should not be surprised that such things happen."[316]

As I see it, SD is the legitimate child of the wretched Swedish political situation. The major parties have failed miserably – and, not least, have failed the lost girls and women in the enclaves who lead lives not unlike those of their sisters in Kabul and Mogadishu.

Germany's problems surface

Berlin, October 2006: "I encourage you Muslim women: come into modern times. Take part in Germany. Then take off the head covering that is a symbol of the oppression of women and male dominance. Take it off and show that you have the same civil and human rights as men."

This statement caused a great stir in both Germany and Turkey in 2006. The words were spoken by a politician in the German national parliament, a woman born in Turkey who had come to Germany at the age of eight. The then 34-year-old Ekin Deligoz, a mother of small children and a member of the Green Party, received a reply to her frank remark: She received death threats from various quarters, and German authorities did not dare to risk waking up one day to an execution in the open street of the kind that the Netherlands had experienced when filmmaker Theo van Gogh was killed on November 2, 2004, in Amsterdam for directing the film *Submission,* written by Ayaan Hirsi Ali, which commented critically on the oppression of women in the name of Islam. Therefore Deligoz instantly was given two round-the-clock bodyguards.

The Turkish press and Islamist-inspired organizations in Germany went on the attack against Deligoz and her statements. The various organizations proclaimed unambiguously that the veil is obligatory for Muslim women while the Turkish press ran what might almost be called a hate campaign against her. Deligoz was accused of "having been turned into a German in Germany." She had "distanced" herself from her "Turkish and Islamic identity" – apparently a cardinal sin.

But the accusations went a great deal further than that. Deligoz was even accused of using "Nazi-like logic." Her comments, it was maintained, had put the Turks down on racist grounds. When it became clear to leading German politicians that what a woman wears on her head can literally cost her her head in today's' Germany, Deligoz quickly won widespread support. The president of the national parliament called the assaults on Deligoz "a serious attack on the core values of our constitution."

Meanwhile, many prominent Muslim women, as well as leading German intellectuals, tried to paint the veil as innocent by calling it a "fashion accessory." Deligoz replied as follows: "If the veil were only a fashion accessory, I wouldn't be living under police protection."[317]

The veil's steady advance in Germany is a symptom of the underlying problems facing Muslims in regard to the matter of becoming full-fledged members of the national state they live in. Several studies of Muslims in Germany in recent years have drawn international attention. Among other current developments in German Muslim communities is an obvious radicalization of young people.

- Fewer than half of young German Muslims say that immigrants should adapt to German culture, which is a much lower figure than that for the number of older Muslims who support assimilation. Forty percent of young Muslims agree strongly that obeying the religion's

324

commandments is more important than democracy.

- The study "Muslimer in Deutschland" (2010) shows that so-called fundamentalist attitudes are extremely widespread. In this context, "fundamental" means a strong belief that has a decisive role for the religion in day-to-day life and a strong attention to religious rules and rituals, in which the tendency is also to distance oneself from Muslims with non-fundamentalist views. At the same time, there is a general tendency to emphasize Islam and undervalue Western, Christian culture. Forty percent of the Muslim German population holds such views.

- Almost half of the young Muslims in schools have such fundamentalist views. Over four-fifths view the Koran as God's direct revelation, and over half of the young people believe that those who seek to modernize Islam are destroying the true faith.

Another extensive 2010 study shows that Muslim boys are more violent than others. Boys who grow up in extremely religious homes are more violent than others, and Muslim boys who are very religious are twice as violent as Christian immigrant boys who are very religious.

Like Sweden and other countries, Germany also contains more and more areas that are defined as no-go zones. Riots and violence are almost out of control. As the head of the German Police Union puts it, the attacks on police are now so common that they are causing the state's monopoly on power to wobble: "There used to be huge fist fights going on when the police arrived. Today they don't really seriously start until the police arrive – and they're against the police." Wendt also says that "there are some streets in Berlin, Hamburg, Duisburg, Essen, and Cologne where you can't walk alone. If an officer stops a speeder, 40 to 70 of his friends are summoned to the spot at lightning speed, and in the face of such a superior force the state unfortunately has to withdraw." The young people have no respect, then, for officers of the law. "The perpetrators don't accept the German legal system and its representatives. Also, it's known all over Germany that these lightning mobilizations are carried out by Turkish and Arab boys. The police are driven away with the words: 'We'll settle this among ourselves. Get lost.' In areas like that, the state's monopoly on power is wobbling." [318]

That the state's monopoly on power is wobbling in a city like Berlin, for example, is also borne witness to by anonymous police officers' statements on German television in 2010. The police there talk about fear of doing their job. They say that they can be surrounded by up to 50 people, typically young men with Arabic backgrounds, who spit, hit, and insult them. Owing to low manpower, the police have to withdraw from the scene. The police also say that they refuse to report assaults directed against them when they are doing their job, out of fear that they will be denied promotions. In 10 years, the violence against the police has risen by 28.6 percent, and since 2006 over 6,000 people have refused to obey police orders, an increase of 55 percent. Rarely are the violent elements convicted.[319]

In 2008, on a public stage, Turkish President Recep Tayyip Erdogan threw salt on the wounds of German integration. In front of 16,000 German Turks in Cologne, Erdogan warned them in the strongest terms against adopting the values upon which German society is built: "Assimilation i a crime against humanity," he maintained, and demanded that Germany set up Turkish-language secondary schools and a Turkish university, preferably with teachers educated in Turkey.[320] His comments caused a political storm.

The German debate about the problems with integrating Muslims exploded in August 2010. The Social Democrat Thilo

Sarrazin, also a member of the board of the German central bank, Bundesbank, published the book *Deutschland schafft sich ab* (*Germany Does away with Itself*). Sarrazin mercilessly criticized Muslims' lack of willingness and ability to integrate, cited their overrepresentation in statistics on violent crime, and wrote: "I don't want us to end up as strangers in our own land, not even on a regional basis." Both Chancellor Angela Merkel and the Bundesbank scrambled to put out the fire. The leaders of Bundesbank said that Sarrazin's comments had "damaged Bundesbank's image." It was said that "discrimination doesn't belong in the bank." Merkel "urged the bank to take action." It was obvious that Merkel wanted Sarrazin fired from the bank's board. [321]

Sarrazin presented his points indelicately, not least when he argued that one of the problems facing Germany was a lower intelligence level among Muslims, and also when he claimed that "there is a special gene for Jews, just as there is a special gene for Basques."[322] The head of Sarrazin's local party in decided to start the process of shutting Sarrazin out, and the president of Deutsche Bundesbank, Axel Weber, wrote letters to the President of Germany, Christian Wulff, encouraging him to discharge Sarrazin.

What, then, were Sarrazin's proposed solutions to the actual integration problems? They include the following:

- "All those who are able to work must commit themselves to working. If not, they should lose their rights to social benefits."

- "All children over three years of age should be in day care. If not, the parents will lose child benefits. Doing homework must be obligatory for weak students, Germans included. Exemptions from education on religious grounds should be rejected, and hijab should be banned in schools."

- Language requirements for acquiring German citizenship must be tightened up, and those who bring new spouses to Germany must be able to support them themselves.

- "Immigration must be changed, so that those who come to Germany in the future must have education and qualifications that will benefit German society."

While Sarrazin was criticized intensely by a broad spectrum of the German elite, he also received support. Among those who took his side were the lawyer, women's rights activists, and author Seyran Ates, who has Turkish roots, and the prominent sociologist and author Necla Kelek, also born in Turkey. He also received massive support in the many online debates that following the publication of the book and the intense media coverage. The impression is that the average German agrees with Sarrazin and that the elite is out of touch with people's daily experiences.

In September of the same year, Sarrazin resigned from the board of Bundesbank. Over one million copies of his book were printed in the autumn of 2010. During this time, Angela Merkel made amends to Sarrazin, in a sort of indirect way. Merkel may have been scared of losing voters on account of the massive popular support for Sarrazin when he stated firmly: "German's multiculturalism has been a complete failure."[323]

France: Citizenship and visible faces

The situation for the largest Jewish population in northern and Western Europe has in no way improved in recent years. On the contrary. In many ways it is dramatic, especially in the wake of the escalating conflict between Israel and Palestine during the last few years, as a result of which hatred for Israel has led to hated for Jews. Several thousand Jews are now leaving France for good every year, most of them for the U.S. or Israel. For example, in March 2007 a group of more than 7,000 French Jews applied for political asylum in the U.S. The application was sent to the U.S. Congress with all the applicants' signatures. The grounds for the application were "the increase in the numberof anti-Semitic acts committed by Islamic fundamentalists," as a result of which a "significant number" of Jews do not feel "safe any more in France."[324]

The asylum application cites the most grotesque action committed against a Jew in France and Europe in recent times – an action that shocked the country. Ilan Halimi, a 23-year-old man with Moroccan roots, was kidnapped and imprisoned by a gang of Islamists who called themselves "The Barbarians." He was brutally tortured for 24 days until the torture took his life. On 29 April 2009, the trial against the 27 gang members began, and the French-born 28-year-old leader of the gang, Fofana Youssouf, "sneered at Halimi's relatives and cried 'Allahu akbar'" (*Allah is great* in Arabic) when he entered the courtroom. When the judge asked him where and when he was born, he replied: "13 February 2006 in Sainte-Genevieve-des-Bois" – the same date and place where Halimi was murdered. Several of the defendants confirmed that they had kidnapped Halimi for one single reason: he was Jewish.

Of the 27 defendants, the gang leader, Fofana, received a life sentence of at least 22 years in prison, while several of his co-conspirators received far more lenient sentences. Several were given only a few months or two or three years in prison. Two were acquitted.[325] Unsurprisingly, Halimi's murder, and the trial with its many lenient sentences, became a national symbol of the increasing harassment of Jews in France.[326]

Deprivation of citizenship

The riots in France's ghettos, and hence also the violence against police and other authorities, continues unabated. There is no sign that this will turn around. President Nicolas Sarkozy knows this, of course, and he has clearly understood that he needs to make a powerful effort if France is going to see better times. After violent riots in Grenoble in the summer of 2009, Sarkozy made such powerful statements in the media that it was impossible to come to any conclusion other than that the situation in the immigrant-heavy areas is out of control. Sarkozy presented a specific and controversial proposal: that it should be possible to rescind the citizenship of people who have become French citizens during the last ten years and who have attacked the police or other officials. The proposal met with strong opposition from the left and from legal experts, who believed that such a measure might violate the French constitution, which says that all citizens are equal before the law, regardless of race, religion, or national origin. Three out of four Frenchmen, however, supported the proposal.

In the autumn of 2010 Sarkozy announced that he was proceeding with the plan to rescind people's citizenship. This announcement was made at a meeting with the ministers responsible for security, justice, and immigration. In October, therefore, French law was changed. Henceforth, someone who kills or performs acts of violence that lead to the death of a police officer or soldier, and who has been granted French citizenship during the last ten years, will be deprived of his citizenship, provided that this action does not render the individual stateless.[327]

While this was taking place, Interior Minister Brice Hortefeux called for the same punishment to be meted out to those who support polygamy and genital mutilation. Sarkozy rejected his proposal. I find this rather surprising, given his initial desire to take citizenship away from people who performed acts of violence against public officials. Surely it must be considered an equally bad, if not worse, offense to ritually mutilate a defenseless child than to assault an officer of the law?[328]

Sarkozy leaves no doubt, however, that his patience in regard to real integration is close to the breaking point. In the same year, 2010, he took on Islamic garb, namely the increasing use of the face-covering garments the burka and niqab: "In our country, we can't allow women to be imprisoned behind a screen, isolated from all social life, deprived of all identity....The burka is not a religious symbol. It is a symbol of subordination, a symbol of debasement....It is not welcome on the territory of the French Republic."[329]

In the summer of 2010, Sarkozy won an overwhelming majority in the national legislature for his proposal. The people supported him, too: eight out of ten Frenchmen were for the ban and on 14 September 2010, Sarkozy also received the necessary support from the entire Senate, with the exception of one vote, for a national ban. Only the French Constitutional Council could put a stop to the ban, which calls for fines of 150 euros for women who wear the burka or niqab in public, as well as a compulsory course in French values. Men who force women to wear clothing that covers them fully will receive a far more severe punishment: a fine of 30,000 euros and a year in jail.

The Constitutional Council issued its decision on the ban. The council's statement mentioned neither the burka nor Islam, but rather noted that it is punishable "to hide one's face in public," and that this ban strikes a "reasonable balance" between personal freedom and the need to maintain other constitutional principles, such as women's rights and public order. Exempted from the ban are "houses of worship open to the public."[330]

During the process leading to the ban, the Islamist preacher Omar Bakri warned Europe about a rise in European support for Al-Qaida should the ban be introduced. Omar Bakri, who was expelled from Britain and lives in Lebanon, may have been somewhat correct in his claim. For a week after the Senate approved of the ban against face covering, the authorities received information about a woman who was supposed to have planned a suicide attack on the Paris Metro.[331] The threats were supposedly made by Al-Qaida and the motive is supposed to have been the ban. When this became clear, France raised its threat level at once, and Bernard Squarcini, the head of France's counterterrorism agency, stated very clearly that it was just a

331

question of time before France experienced a terrorist attack on its own soil: "We are expecting an attack on our territory."[332]

It remains to be seen whether Squarcini is correct and France will be thus be the next European country to experience a terrorist attack on its own soil, which undeniably would be a feather in Al-Qaeda's cap. Such an attack would also have a profound impact on the French state – that open, free democracy founded on absolute secularism.

The Redeker case

It will not necessarily be the burka ban that provokes terrorism on French soil. Robert Redeker, a well-known philosopher and author, published an op-ed in *Le Figaro* on September 19, 2006, under the title "How should the free world deal with the Islamists' threats?" The piece was a defense of the pope's famous speech, given at the University of Regensburg earlier that month, in which the pope mentioned genuinely brutal aspects of Islamic history. In his piece, Redeker wrote that "Jesus is the master of love, Muhammed is the master of hate."

The next day, Redeker was named "the Islamophobe of the moment" by Yusuf al-Qaradawi on the Al-Jazeera TV channel, watched by tens of millions of viewers. Redeker instantly began to receive personal threats by e-mail. Meanwhile, though he did not know it, terrorists were planning to eliminate him. The French intelligence service had tracked down a coded electronic message that read, in part, as follows:

First the pig's name: Redeker, Robert. And on to the second: a photo, so we won't forget his face. And third, this arrogant liar's address:...Fourth: Where does he work? Near Toulouse in Saint-Orens-de-Gameville, where he teaches philosophy at the Pierre-Paul Riquet secondary school....Fifth: Where is Escalquens? Not very far from Toulouse, about 15 kilometers southeast of the city.

Thus ended Redeker's and his family's freedom. After this, they had to live underground, at a series of addresses, under police protection.

One Must Try to Live is the expressive title of Redeker's book about his life after the *Figaro* op-ed. When he visited Copenhagen in 2009 to address the Free Press Society, he arrived at the airport with four bodyguards.

Yet another new Danish policy

Denmark will never again be what it once was – that is, before 2005. The world-famous cartoons will doubtless haunt the once small and happy country, which used to enjoy a deep sense of community, for a long time. In the wake of the 2006 riots there has been one event that will definitely go into the history books: the murder attempt on the retired grandfather Kurt Westergaard, who drew the most famous of the cartoons – Muhammed with a bomb in his turban.

On New Year's Day 2010, Westergaard escaped death with a cry for help in his own home in Århus. Westergaard was home alone with his five-year-old grandchild when an axe-wielding man of Somali ethnicity broke in through the door. In a fraction of a second Westergaard had to make a horrible decision: should he stay in the living room and try to protect his grandchild and himself with just his fists, or should he rush into the specially fortified bathroom that the authorities had provided him with for security reasons after the cartoon crisis? He saw that he would not be able to take the child with him, and he had been told by the police that any terrorists would be out to get him, not his family. So Westergaard retreated alone into the bathroom, with the intruder hot on his heels. The man tried unsuccessfully to break down the door. The child was untouched, but Westergaard was as close to death as it is possible to be.

Since that time, Danish intelligence has provided Westergaard with bodyguards 24 hours a day, 365 days a year. And he will have to live like this for the rest of his life.

The reaction by the Danish public, politicians, and media can described as a mixture of alarm, despair, and outrage. It turned out that the would-be murderer was a 28-year-old Danish Somali with ties to Al-Qaida, and that he reportedly belonged to a network of would-be terrorists that had a foothold in Denmark. On 9 July 2010, he was prosecuted for terrorism and attempted murder, and the prosecutors further asked for him to be expelled from Denmark since he is not a Danish citizen.[333]

Hardly any person in Denmark today is as highly regarded as Westergaard. His quiet humour, his always optimistic tone, his jovial manner, which is so utterly free of self-importance, combined with his steadfast defense of freedom of expression, has possible made him more popular among the Danish people than even the highly popular Queen Margrethe.[334]

For my part, I do not think I have ever felt more honoured than when I was invited to Copenhagen in 2007 by the Free Press Society to present the Sappho Prize for journalism to the man responsible for the Muhammed cartoons, *Jyllands-Posten*'s culture editor, Flemming Rose. I had written the speech beforehand and sent it to the head of the Free Press Society, Lars Hedegaard. When I landed at Copenhagen Airport on 27 March, Hedegaard met me in the arrivals hall with a broad smile and with that day's issue of *Jyllands-Posten* in his hand. Hedegaard had arranged for my entire tribute to Rose to be published in *Jyllands-Posten* – illustrated by the newspaper's then editorial cartoonist, Kurt Westergaard.

There is no doubt that Denmark, in the wake of the cartoon crisis, has been a highly prioritized target of international terrorism, and that Al-Qaida and similar groups have a hard time forgetting and forgiving Several planned terrorist attacks have been prevented at the last minute, and in Al-Qaida's first English-language magazine, *Inspire*, which came out in 2010, three Danes appear, along with six people from other countries, on the terrorist group's international death list: Kurt Westergaard, Flemming Rose, and *Jyllands-Posten*'s former editor-in-chief Carsten Juste. One of the most important articles in the terrorist magazine is about the cartoons, and the message is that all Muslims are obliged to wreak revenge on those who have insulted the prophet. The article is followed by a full-page death list, illustrated by a shining pistol.

According to the American terrorist researcher and former CIA man Bruce Riedel, the article shows that Al-Qaida is actively trying to keep the focus on Denmark as one of the world's most obvious terrorist targets: "It is clear that Al-Qaida is focused on attacking Danish targets because of the cartoon crisis. Last year the terrorist network planned a massive attack against Denmark with the help of the American David Headley. It was called off when he was arrested. But it is likely that both Al-Qaida's central leadership in Pakistan and Al-Qaida's division in Yemen will try to go after Denmark again."[335]

The burka debate

Facial coverings have led to widespread debate in almost all northern and western European countries in recent years, and Denmark is no exception. The Danish Syrian Naser Khader, who now belongs to the Conservative People's Party, proposed a ban in the summer of 2009, and a broad debate ensued. But the debate was killed off by the judicial bureaucracy. The next year, judicial officials wrote to the Folketing that they were "most inclined to think" that "considerable doubt" could be raised as to whether such a ban would be consistent with the constitution and with the European Convention on Human Rights (ECHR). Then the Minister of Justice, who belongs to the same party, said that "it goes without saying that neither I, as Minister of Justice, nor a party like the Conservative People's Party can make a proposal that raises this kind of legal question."

Karen Jespersen, who belongs to the Liberal Party, which is part of the current government, and heads up the integration committee in the Folketing, was (to put it mildly) less than satisfied. She pointed out that France had evaluated the situation differently, deciding that out of "concern for public order which

335

is also mentioned in the ECHR (article 9, point 2)," religious freedom can be curtailed. But in Denmark the jurists had not done their jobs, as their counterparts had done in France, Jespersen believed, given that the French jurists had made an *argument* for restricting religious freedom by banning face coverings. Thus the politicians were given an entirely different interpretation on which to base their independent judgment. When the French Minister of Justice presented the proposal for a ban, she emphasized that the burka and niqab violate human dignity and equality, and that these "garments", which should instead perhaps be regarded as uniforms, can also present a security risk. A major argument was that the "garments" contravene the very principles on which France was founded: liberty, equality, and fraternity.

In an op-ed in *Jyllands-Posten* on 16 August 2010, Jespersen continued her argument as follows:

> We have freedom of religion in Denmark. This means that one must not be discriminated against on the basis of one's religion. But §70 [of the Danish Constitution] does not mean that one can do everything in the name of religion. As the Court of Human Rights has made clear: religious freedom "does no protect any action whatsoever that is motivated or inspired by a religion or a conviction, and does not always guarantee the right to conduct oneself in a way that is dictated by a religious conviction." This is emphasized in two judgments mentioned by the Minister of Justice himself (Dogru *vs.* France, Sahin *vs.* Turkey). The point is clear: you can't necessarily dress in any way you want, in any context you like, and defend it by crying religious discrimination.

In the autumn of 2010, Jespersen promised a fight, and the result of this ongoing struggle can, as I see it, go both ways. In Denmark, as in most other European countries, a very intense conflict is underway about the *interpretation* of human rights, and especially about which human rights should have priority over others. Briefly put, the debate is about women's freedom and an open society *vs.* unrestricted religious liberty.

Denmark plays in its own division when it comes to immigration and integration policies in Europe. The country's politicians and intellectuals, however, don't disguise the fact that even in Denmark integration "is an uphill battle" (to borrow a phrase that is frequently used behind the scenes by leading Danish politicians). The justice system in Copenhagen released statistics for 2009 which showed that 15- to 17-year-old boys with immigrant backgrounds are strongly overrepresented in crime figures: 73 percent of the boys and young men who had been arrested during that year had foreign backgrounds. Most of the charges involved robbery, but there were also many crimes of violence, weapon possession, and arson, and a high percentage of the perpetrators had been taken into custody owing to the seriousness of their crimes.

The Danish police describe a dramatic rise in crimes committed by young immigrants.[336] That there is a strong correlation between these crimes and Muslim immigration can also be observed in the crime statistics. Figures from Statistics Denmark (2009) demonstrate that even when social circumstances are taken into account, individuals with backgrounds in Muslim countries are heavily overrepresented among the perpetrators of serious crimes, while persons with other non-Western backgrounds are underrepresented. If we place the average rate of criminality in Denmark at 100, Thais are at 76, Filipinos at 59, and Chinese at 37. Toward the other side of the scale are Moroccans and Turks at 187 and 184 respectively, while at the far end of the scale are Somalians at 277, Moroccans at 255, and Lebanese at 243.[337]

When one takes into account the large numbers of young people with immigrant backgrounds – especially from Muslim lands – who are now growing up in Copenhagen and other Danish cities, and the ongoing establishment of ghettos, it is hard not to see dark clouds on the horizon.

To be sure, Denmark's new immigration rules of 2001, in combination with later measures, have led to higher employment levels among non-Western immigrants. There is nonetheless a clear acknowledgment that the costs of immigration are not economically sustainable. The welfare state cannot easily be preserved without radical new changes. This awareness exploded like a bomb in 2008. In the report for its third quarter, the Danish National Bank (DN) presented figures that startled Europe and that confirmed Finance Minister Thor Pedersen's 2005 statement: "...integration is Denmark's greatest welfare reform." DN reported these cold facts: it is only the (unrealistic) "superimmigrant" that enriches Denmark (or other European countries) economically. The superimmigrant comes to Denmark fully educated and dives right into full-time work and pays as much tax as an average Dane. She or he does not bring any family to Denmark, and leaves the country before retirement age.

If 5,000 non-Western persons immigrate over the course of a year, it will cost the Danish state 10 billion kroner annually in additional expenses, while for 5,000 Westerners the additional expenses come to 500 million kroner, DN ascertained. If Denmark achieves "perfect immigration," on the other hand – meaning that immigrants in Denmark today contribute just as much to the work force and pay just as much in taxes as Danes – the Danish state will save 23 billion dollars in expenses every year.

But doesn't Denmark, with its low birth rates, need (like other European countries) more people to enter the work force in the years to come, especially now that the population is growing steadily older, as politicians nearly across the political spectrum maintain? Yes, we need more workers, not least in nursing and other such professions. But we do not need family immigration, low employment rates, and high welfare consumption. As DN showed, it is only "superimmigration" that is economically profitable, and "perfect integration" of immigrants and their descendants is the only proper medicine.[338]

In May 2009 another report caused a sensation in Denmark. The independent analysis institute DREAM calculated the state's expenses on immigrants and Danes.[339] DREAM divided the population into five categories: Danes, immigrants from "less developed countries" (i.e., non-Western countries), the latter's descendants, immigrants from "more developed countries" (i.e., Western countries), anf *their* descendants. The figures showed that every year a Dane costs the state 5,500 kroner; a non-Western immigrant, 29,600 kroner; and a non-Western descendant, 29,000 kroner; while a Western immigrant, who is likely to be educated and to have come to Denmark to work, contributes 13,500 kroner to the state. Descendants of Western immigrants, however, cost the state 8,500 kroner a year.

The new integration minister, Birthe Rønn Hornbech, sent out a trial balloon in September 2010 which was probably a consequence of the study by DN and DREAM and the analysis by Cepos. She warned of a radical new immigration policy: "The time is right for a departure from, and a revolt against, the Aliens Law that we passed in 2001, because the world is quite different today. We have managed to stem what we wanted to stem. Now it's about a development agenda. We can't afford to exclude good workers, and we will have a lack of workers within a few years. In the future, the clear and new guiding principle of Danish immigration policy will be to prioritize those who can contribute to the growth and prosperity of Denmark." She continued with these words: "I know that it's entirely new to hear a message like this from me. But I have become so preoccupied with Denmark's need for growth that I now see myself as the head of a ministry of development. I have begun to read the newspapers in another way. Development is the entire foundation of the welfare society. Therefore, in future legislation on aliens we will focus entirely on the development agenda and the future of the welfare society."[340]

And so it was done. On 7 November, the government entered into the agreement entitled "New times. New demands" with the Danish People's Party (DF), an agreement that will stop all immigration of non-Western spouses who do not have the skills to join the work force, embrace Danish values, and integrate into Danish society. Before immigration, for example, a new foreign spouse must provide documentation of higher education and/or solid work experience and relevant language skills. Applicants will be subjected to a point system whereby extra points will be given if they can speak a Scandinavian language and do not settle in a ghetto. The couple will also be required to have a much stronger connection to Denmark than to any other country.

Previously, Denmark had the 24-year-old rule and a relatively weak connection requirement that applied to the foreign party; now, it will be an unconditional requirement that the foreign party will be required unconditionally to display clear indications that he or she is qualified and willing to contribute positively to Danish society.[341] In addition, the requirements placed upon the Danish party will be further sharpened; for example, one must not have been convicted of terror-related crimes, must not be in debt to the government, must not have received welfare payments during the last three years, must have been working full-time during the last few years, and must pass a Danish test.

Furthermore, the government and DF have asked for a report on the economic consequences that would have resulted if the nation's policy had *not* been changed in 2002. An accounting will also be made of what Danes and immigrants, and various immigrant groups, contribute to or cost the Danish state.

These retrenchments – which, given the current European situation must be described as dramatic – have been made even though Denmark halved its non-European marriage immigration after the reforms introduced in 2002, and even though the pattern changed in such a way that the majority of immigrants now belong to national groups that have a good record of participation in the Danish labour market.[342]

There is no doubt that the Danish political leadership knew very well why these measures were necessary: the welfare state and the Danish sense of community were approaching the precipice.

Is Norway closing in on Denmark?

An intense struggle took place in the Norwegian government in 2006 and 2007 about a new family-reunification policy. The struggle was between the Labour Party (Ap) and the significantly smaller Socialist Left (SV), its major partner in the governing coalition. No matter which measures Labour proposed in an effort to limit undesirable marriage immigration, SV rejected them. Neither arguments from a feminist standpoint (regarding, for example, the importation of young, vulnerable housewives) – arguments which SV itself usually employs successfully in other fields – or arguments related to the ways in which current rules encourage the forced marriage of young people won SV over.

The desperation increased within the Stoltenberg camp, that is to say, at the centre of power: like the Danish government, Prime Minister Stoltenberg and company understand that marriage immigration isn't economically sustainable.

In the spring of 2007, Labour's blood was boiling over SV's irresponsibility. HRS was contacted privately by a member of the government: "SV refuses to accept any proposed change," this individual said. "We have to put something on the table that they can't say no to." The member of the government came to our office, and in the course of a three-hour discussion we drew up what we called the five-year rule: that persons living in Norway must have worked and/or studied for five years after primary and secondary school before they can apply to import a new spouse to Norway from countries outside the EU.

We thought that the rule was ingenious and very difficult for SV to reject: it is, after all, in everybody's interest that young and unqualified immigrants in the country work or study, and especially that young non-Western immigrant become, in this manner, active members of and contributors to society as a whole. Such a proposal would promote integration and improve the economic health of the welfare state. All in all, a humanitarian proposal.

The politician got the Labour leadership on board immediately, and the third party in the government, the Centre Party (Sp), accepted the new rule too, on the condition that the requirement be lowered to four years (probably a purely political move). SV, however, again put its down, and instead of taking the proposal (which the Progress Party supported) to the Parliament, Stoltenberg chose to bury it and thereby keep the peace with SV.

The national election in 2009, however, put a stop to SV's opposition. Support for the party went down three percentage points to six percent, while Labor received 32 percent of the vote and Sp 8 percent. SV's power had declined, and the new Stoltenberg government's political platform, the Soria Moria II Declaration, included the four-year rule. As of 1 January 2010, the rule applied to all those who have come to Norway through family immigration or as refugees or who have been granted residency on humanitarian grounds. While the present government remains in power, the rule will apply to all citizens of Norway.[343]

Leading figures in the Danish government and Folketing were very pleased that Norway showed, in such a manner, that it was beginning to follow in Denmark's footsteps. HRS also felt that the new political course in Norway constituted a nod of respect to the oft-maligned Kingdom of Denmark.

A new government in 2013?

Yet this new measure will not help. Far more desperate remedies are needed, remedies of the ort instituted in Denmark in 2010. Prime Minister Jens Stoltenberg, it seems to me, is seeking to legitimize a powerful tightening of the laws. In May 2009, he established the so-called Brockmann committee, whose task is to analyze the consequences of immigration for the future of the welfare state. The committee's mandate states that "a high level of participation in the labour force is a necessary condition for the welfare society." It also states that "[i]ncreased international mobility requires increased knowledge of and a better understanding of the connection between migration and the future development of the welfare model and welfare arrangements – in order to provide a more solid foundation, the next time around, for a complete development of policy....The committee shall also describe how the formulation of Norwegian welfare rules can affect the flow of migration." It further says that the committee shall "determine whether there are aspects of the immigration policy that are particularly relevant to the future development and formulation of the Norwegian welfare model."

In a list of bullet points, the mandate leaves no doubt that what is at issue here is the connection between immigration and the sustainability of the welfare state:

> The committee is particularly requested to determine:
>
> - Whether the universal welfare rules, together with the specific means of integration, help to achieve the highest possible level of employment.
>
> - What significance increased mobility has for the relationship between welfare production and welfare consumption.
>
> - Whether a greater ethnic and cultural diversity can be assumed to affect attitudes toward and exploitation of current welfare arrangements. This requires that the committee examine more closely the necessary conditions for the legitimacy and sustainability of the rules, as well as norms and the establishment of norms."

343

The committee is also supposed to evaluate developments in relevant neighbouring countries, such as Denmark.[344]

The Brockmann committee will deliver its report in May of 2011. I expect that the report will be so explosive that at the next national election campaign in 2013, a radical new immigration policy to ensure the sustainability of the welfare state will be a major plank in the Labour Party's platform.

Opinion polls held in the autumn of 2010, however, show that two other parties, the Conservatives (H) and the Progress Party (FrP), stand a good chance of taking power in 2013. The Progress Party has made it perfectly clear that it wants to copy the Danish policy. The Conservatives, on the contrary, show no interest in tightening the policy on family reunification. The party seems to be split internally on two levels: after having given many talks to local Conservative Party groups in the last four years, I am in no doubt that the party's grass roots – as well as the Young Conservatives – have a realistic view of the costs and challenges of immigration and would therefore welcome a new Norwegian policy similar to the current Danish policy. The party leadership, then, is out of touch with the grass roots.

But in addition to this, the leadership is itself divided into what can roughly be described as two wings: the highly liberal globalists and the more traditional conservatives. Perhaps the most prominent globalist among the leading members of the Conservative Party is Kristin Clemet, who has served several times as a cabinet member and who is now the administrative director of the think tank Civita. At a seminar on the welfare state and immigration in 2010, Clemet made it clear that she was in favour of free movement of people from country to country. In her ideal world, the globe would find itself in a "win-win situation," as she put it: Europe's population is shrinking, while millions of young people in the third world need work. Thus: open borders.

Clemet underscored the moral aspect of immigration: as she put it, we in Norway and the rest of Europe belong to "an international overclass." She further argued that "it is a human right to leave one's country," thus ignoring article 8 of the European Convention on Human Rights, which says that a state can take action when it is "necessary in a democratic society in the interests of national security, public safety or the economic well-being of the country, for the prevention of disorder or crime, for the protection of health or morals, or for the protection of the rights and freedoms of others."

Her conclusion was that Europe is following a "rather cruel policy."[345] She didn't touch upon the question of how the sustainability of the welfare state would be ensured if an open-border policy were to be pursued. Among the more classical conservatives, especially in the circles around the rising political talent Torbjørn Røe Isaksen, I see a promise that common sense, realism, and responsibility will triumph over feelings.

At the same seminar it was also made crystal clear that Stoltenberg can expect powerful political resistance within his party if he wants to curb immigration. Anette Trettebergstuen, a member of the party's central board and of Parliament, said that immigration "enriches the welfare society and the welfare society is dependent on immigration." She also believed that those who say that "immigration is a threat to the welfare state, they should just be dismissed." She did not present a single statistic to support her argument.

The struggle over values

In recent years, certain elements of Norway's Muslim community, which makes up about three percent of the population, have dominated the media. No other religious group's self-appointed or chosen leaders and front men demand anywhere near as much attention or demonstrate so clearly that they are dissatisfied with our freedoms. How, people ask me with concern, will our society fare when Muslims make up 10 or 20 percent?

12 February 2010 became a red-letter day and a powerful reminder of the kind of forces that are on the march in Norway.

At University Square in Oslo, where the Nazis held rallies in the 1930s, 3,000 Muslim men demonstrated, many of them dressed according to the code of the prophet Muhammed: a long coat, ankle-length baggy pants, and head coverings, plus full beards. The occasion was an article in the newspaper *Dagbladet* about an unknown Internet user who had linked to a caricature of Muhammed as a pig on the Facebook page of the Norwegian Police Security Service (PST). Even though the drawing was removed by the PST when it was discovered, *Dagbladet* ran this as a front-page story, illustrated with the pig drawing.

This was the prelude to the mass demo on 12 February, at which one of the speakers, a Norwegian-born Muslim dressed like an Islamist, issued a warning to Norway, saying (among much else): "When will Norwegian authorities and their media understand how serious this is? Maybe not before it's too late. Maybe not before we experience an 11 September on Norwegian soil. This is no threat; this is a warning."[346] The young man who made this threat, Mohyeldeen Mohammad, and who was then studying sharia at the Islamic University in Medina, Saudi Arabia, was one of the demo's planners.

The most disheartening aspect of the demonstration in Oslo was not that this pure Wahabbist, with his thoroughgoing Saudi style and spirit, threatened a new 9/11. What was really unsettling, as I see it, was the *number* of people who showed up for the rally and the fact that so many of them, by their actions and attire, showed their support for sharia. It was the epitome of darkness, displaying itself in broad daylight. These days, more and more extremists do not hesitate to show their true – and morally repulsive – colours in public. I fear this is a sign of something that can cause problems to spin out of control: young Muslims confused about their identity will be fascinated by the exceedingly clear message such Islamists put out. These young people are offered a full package – sharia as the answer to all of life's and society's challenges. And they are given the chance to join a "nation" of their own – the umma – to replace the national identity.

Such a development has obviously taken place at Oslo University College, where the student group Islam Net has its headquarters.[347] After only two years' work, Islam Net has become Norway's largest membership organization for Muslims, with over 1,200 paying members. Its goal is to clear up "general misunderstandings about Islam," "misunderstandings among non-Muslims," and "misunderstandings among non-Muslims with higher education," and to convert non-Muslims to a conservative and controversial interpretation of Islam by means of the so-called "convert school" it has set up.[348] Islam Net itself leaves no doubt that it is an Islamist group. A key ideologue for the group is the Indian Islamist Zakir Naik, who is regularly promoted on Islam Net's website. Naik is regarded as so extreme that he is denied entry into both Britain and Canada. Here are the statements that caused him to be banned from these two countries in 2010: "Every Muslim should be a terrorist." And: "If he [Osama Bin Laden] terrorizes the terrorists, if he terrorizes the terrorist America, because the U.S. is a terrorist, I support him."[349] Naik has also claimed that it is "obvious" that George Bush was behind the terrorist attack on the Twin Towers. He also believes that apostate Muslims should be punished with death. Other speakers whom Islam Net has flown in from abroad have also preached an Islamist and literalist Islam. So far, Islam Net has not, to my knowledge, invited a single speaker who comes close to promoting open democracy based on human rights.

Nor, as far as I know, does any other student organization in Norway manage to draw so many people to its events as Islam Net does. On November 7, 2010, Islam Net invited the former rapper den Loon, an African-American who converted to Islam in 2008 and who has taken the name Amir Muhadith. Muhadith now comes off as a full-fledged Salafist, and between 700 and 800 people showed up for the event at the college, which had separate entrances for men and women. The head of Islam Net, the Norwegian-born Fahad Qureshi, who also comes off as a Salafist, explained this gender separation as follows: "If women want separate entrances, I think they should get them....Many want it. It is usual if you come from Pakistani or Somali cultures. Gender separation in the auditorium was discussed at the meeting, and I asked if it was true that the women wanted to sit with men. The answer was a loud no from all the women in the auditorium. It is sickening, and it is oppressive to women, to force women to sit with men against their will." When it was pointed out to Qureshi that "it is usual for men and women to sit together and use a common entrance," he replied as follows: "Yes, Norwegians maybe aren't offended by it. But if you have another culture, it's different. I think people should accept it. It would be an offensive act on the part of the college if it didn't allow people choose to sit separately."[350]

This, then, is just how "Norwegian" the Norwegian-born Qureshi and his "sisters and brothers" are. These are students who in a few years will occupy key positions in Norway. As a number of international experts have pointed out, it isn't terrorists who constitute the greatest threat to European society, but the increasingly Islamist-inspired young people who are working hard to turn our secular society into one governed according to sharia law – and who are employing non-violent but long-term ideological methods to achieve this end. Non-violent Islamists, in short, are more dangerous than violent terrorists.

It has also been very unsetting to follow developments in Norway's umbrella organization for the Muslim faith community, the Islamic Council (IRN), for example its positions on the death penalty for homosexuals. At an open debate in 2007, IRN's then second-in-command, Asghar Ali, refused to reject the death penalty for gays in Iran.[351] During the debate, he was challenged repeatedly to state his view of Iran's death penalty for gays, and his answers shifted between "I don't know" and "I can't answer that."[352] The story quickly resulted in waves of antipathy toward Ali, who then issued a press release: "As a Norwegian Muslim, naturally I reject all forms of violence and persecution of people based on their religion, skin colour, sexuality, and ethnicity. This also means, of course, that I reject the death penalty for homosexuals," wrote Ali.

At first glance this might seem trustworthy, if only he hadn't said: "As a *Norwegian* Muslim…" He was, then, speaking as a "Norwegian Muslim," and as a Muslim in Norway he is obliged under sharia to obey the laws of the country in which he lives. In a single sentence, then, he took a linguistic somersault – he rejected he death penalty on account of Norwegian law, but at the same time did *not* reject it as a Muslim, thereby maintaining his support for the sharia-decreed death penalty for homosexual acts.

It must also be mentioned that one of the participants in the same debate was the then medical student (now doctor) and former leader of the Muslim Student Association and Pakistani Student Association, Muhammad Usman Rana. He also made use of the sharia tactic: "As a Norwegian Muslim I consider the death penalty entirely out of the question, and that applies also to the death penalty for homosexuality," Rana told NRK after the debate at Humanismens Hus. "I also said this during the debate. But in a theological discussion I will defer to academic scholars of Islam abroad. I am not going to get into that discussion."[353] I call such conscious manipulation, which so many journalists and politicians unfortunately allow themselves to be seduced by, "sharia talk".

IRN refused to say whether it is for or against the death penalty in Iran, and sought the guidance of the European Council for Fatwa and Research (ECFR), whose misanthrophic mentality is discussed in chapter 6 of this book. Now, three years later, ECFR has still not provided IRN with a ruling on the death penalty question and thus the government-supported IRN still has no official position on it.

In the Western humanistic tradition, one would expect that rejecting the murder of people on the grounds of whom they love and have feelings for would be automatic.

There is no doubt that Norway is being divided increasingly along religious lines. The picture of a people who stand shoulder to shoulder has cracked. Precisely for this reason, the government is trying to shape a new way of thinking about Norwegian society. There is talk about "the big we" – a new Norwegian community in which there will be room for a broad diversity of expression and lifestyles. Yes, diversity is essentially a good thing. But i can seem as if the lesson of history about what binds a nation together has been forgotten.

Barometer of values

The situation is undeniably this: Islam is on the march. You can see it grow, from year to year, with the naked eye – whether it is the spread of hijab in public spaces, men with beards and ankle-length baggy pants, or the construction of flashy new mosques. I notice more and more uncertainty and anxiety on the part of "ordinary" people who feel like strangers in their own country. People wonder: what is the goal of this project? Do we, as a nation, not have a right to pass on our own cultural heritage, our traditions and values, to our children and grandchildren? Will we, in the name of tolerance, give in to the demands of "the others" as their numbers grow and as they become increasingly visible and vocal?

A major politician put it this way in a private conversation with me: "What do you think will happen to liquor licenses in Oslo on the day the majority of members of the city council are Muslims?" Another politician who has been a high-profile figure for two decades put it even more bluntly when I asked, in a private exchange: "What do you think of the immigration from the Muslim world?" The answer was concise and so merciless that I was taken aback and unable to speak: "What have they given us?" (And no, neither of these two politicians belong to the Progress Party, which of all Norway's parties is considered the most critical of immigration.)

Let it be said: of course there are many Muslims in Europe who get along just fine, who get the same chills down their spines that Europeans get when they think of sharia and the lack of freedom that traditional Islam brings with it. But we know who has the most power in the public square, who has the power "on the inside" over the "ordinary Muslim," who is best organized and has managed to develop exceptionally strong and close ties to government leaders. It is not the secular Muslims, those who want a Europeanized Islam – that is, a privatized Islam isolated from political and judicial influence. It is, in other words, not the generally secular, well-integrated, and well-educated Persians from Iran who hold the cards in the Muslim communities in Europe. (One thought, moreover, has occurred to me many times: can anyone point to a single mosque in Europe that was established by Persians? Interesting, no?) Persians have generally become a part of mainstream European culture. They have assimilated into our values, even as they have preserved traditional from Persian culture which do not conflict with human rights.

As a rule, then, Persians have been an immigration success, an enriching presence, who take full part in European society, in opposition to the large groups of immigrants from the tradition-based countryside in other Muslim nations. It is precisely their unwillingness (and inability?) to become a natural part of European society, to appreciate such cardinal values as equality, religious liberty, and freedom of speech, and to embrace a life based on personal freedom, participation in society, and taking one's share of the responsibility for the community, that I think is decisive in understanding people's increasing concern about the future.

For at some point or another, Europe must put its foot down – if we are going to be able to preserve the society we know today. There are, for example, limits to how many minarets we can live with, how many hijabs and baggy pants Europe's streets can tolerate, for our public spaces can become as unfree as the streets in a country like Pakistan. It is about standing up to maintain our core culture, a successful culture that is the very reason why Muslims stream to our continent, and why the stream is not flowing in the other direction. My clear impression is that the attitude of the people of Europe is: you are welcome to come to Europe to be a part of us, but don't come here to overturn our culture and our values. Norway will no longer be Norway, and the West will no longer be the West, if our core culture is not preserved, and Christianity is an inextricable part of that culture. Whether one likes or dislikes religion, this is an indisputable fact, as Ayaan Hirsi Ali so brilliantly explains in her most recent book, *Nomad*.[354]

If Islam were to become our core culture, most people understand – if they make the effort – that the Norwegian way of life would be over, unless something takes places that seems more and more like an impossibility: namely, a revolution (in the true meaning of the word) within Islam that would turn all inhuman actions by Muhammed into pure storytelling, just as the Christian world turned its back on the inhuman aspects of the Old Testament. Of course such a revolution would require all of the violence and hatred in the Koran to be stricken from that book for ever. But Islam has failed for around 1,000 years to carry out such revolution. This is, after all, the main reason why people are pouring out of these failed states. The big question of our time, therefore, is this: how can Islam in Europe come to assume a form that is the very opposite of the form it takes in the Muslim world?

Naturally, Norway should not accept any cultural or religious phenomenon that finds its way here. But where to draw the line? There is no one answer to this question. The answer will vary according to the nature and strength of the challenge. But if we compromise our core culture, and relativize it, and support a constitution that is a long, dusty catalogue of rights, we can end up with democratic ideals that that are nothing more than empty slogans and that do not provide us citizens with a real map or compass by which we can steer our society in terms of values. And what can come to happen in crisis situations if the people do not have a real sense of community? How can we ensure a broad sense of belonging if freedom of speech is really threatened or if we are subjected to a terrorist attack? Can we risk acquiring the civil war-like conditions that we see in Europe's no-go zones?

People must also have feelings – of a positive kind – about one another. Last winter I had a thought-provoking experience in downtown east Oslo on the way home from work. A thin layer of snow covered the patches of ice on the streets. A Somali woman dressed in ankle-length hijab slid as I passed her. I instinctively reached for her and managed to cushion what could have been a bad fall, and of course helped her to her feet again. I asked if she was all right, but she hurried on with a completely expressionless face. Not a single gesture, not a single glance at me. I was left standing with an empty and alienated feeling, completely rejected as a fellow citizen.

There doesn't seem to be a broad political understanding in Norway and the EU system of a society's and a culture's need for the people living in it to have a sense of shared belonging. There doesn't seem to be an understanding that the national culture, with its folk songs, traditional holidays and holy days, the flag and national anthem, is something entirely different from a general constitution based on ideals of equality, a text that cannot replace a feeling of community. A viable society is about things close to home, about traditions, about tangible things, about something as obvious as a shared language and a sense of belonging to the country, whether it is one's fatherland or not. And it is also about church spires and the rituals and traditions that have their place within the church. The people cannot be bound together by measures adopted by politicians. It takes more than that: trust between citizens, loyalty to the country, and a shared understanding of the freedoms upon which the society is built and the responsibilities that each individual has to the community. Edicts by politicians to tolerate something one has absolutely no fondness for, moreover, will only strain the national culture. You can't make tolerance grow by pointing fingers or moralizing.

In light of the immigration from the Muslim world, it is very important to be aware of the history of our Western democracy. It was not the case that we adopted democracy, with all of its magnificent values, and then developed a sense of community. It was the other way around. Our free society is a historical result of a society based on mutual trust, a shared culture in which Christianity played a central role. Norway would not have acquired its constitution at Eidsvoll in 1814 if the country had been divided along cultural and religious lines. It was a country founded on a shared culture and religion which could reach agreement on a shared text upon which the country would be built. It is thus shared cultural norms, and not theoretical and abstract ideals of equality as spelled out in international conventions, that make people stand shoulder to shoulder and contribute to society. A liberal democracy such as Norway is not and never has been self-preserving.

It also seems to be very difficult for the great majority of our politicians to admit that Islam is as much an *ideology* and a *social system,* a religion of laws with political ambitions. To an extraordinary extent, Islam and Christianity are still treated by the Norwegian state as identical twins. This grossly mistaken view may end up costing us dearly.

The greatest of these

Few prominent individuals have emphasized the difference between Islam and the Western Christian world more clearly than Ayaan Hirsi Ali, who, having grown up in Somalia, Kenya, and Saudi Arabia, and spent her adult life in the Netherlands and U.S., must be acknowledged to have the requisite experience to pronounce on these matters. When she visited Norway in connection with the publication of the Norwegian edition of her book *Nomad* in November 2010, she first pointed out this: "In one European country after another the population growth speaks clearly: in 2020, 15 percent will be Muslims. In 2050 – give or take a few years – 50 percent will be Muslims. The question then is whether the European societies will still be free, equal societies based on individual rights and political

354

democracy, or whether they will be marked by groupthink, major tensions, and perhaps civil war-like conditions, as we see in many Muslim countries today."[355] These are very brutal words, but the scenario is not at all unrealistic.

Hirsi Ali then offered what she thinks may be the solution: "The only solution is for Muslims to give up thinking in terms of clans and tribes and become fully assimilated in European societies. The idea of the so-called multicultural society must be given up, as the German chancellor Angela Merkel recently stated. In order to achieve this, we have to liberate the Muslim women from the power of their husbands, fathers, and male family members. If the Muslim women are liberated, we will crush the Muslim patriarchy's foremost bastion, namely control over women."

Then she came to the key question: can Islam become an integrated part of the West? Hirsi Ali replied: "First of all, Islam has to an extreme degree conserved the mentality of the pre-modern patriarchal tribal society as it existed in Arabia in the 7th century. Second, the religion places an unbalanced emphasis on the hereafter – that is, on what happens after death. This death culture draws thoughts away from how society can be improved here and now....Finally, the case is that Muslims look back to Islam's golden age, when it ruled an empire from India to the Atlantic. That the empire collapsed, they claim, was the fault of Islam's enemies, and they take on a destructive victim role. Together, these are three elements that I think have been decisive in shaping a Muslim world most of which disconnected from modern developments."

But can't a modern interpretation of the Koran modernize Islam? Hirsi Ali doesn't buy it: "The problem is that two strong forces in the Muslim world are absolutely literal: it is about the ruling class in the Arabic countries, and it is about the extreme fundamentalists. Those who claim that one can interpret away the difficult chapters of the Koran meet with massive opposition from both of these powerful forces. The Muslims are unfortunately brought up, from when they're very small, to believe without reservation in what Allah and his prophet Muhammed say. When the Koran unambiguously legitimizes violence against people with other beliefs and clearly states that a woman's testimony is worth half of a man's, it's not something you can reinterpret without making both Allah and his prophet look like meaningless figures. The so-called new interpretation ends up in a blind alley."

Hirsi Ali's thoughts are somber. Perhaps it is out of sheer defiance (or despair?) that I hesitate, at present, to endorse her short-term predictions. To do so is simply too painful. At the same time I no longer doubt that Europe (with the exception of Eastern Europe) is in the process of giving birth to an Islamic state. I would predict that this state will be born in some part of Britain, where (for example) the judicial authorities – without debate – introduced five official sharia courts in 2008.[356]

Still, I continue to hope that the struggle for values that lies ahead of us will be won by the spirit of the Enlightenment. This hope springs out of the fact that Europe, on three occasions in recent history, has managed to conquer the forces of totalitarianism, inhumanity, darkness. Nazism, fascism, and Communism alike were obliged to give way to that which is the greatest of all: freedom.

H.S., 1 December 2010

Selected Literature

Amara, Fadela, *Varken hora eller kuvad*, 2005

Berman, Paul, *Terror and Liberalism*, 2003

Björkman, Ingrid, Jonathan Friedman, Åke Wedin, and Jan Elferson, *Exit folkhemssverige – en samhällsmodells sönderfall*, 2005

Brox, Ottar, Tore Lindbekk, Sigurd Skirbekk (eds.), *Gode formål – gale følger? Kritisk lys på norsk innvandringspolitikk*, 2003

Brix, Helle Merete and Torben Hansen, *Islam i Vesten. På Koranens vei?*, 2002

Brix, Helle Merete, Torben Hansen and Lars Hedegaard, *I krigens hus. Islams kolonisering av Vesten*, 2003

Dahl, Tove Stang, *Den muslimske familie: en undersøkelse av kvinners rett i islam*, 1992

Enzenberger, Hans Magnus, *Skrekkens menn. Om den radikale taper*, 2006

Esposito, John L., *Islam: The Straight Path*, 2001

Fallaci, Oriana, *The Rage and the Pride*, 2003

Fallaci, Oriana, *The Force of Reason*, 2004

Hirsi Ali, Ayaan, *The Caged Virgin*, 2006

Khan-Østrem, Nazneen, *Min hellige krig*, 2005

Lewis, Bernard, *What Went Wrong? Western Impact and Middle Eastern Response*, 2002

Lien, Inger-Lise, *Ordet som stempler djevlene*, 1997

Mawdudi, Abu Ala, *Purdah and the Status of Women in Islam*, 1991

Mernissi, Fatima, *Beyond the Veil: Male-Female Dynamics in Modern Muslim Society*, 1985

Mumtaz, Khawar and Farida Shaheed, *Women of Pakistan: Two Steps Forward, One Step Back?*, 1987

Pittelkow, Ralf, *Efter 11. september. Vesten og islam*, 2002

Pittelkow, Ralf, *Forsvar for nationalstaten,* 2004
Pittelkow, Ralf and Karen Jespersen, *De lykkelige danskere,* 2005
Pittelkow, Ralf and Karen Jespersen, *Islams magt. Europas ny virkelighed,* 2010.
Qutb, Sayyid, *Milepæler,* 2004
Roald, Anne Sofie, *Er muslimske kvinner undertrykt?,* 2005
Storhaug, Hege, *Mashallah. En reise blant kvinner i Pakistan,* 1996
Storhaug, Hege, *Hellig tvang. Unge norske muslimer om kjærlighet og ekteskap,* 1998
Storhaug, Hege and Human Rights Service, *Human Visas,* 2003
Vogt, Kari, *Kommet for å bli. Islam i Vest-Europa,* 1995
Vogt, Kari, *Islam – tradisjon, fundamentalisme og reform,* 2005
Warren, Ibn, *Hvorfor jeg ikke er muslim,* 2003.

Notes

[1] I have corrected some errors in usage and sentence construction; otherwise the letter is just as Anooshe wrote it. The entire letter [in the original Norwegian – *trans.*] can be read at Dagbladet.no and on the Human Rights Service website, rights.no.

[2] Those who wish to read more about the murder of Anooshe can find a great deal of material online. The most extensive coverage is at Dagbladet.no and rights.no.

[3] I'm not taking into account here the new situation involving such matters as residency permits and family reunification for Poles and other European groups, since immigration within the European Economic Community is not a topic of this book.

[4] On several occasions, HRS has ordered statistics from Statistics Norway on marriage immigration from Norway's major immigration countries. The last set of statistics are from 2005 and concern 18 immigrant groups in Norway, from Bosnia, Chile, China, Eritrea, Ethopia, Gambia, India, Iran, Iraq, Morococo, Pakistan, the Philippines, Serbia and Montenegro, Somalia, Sri Lanka, Thailand, Turkey, and Vietnam. We wanted to know how many people in these resident groups in Norway married in the year in question, whether they married a Norwegian resident with the same national background as themselves, with another foreign background, or with a Norwegian background. The statistics had to be divided according to sex and between first- and second-generation immigrants; they also had to show the average age of both the spouse living in Norway and the spouse being imported from abroad. It is important to note that (for example) a boy of 20 may just as easily be a first- as a second-generation immigrant. What matters is whether he was born here or abroad. This material was published in January 2006 in the report "Ekteskap blant utvalgte innvandrergrupper" (Marriage in selected immigrant groups), which can be read at rights.no.

[5] To be precise, Statistics Norway says that it expects that those in the group who have married "abroad" have married, almost without exception, in their families' homelands. There can be exceptions – for example, a Norwegian Pakistani who

has gotten married to a Pakistani in the U.S. Such exceptions, however, do not significantly alter the general pattern of the statistics. The Norwegian Directorate of Immigration's annual statistics on newly immigrated spouses from Pakistan, moreover, are highly consistent with Statistics Norway's marriage statistics.

6 Statistics Norway has on several occasions asserted this hypothesis. Their argument is that there are still many members of the second generation who are of marriageable age but who have not yet married, and that many of these will likely marry in Norway. This is a hypothesis, and whether it is true or not will not be established for a decade or so. My hypothesis is that the overall pattern of fetching spouses from one's family's homeland will continue in the second generation because integration is still going slowly, and because statistics from other European countries show high levels of fetching marriage among the children of immigrants. Among major groups, the percentage of marriages with cousins in the family homeland actually increases in the second generation. I will return to this in Chapter Two.

7 See, for example, "Vil avlive innvandrermyter" ("Wants to Kill Immigration Myths") in *Bergens Tidende,* 15 July 2005.

8 The reader can confirm this by looking at Statistics Norway's own report: "Rapport 2004/I," page 46.

9 After HRS asked to see this material, we were permitted to do so in the autumn of 2005. On the basis of the data we examined, we published, in December of the same year, the report "Gift til Norge med slektning" ("Married to Relatives in Norway"), available at rights.no.

10 The Children's Law was changed on 19 December 2003. The law now invalidates marriages arranged on behalf of children.

11 See, for example, the interview with the Norwegian-Pakistani Jeanette and the Norwegian-Moroccan Nadia in *Dagbladet,* 26 January 2002, under the headline "Vi krever handling!" ("We demand action!").

12 HRS is not an aid organization. On rare occasions, however, we involve ourselves in specific cases. We do so when individuals' cases are not being followed up by the authorities and when the specific situations may reveal conditions that are of political significance.

13 In the essay "Fra turistvisum til ekteskapsvisum" ("From tourist visa to marriage visa") in Brox, Lindbekk, and Skirbekk, eds., *Gode formål – gale følger?,* I have documented the immigration situation circa 1970 from non-Western countries to Norway.

14 "Data om utenlandske statsborgere" ("Data on foreign citizens"), Kommunal-og arbeidsdepartementet (Ministry of Local Government and Labour), 1983.

15 This woman was on disability mainly because of anxiety problems. During a 2003 conversation with her, it became clear that she bitterly regretted what she had gotten herself involved in, especially because she had been physically and sexually abused by both Mina's husband and his brother, with whom she entered into this pro forma marriage. That she had reported the rapes was confirmed by a police source, but the report was shelved because there was a lack of damning evidence.

16 The reason why I didn't delete her text messages was my fear that she might be killed, and that the text messages might prove useful to police investigators.

17 Based on research in Pakistan and England, Katharine Charsley concludes that Pakistani men who immigrate to Britain to live with their British Pakistani wives have cultural and gender-related conflicts that result from moving in with a woman and her family. Violence in such marriages is therefore widespread, Charsley writes in the article "Vulnerable Brides and Transnational Ghar Damads: Gender, Risk and 'Adjustment' among Pakistani Marriage Migrants to Britain," *Indian Journal of Gender Studies,* 12:2 & 3, 2005.

18 The doctor has confirmed this state of affairs in conversations and by referring us to a written statement in which she told the father that Mina might be in danger of an honour killing.

19 The woman who had reported Mina's husband for rape is the same one who entered a pro forma marriasge with a brother of Mina's husband who was twenty years her junior.

20 Two employees in the Barnevernet are now working with Mina's children in an effort to unlearn them this game.

21 Ayaan Hirsi Ali chose to resign from the Dutch Parliament in May 2006. She was at that time receiving more death threats than any other public figure in Europe. After a long struggle with Dutch authorities, she was able to live in an ordinary apartment complex with twenty-four-hour bodyguards. The neighbors went to court to force her to move out because the presence of the guards resulted in noise and a feeling of insecurity. While the neighbors won the day in court, a TV documentary was aired in which it was reported that Hirsi Ali had given a false identity when seeking asylum in the Netherlands in 1992, in order to ensure that she would not be forced to return to Kenya where she had legal residency. This information was far from new; she had herself publicly discussed this on many occasions. But only now did the Dutch authorities react, and cabinet minister Rita Verdonk sought to revoke the citizenship she had received in 1997. In the documentary Hirsi Ali's family also maintained that she had not

been forced, but had freely agreed, to marry a cousin in Canada. Hirsi Ali rejected this claim, but decided to leave both Parliament anad the Netherlands and move to the U.S., where she had already gotten a job in a leading think tank, the American Enterprise Institute.

22 "Sej kamp mod import av ægtefæller," *Ugebrevet* A4, no. 33, 29 September 2003.

23 Eyvind Vesselbo, "'I går, I dag, I overmorgen.' Indvandrerrapport III," Ishøj Kommune 2000.

24 Data from Statistics Netherlands (CBS), presented in the report "Trouwen over de grens – Achtergronden van partnerkeuze van Turken en Marokkannen in Nederland," Erna Hooghiemstra, Sociaal en Cultureel Planbureau, The Hague, May 2003. The report has an English summary.

25 This information is from Katharine Charsley's article "Vulnerable Brides and Transnational Ghar Damads: Gender, Risk and 'Adjustment' among Pakistani Marriage Migrants to Britain," *Indian Journal of Gender Studies,* 12:2 & 3, 2005.

26 In 1997 the then Labour government revoked the so-called Primary Purpose Rule, which said that if the main intention underlying a newly established marriage was to migrate to England, the entry visa would be denied. After this rule was revoked, marriage immigration nearly tripled. The annual figure of 150,000 is from telegraph.co.uk (16 April 2006).

27 *Weekendavisen,* no. 15, 12-13 April 2006.

28 Ibid.

29 In November 2003, the then government introduced an absolute support requirement for people under 23 years old of 160,000 kroner a year in income. The purpose was to protect young people against forced marriage. HRS and others warned the government that such a requirement could have negative consequences, notably that young people could risk being taken out of school in order to work and thereby finance their own forced marriages. Hera was one of the victims of this new policy. She had finished secondary school when she was married off to a cousin. She had been accepted to a college, but was forced to go to work.

30 This information came from a source in 2005 who insisted on anonymity but agreed to allow the information to be made public.

31 Telegraph.co.uk, 16 November 2005.

32 Ibid.

[33] "Birth Defects and Parental Consanguinity in Norway," *American Journal of Epidemiology*, Vol. 145, No. 5, 1997.

[34] William Jankowiak and Edward Fisher, "A Cross-Cultural Perspective on Romantic Love," *Ethnology* 31:22, 149-155, University of Pittsburgh, 1992.

[35] In 2003 I gave a lecture about these problems to employees of the Hundvåg and Storhaug social security office in Rogaland and of the county social security office in Oslo. (The latter lecture was also attended by employees of social security offices in the county of Østland.)

[36] Between November 2005 and January 2006 I held a total of five lectures for the National Police Directorate and the National Police Immigration Service. It was these encounters that led to my receiving this information.

[37] This information, too, came to our attention as a result of a lecture given under the auspices of the National Police Directorate in November 2005, and several lectures given under the auspices of the National Police Immigration Service in December 2005 and January 2006.

[38] Ibid.

[39] The account of Samira's story is based on conversations in Tromsø in 2003 with her friends, teacher, principal, father, and the police

[40] HRS was contacted in December 2002 by Samira's principal, Nina Breines Johnsen. On our agenda was the topic of shipping children abroad. Together with Johnsen and the school principal, therefore, we agreed to use Samira as a test case to discover the possibilities and limitations of current law and practice. The full story of our effort to get the government to pay attention to Samira's case can be read in the report "Ute av syne, ute av sinn. Norske barn i utlandet" ("Out of Sight, Out of Mind: Norwegian Children Abroad"), HRS, 2004.

[41] The reply, dated 27 April 2004, came after a six-month wait.

[42] Both I and HRS director Rita Karlsen took part in this conversation in Tromsø.

[43] Correspondence between HRS and the Parlimentary Secretary in the Ministry of Local Government and Regional Development, Kristin Ørmen Johnsen.

[44] Almost without exception, the tracking service accepts assignments only from the families of people being searched for. They made an exception for Samira, and defined her friends as being those closest to Samira.

45 Sent 7 October 2003. The document sent by HRS to the police can be read in "Ute av syne, ute av sinn," on pages 13-25.

46 Police chief Truls Fyhn replied to this in writing: "I have gone through the documents you sent, and compared them with our own documents. After careful deliberation I have come to the conclusion that we cannot do anything more about this case, for which I apologize to HRS. My decision is based on an evaluation as to whether there anyone has committed a punishable act. There are indications that Samira's father has told untruths to the police, which, from an objective viewpoint, is punishable, but this, however, is not a sufficient reason to follow up the case, in that an investigation of him would obviously not have any importance in relation to the principal case, namely to get Samira back. I have also placed considerable emphasis on the fact that a follow-up on our part will involve a use of resources that is not justifiable in relation to what we can reasonably expect to accomplish. Whatever way we look at it, it cannot be the police who solve problems such as the matter in hand. I would rather not say anything in regard to the question of which Norwegian authorities should have responsibility for ensuring that Samira and others in the same situation return here."

47 Samira was the main story on NRK's "Lørdagsrevyen" ("Saturday Review") program on 8 November 2003.

48 The meeting took place on 29 September at Solberg's office.

49 It is known that Somalians fetch children who are not their own to European countries, and the phenomenon appears to be especially widespread in this group.

50 The story was first reported in *BT* on 21 April 2003. The newspaper revealed both Samira's situation and the extensive swindling of the social security department by Somalians in Denmark, who among other things take their children out of school for several months and send them to imaginary parents in Britain. In this way they can collect child benefits in both Denmark and Britain.

51 *BT,* 25 April 2003.

52 She is one of the few people I have met who, despite such experiences, have avoided life-inhibiting psychological damage and managed very well in life.

53 Kåre Vassenden of Statistics Norway performed a study in 1997 among Norwegian-Pakistani seventeen-year-olds. Of the then 268 seventeen-year-olds of the second generation who lived in Norway in 1996, fully 40 percent have had at least one foreign stay recorded in the national register during their lifetime – that is, trips involving at least six months' intended absence from Norway. In the

same age group, among the first generation, 20 percent had one registered foreign stay after moving to Norway for the first time. Vassenden concluded as follows: "It happens in all immigrant groups that some move to Norway several times, but only among Pakistanis is the phenomenon downright widespread."

[54] The guide "Norske familier i utlandet," Ministry of Children and Equality, March 2005.

[55] The reason why the majority of children sent out of the country are Pakistani is that Pakistanis are the largest immigrant group in Norway, that many Norwegian-Pakistanis have acquired sizable residential properties in Pakistan, and that contact with Pakistan is close.

[56] Confirmed by embassies, such as those in Gambia, Morocco, and Pakistan. The embassies base this on the increased number of applications for passport renewals for children residing in the countries in question.

[57] This situation also can be found in Turkey and Morocco: most of the immigrants come from one area. In Morocco it is the city of Nador and the surrounding Berber villages, and in Turkey it is the city of Konya and the surrounding Kurdish villages.

[58] A Norwegian-Pakistani visited Idara Minjah ul-Quran in Norway to ask whether they could recommend a Koran school in Pakistan for girls. This school was especially recommended as a school with high standards and a high level of professionalism, and it was also said that Norwegian-Pakistani children went there, and that many others had gone there. Other Norwegian-Pakistanis were able to name specific girls from Norway who attended the school in the winter of 2004.

[59] The description of the tour of the school is provided by HRS director Rita Karlsen. None of the rest of us –Halvor Tjønn of *Aftenposten*, interpreter Humera Ejaz, and myself – was allowed to enter the school.

[60] Our interpreter reacted especially strongly to the fact that the girls were under male supervision. The reason was that the sexual abuse of children is widespread in Pakistan, including in schools, as has been reported by many of the country's English-language media. The well-known, independent human-rights organization Human Rights Commission of Pakistan (HRCP) has also reported on the sexual abuse of children at religious schools on several occasions. HRCP receives financial support from Norway and several other Western countries. Their very good annual reports can be read at www.hrcp-web.org.

[61] When Norwegian-Pakistanis began to build residences in Pakistan, most of them did so in their native villages. Now it is a status symbol to build a residence

either in the Kharian Cantonment, which is the name of the military area in Kharian, or in the capital, Islamabad.

62 Norwegian-Pakistanis in the region say that a plot of the usual size can cost up to a million Norwegian kroner and that the house can cost an additional one to two million kroner. I cannot vouch for the precision of these estimates.

63 Because the principal's comments are so controversial, he will remain anonymous.

64 Sources in Norway told us about the girls before our trip to Pakistan.

65 We captured this tableau on film.

66 Fifty percent of the children who are enrolled in public schools drop out during the first five years. Thirty percent drop out during the next few years. On average, boys go to school for 1.9 years and girls 0.7 years, according to statistics from the Human Rights Commission of Pakistan.

67 About half of the national budget goes to the military, mainly because of the conflict with India over Kashmir. Virtually all other Muslim-dominated countries in the world are better off than Pakistan, whether one is talking about education, health, or the economy, according to reports from UNDP. The significantly lower level of expenditure on education over so many years is seen as one of the main reasons for the catastrophically low level of development in Pakistan. All of the other countries in the region, such as India, Bangladesh, Nepal, Bhutan, and Sri Lanka, have a higher level of development than Pakistan.

68 Human Rights Commission of Pakistan, various annual reports.

69 Ibid.

70 Zia ul-Haq overthrew the democratically elected Zulfikar Bhutto in 1977 and executed him in 1979. Ul-Haq governed the country with a brutall hand up to 1988, when he died in a helicopter accident which is popularly viewed as a "holy conspiracy between Allah and the CIA." Intellectual democrats in Pakistan view ul-Haq as the most destructive leader the country has ever had, because of the strong Islamization he forced upon the country, and which was especially manifested in Pakistani criminal law. The law remains essentially the same today. For example, women who cannot prove a rape are convicted of infidelity.

71 The truth is that Jinnah warned in the strongest terms against allowing religion to be the foundation for the nation. He noted the conflicts that would arise: Which kind of Islam should be followed? Who should interpret Islam? The movement for the foundation of Pakistan did not have an ideology of its own.

Not until 1962, during a parliamentary debate, did a member of the Islamist party Jamaat-i-Islami propose that Pakistan's ideology be defined. The same Islamist forces, including the leading Islamic ideologue, Mawdudi, opposed the foundation of Pakistan.

[72] Pakistan has a number of minorities. About two percent of the population is Christian, while one percent is Hindu. Another minority is the Kalash people in the north, who are animists.

[73] My discussion of the Islamization of teaching plans and schoolbooks is based on material in the respected *South Asian Journal: Quarterly Magazine of South Asian Journalists & Scholars* (October-December 2003), in which the educationist and physicist A.H. Nayyar at Quaid-e-Azam University in the article "Islamisation of Curricula" presents specific national teaching plans for various subjects at the various grade levels.

[74] The first known civilizations were Mohenjodaro, Harappa, and Taxila, which existed about 2500-3000 years before Islam.

[75] For example, a new national grade-school teaching plan in Urdu says that the pupil should "be aware of the blessings of Jihad, and must create yearning for Jihad in his heart." This is also according to the above-mentioned article by A.H. Nayyar.

[76] The most democratic period in Pakistan was under the popularly elected prime minister Zulfikar Ali Bhutto (1971-77), who led the Pakistan People's Party. Bhutto was loved by the people for his attempt to lift up the poor. He raised the status of women, too. But he also founded the Federal Security Force (FIS), which answered to him personally. Though the motive may seem noble – he wanted to stem the military's considerable influence – this didn't help as long as Bhutto used the FSI to suppress his political opponents, several hundred of whom were imprisoned and mistreated.

[77] In 2002, there was an election for the national assembly. Six religious parties formed an alliance, Muttahida Majlis-e-Amal (MMA), and thus got many representatives elected to the national and regional assemblies. Both nationally and internationally, it is feared that MMA will further the Talibanization of Pakistan.

[78] The family told us this through a translator in February 2004. HRS has photographically documented the Drammen man's living situation and residence.

[79] Ayaan Hirsi Ali, the Somali-born member of the Dutch Parliament, also tells of having been brought up with this blind and irrational hatred (*The Caged Virgin*, p. 38). She did not meet Jews for the first time until she came to the Netherlands

as an adult. She writes: "the first time I saw a Jew with my own eyes, I was surprised to find a human being of flesh and blood."

80 Asma Jahangir, who has led the Human Rights Commission for many years and served as a Supreme Court lawyer and a special rapporteur for the UN, is one fo those who describe Pakistani views of women in this way. Because of her political and legal work she has lived with armed guards twenty-four hours a day since I first met her in 1993.

81 There are government-run crisis centres, but they are largely in a pitiful state and also unsafe. It is reported that women's families bribe personnel to get them out, that women are forced into prostitution and subjected to other forms of abuse. There are, however, other centres that are run properly by voluntary organizations.

82 Young Norwegian-Pakistani girls and boys, too, are inhibited in their daily lives by this attitude toward socializing between the sexes. They say that simply to be observed at a streetcorner in a conversation with a passerby of the opposite sex leads, as a rule, to gossip that one is having a relationship with that individual.

83 Annual reports by the Human Rights Commission and Pakistan, for example, make this clear.

84 Human Rights Watch: "Crime or Custom? Violence against Women in Pakistan" (1999).

85 Communicated to me in an interview by Aziz Siddiqui of the Human Rights Commisssion of Pakistan in 1997.

86 Human Rights Commission of Pakistan (2003).

87 I know several such elite families. Their relationships to values and norms is overwhelmingly comparable to our liberal values in the West. But they are compelled to deal with the society they live in, and thus must (for example) take precautions with regard to girls' and women's movements in public and the lack of tolerance for dissenting views.

88 I have seen a photo taken at a Karachi art school in the late 1960s. It might well have been taken in Paris. The female Pakistani painters had their hair cut short or had somewhat longish modern hairdos, and wore tight, short-sleeved Western dresses. At an art school in Lahore in 2004, I encountered another world, in which some of the young women were entirely covered, while most of the others wore traditional Islamic attire.

89 The estimate was presented at a meeting between HRS and embassy personnel

in January 2004. The embassy had two alternative replies, one short and one long. The short one was: We don't know what the number is. The long answer was based on how many people renew their passports at the embassy or add their children to their own passports. In 2003, the embassy had about 500 such cases, which suggests that there may be 4000-5000 Norwegian citizens in Pakistan at a given time. This number is not broken down by age or sex, and therefore a new hypothesis is that a high percentage of the individuals involved are children. The embassy believes that the "most correct" answer is the following: "There are many children who are Norwegian citizens in Pakistan."

[90] "Norske barn i utlandet," SSB Notat (2004/7).

[91] The parliamentary secretary in the Ministry of Local Government and Regional Development said the following to *Aftenposten,* 20 December 2004: "The report from HRS was accompanied by an estimate that seems relatively high; therefore, we want to ensure the quality of the figures. We are glad that we have secured tangible figures."

[92] "Rapport om en styrket indsats mod genopdragelsesrejser og andre længerevarende udlandsophold af negativ betydning for herværende børns skolegang og integration," Ministeriet for Flygtninge, Indvandrere og Integration, June 2006.

[93] Estimate accepted by the World Health Organization, among other institutions.

[94] Based on statistics purchased by HRS from SSB in June 2006. These figures do not include girls from (for example) Kurdish regions in Turkey, Iraq, Syria, and Iran, where genital mutilation also takes place. The reason is that Norway does not collect data based on ethnic identity.

[95] According to the report "Female Circumcision," a colLabourative project between the London Black Women's Health Action Project and the London School of Hygiene and Tropical Medicine (March 1998), about 50 percent are mutilated after settling in Britain or after being born in Britain. Experts in Scandinavia also estimate that about 50 percent are mutilated after migrating. But the head of the British organization Forward, Adwoa Kwateng-Kluvitse, believes that far more than 50 percent of the girls in question are mutilated (Dagbladet.no, 29 August 2005).

[96] World Health Organization, 1995.

[97] Law of 15 December 1995, no. 74.

[98] *Göteborgs-Posten,* 26 June 2006.

99 I believe it must be acknowledged here that some forms of Type 4 genital mutilation can be difficult to observe. But Type 4, as noted, is not common.

100 See, for example, *VG,* 3 June 2005.

101 Astrid Meland's articles about the trip appeared on Dagbladet.no.

102 The entire history about the trip to Gambia can be read in the report "Norskfødte jenter kjønnslemlestes" (HRS R-2 2005).

103 Mernissi, 1985:45.

104 Mernissi, 1985:148.

105 Mernissi, 1985:60.

106 Retstidende 1974, p. 1121.

107 A fatwa is a passing of a sentence by an expert in Islamic law.

108 Kari Vogt, 2005:121.

109 The group is called Bedari Women. Another group is called Sahil (sahil.org).

110 In the report "Ungdom, fritid, organisasjonsliv og deltakelse" (Fafo 2005), which contains interviews with 3000 young people in Oslo, it emerges that Pakistani girls, in particular, participate infrequently in organized leisure-time activities, with the exception of religious activities. Many of them said that they wished to take greater part in such activities. The higher the parents' financial status, the less likely the Pakistani girls were to participate in such activities.

111 In 2003, 26 percent of Norwegian-Pakistani women were employed. For women from Iraq and Somalia, the employment rate was 19 percent. For women from Sri Lanka, Vietnam, Thailand, and India, the employment rates are 50 percent or higher (figures from the SSB statistics bank, 2005).

112 This view is preached, for example, by the the Islamic Cultural Centre in Norway. See islamic.no and the article "Kvinners stilling i Islam."

113 Islamonline.net is run from Cairo and has over 100 employees (Kari Vogt, 2005:109).

114 The fatwa can be read at the fatwa bank at www.islamonline.net, 7 February 2004. Here al-Qaradawi cites the hadith and expresses his personal support for this position in the modern world.

115 See the website of Det Islamske Forbundet, islam.no.

116 It is worth noting that the word for rape in the Urdu language means "honour robbery" – the point being that the man has robbed the women's, and thus her family's, honour.

117 The change was approved on 6 June 2003 by a Local Government and Regional Development committee of the Norwegian Parliament, by means of "Dok.8:122 (2002-2003)," under pressure from HRS.

118 I am aware that if a majority of the members of the Norwegian Parliament were personal Christians, it would have consequences for Norwegian law; for example, abortion would be outlawed and the same-sex partnership law revoked. These changes would have been justified with reference to Christian morality. But it is entirely unrealistic to imagine that such politicians would base Norwegian laws and punishments on Old Testament prescriptions, on the grounds that the latter are divine and thus eternally valid.

119 Many non-Muslims in the West associate sharia with the brutal methods of punishment such as amputation, whipping, and stoning. For most believing Muslim, the question of whether they reject sharia is an impossible one to answer with a simple yes or no. To reply with a categorical yes means that one, equally categorically, rejects Islam itself, since sharia is a divine presence at the heart of the life of believers.

120 Muhammed Naceri is a member of the Morocco Council of Religious Scholars. The quotation is taken from the website No to Political Islam (www.ntpi.org).

121 No other countries that belong to other great religions have gotten together to formulate a religious (and political) reply to the UN's Declaration of Human Rights.

122 Cairo Declaration on Human Rights in Islam, approved on 5 August 1990 in Cairo by 45 member countries of the Organization of the Islamic Conference (OIC). OIC has 57 member countries, and has a permanent delegation at the FN (Wikipedia.org). In 1981 a similar Islamic human-rights declaration was approved, the Universal Islamic Declaration of Human Rights. I have chosen to focus on the more recent of the two declarations.

123 In 2002, the United Nations Development Programme published the first report in the series "Arab Regional Human Development Report," with the title "Creating Opportunities for Future Generations." In 2003 it was succeeded by "Building a Knowledge Society," and in 2004 by "Toward Freedom in the Arab World." This year yet another report, focusing on opportunities for women, will be published.

[124] See the report "Building a Knowledge Society," p. 118-121.

[125] It would not be correct to place all the blame for the extensive problems that have afflicted the Arab world on conservative Islam. Some would argue that entirely different causes underlie the stagnation, oppression, and the dramatic democracy deficit – for example, that Western capitalism has systematically undermined development in the region, that the strongly state-centralized economies promote clientalism and prevent popular participation in political processes, and that the Arab states did not establish themselves through war and power games but were rather created by the great powers in negotiations after World War I. See, for example, the article in the Danish newsmagazine *Ræson:* "Hvorfor er det så lidt demokrati I de arabiske lande?" (7 February 2005).

[126] The belief of leading Muslims of those times that the end of the road had been reached reminds one of the history professor Francis Fukuyama's book *The End of History and the Last Man* (1992). After the fall of the Berlin Wall, Fukuyama believed that we had reached the end of history itself: the liberal Western democracies and capitalism had won, and the victory marked the culmination of humankind's ideological development. It may safely be observed that Fukuyama's theory was exceedingly bold.

[127] As quoted by Ibn Warraq (2003:429).

[128] Kari Vogt quotes woman criticism from considerably earlier dates. She refers to a "brief text" by the philosopher Ibn Rushd (1126-98): "Our social system does not give women any chance to show what they are good for. Their fate is concerned exclusively with giving birth and taking care of children. This condition of subordination destroys women's ability to do something great. Their lives develop like the lives of plants" (2005:117ff).

[129] In the case of Pakistan, the criticism of the West for supporting dictators is largely justified. Pakistan's worst dictator, Zia ul-Haq (1977-88) was protected by the U.S., because the U.S. needed Pakistan as an ally in the struggle against the Soviet Union during the latter's invasion of Afghanistan.

[130] Memri.org, 6 December 2002.

[131] "The Islamization of Europe," article by the British political analyst David Pryce-Jones, *Commentary*, No. 5, Vol. 118, December 2004.

[132] "The Muslim Brotherhood's Conquest of Europe," *Middle East Quarterly*, Winter 2005.

[133] The largest Muslim organization in Sweden is Sveriges muslimska förbund, with 70,000 members. Its leader is named Mahmoud Aldebe, and he confirms that supporters of the Brotherhood belong to his association: "They are

everywhere in our mosques," Aldebe said on "Uppdrag granskning" on the Swedish television network SVT1 on 2 May 2006.

[134] "Livingstone invites cleric back," bbc.co.uk, 12 July 2004.

[135] *Berlingske Tidende,* 6 February 2004.

[136] *The Americsan Thinker,* 3 May 2004.

[137] "The World Muslim League: 'Agent of Wahhabi Propagation in Europe,'" *Terrorism Monitor,* 6 May 2005, Jamestown Organization.

[138] Euro-islam is the principal theme of his book *To Be a European Muslim* (The Islamic Foundation, 1998).

[139] For example, the college principal Nazneen Khan-Østrem, who writes in the book *Min hellige krig:* "Tariq Ramadan is a great inspiration. For me, too" (2005:101). *VG*'s journalist Kadafi Zaman also wrote warmly about Ramadan, as did Basim Ghozlan of Det islamske forbundet.

[140] For example, Caroline Fourest's book *Frère Tariq: Discours, stratégie et méthode de Tariq Ramadan,* and Fiometta Venners's book *OPA sur l'Islam de France: les ambitions de l'UIOF.*

[141] *Berlingske Tidende,* 6 February 2004.

[142] Quoted from Jens Tomas Anfindsen's op-ed in *Dagbladet,* 17 July 2005.

[143] Salafism is directly tied to Wahhabism. There are, in short, violent and non-violent forms of salafism.

[144] The list of lecturers that weekend also included Oddbjørn Leirvik, priest and now associate professor in interreligious studies at the Faculty of Theology at the University of Oslo. The seminars are announced on the website of the Islamic Association (Det islamske forbundet), islam.no.

[145] The article "What Is Behind the Veil" gives a good idea of the book's contents and ideological foundation (muslim-canada.org/purdah.htm).

[146] John L. Esposito, 2001:255.

[147] The history behind this law is that one of Muhammed's wives, Aisha, was suspected of having an affair. It became the subject of gossip, and Muhammed responded by requiring that for an act of adultery to be considered proven, four honourable Muslim men must testify to having witnessed it.

148 Dagbladet.no, 8 July 2006.

149 The report "To moskeer i Norge – med blikk på kvinners status," Human Rights Service, R-2 2006.

150 Human Rights Service, R-2 2006.

151 In Denmark, Minhaj ul-Quran has been shown to be an extremist organization. In the book *Islam i Vesten. På Koranens vej* (København 2002) one chapter by Helle Merete Brix is devoted to Minhaj ul-Quran and its leader, Tahirul Qadri. Qadri's Islamist, totalitarian ideology is revealed in his own writings, in which he supports sharia death sentences and the cutting off of hands and feet. Qadri also supported Zia ul-Haq's introduction of the Hadood Ordinance, personally selects leaders of the movement in various European countries, and regularly visits congregations in Europe, including Norway.

152 Both of these congregations have websites, minhaj.no and islamic.no, and both strongly promote their respective leaders in Pakistan.

153 Human Rights Service, R-2 2006.

154 *Dagbladet,* 2 February 200.

155 Cultural statistics from Statistics Norway show that 83 Muslim congregations were registered in Norway as of 1 January 2004.

156 Fadime Sahindal's murder in January 2002 unleashed a debate about whether Muslim women can wed non-Muslims. The then leader of Norway's Islamic Council, convert Lena Larsen, addressed the question on NRK television by categorically insisting that Islam forbids such marriages. I did not note the date.

157 "Freedom in the World" (2006), Freedomhouse.org.

158 "På tro kan demokrati ikke bygges," opinion piece by professor Mehdi Mozaffari, *Berlingske Tidende,* 15 July 2005.

159 *Kristelig Dagblad,* 6 March 2006.

160 *Weekendavisen,* no. 16, 21-27 April 2006.

161 *Ugebrevet A4,* no. 12, 27 March 2006. The study was carried out for *Ugebrevet* by Catinét Research.

162 *Berlingske Tidende,* 27 June 2003. The study is based on interviews with 900 young people.

163 *International Herald Tribune*, 15 July 2005.

164 *The Daily Telegraph*, 19 February 2006.

165 *The Daily Telegraph*, 23 July 2005.

166 *The Times*, 5 March 2005.

167 TNS Gallup, April 2006, performed for TV2.

168 *Dagens Nyheter*, 5 July 2005.

169 I think the term "enclave" is more appropriate for such areas than "ghetto." The latter term is associated in many minds with social decline, while "enclave" means an area that is dominated by immigrants and characterized by significant integration problems. It does not necessary indicate that the neighbourhood and its infrastructure are in decay, even though this is often the case.

170 The following is based on Aje Carlbom's article "På vej mod integration i etniske enklaver," *Social Forskning*, theme issue, March 2005.

171 Pictures of such an event were shown on Fox News, 26 November 2004.

172 *Sydsvenskan*, 18 April 2006.

173 *Svenska Dagbladet*, 5 December 2004.

174 *Expressen*, 21 August 2005. The source of the information is a report from Det nasjonale Brottförebyggande rådet.

175 *Dagens Nyheter*, 23 April 2005.

176 *Dagens Nyheter*, 15 June 2005.

177 *Berlingske Tidende*, 21 January 2006.

178 Opinion piece by Södersten in *Dagens Nyheter*, 28 December 2003.

179 This study was done on assignment from the Swedish government in 2002. See *Jyllands-Posten*, 14 August 2004.

180 *Sundsvall Tidende*, 3 October 2005.

181 Studieförbundet Näringsliv & Samhälle, "Arbete? Var god dröj! Invandrare i välfärdssamhället" (2002).

182 This seven-page letter to the Swedish Parliament can be read at svt.se, 27 April 2006.

183 Mikael Tossavainen's raport "Det förnekande hatet: Antisemitism bland araber och muslimer i Sverige" (2003), here quoted from DN.debatt, 20 October 2003.

184 See Ralf Pittelkow (2002:121). Pittelkow refers here to the book *Deutschkei* by the German-Turkish Betigül Ercan Argun, which has been translated into English as *Turkey in Germany* (Routledge, 2003).

185 Pittelkow (2002:122).

186 *International Herald Tribune,* 15 July 2005.

187 This figure is presented by Kelek in an article she wrote for "Materialen und Informationen zur Zeit – Politisches Magazin für Konfessionslose und Atheistinnen" (no. 1 – 2005). The figure is referred to in the book *Allahs Frauen – Djihad zwischen Scharia und Demokratie* by Hans-Peter Raddatz (Munich 2005). An acquaintance of mine, the Danish historian Torben Hansen, reviewed the book at sappho.dk. I was unable to reach Kelek before the present book went to press in order to get more detailed information relating to this figure.

188 Selecting the youngest son in the family to kill a sister is a familiar phenomenon in Turkey and elsewhere. The reason is that young felons receive milder punishment.

189 Seyran Ates, a lawyer of Turkish ancestry, estimates that half of young Turkish women are forced to marry (*The New York Times,* 4 December 2005). There is no public documentation on the extent of forced marriage in Germany or any other European country.

190 There is extensive material about this honour killing available online. See, for example, *Berlingske Tidende,* 8 March 2005; *The New York Times,* 4 December 2005; and bbc.co.uk, 14 March 2005.

191 See interview with Necla Kelek in *International Herald Tribune,* 1 December 2005.

192 The estimates vary between five and ten million. There is actually no one who can say how many people with immigrant backgrounds live in France. There are historical reasons for this, namely the registering of Jews during World War II. The French philosophy about immigrants and integration is this: If you have French citizenship, you are by definition French and therefore registered as French. Everyone is equal according to the French republic's values. This makes

it very difficult, of course, for French authorities today to get an overview of the integration situation so that they may come up with solutions to the extensive problems they face. See, for example, *Jyllands-Posten,* 11 April 2005, and *Weekly Standard,* 17 July 2002.

[193] Samira Bellil, *Dans l'enfer des tournantes,* Paris 2002.

[194] Fadela Amara, *Varken hora eller kuvad,* Stockholm 2005.

[195] BBC.co.uk, 8 April 2006; Time.com, 2 October 2004; and Signandsight.com, 22 November 2006.

[196] SignandSight.com, 22 November 2005.

[197] Fadela Amara (2005=. Samira Bellil died the next year of stomach cancer, aged 31. At the time she had been rejected by her family and neighbors because she had talked publicly about the shameful conditions for girls in the enclaves.

[198] Times Online, 4 December 2004.

[199] CBS News, 16 May 2004.

[200] *Time,* 24 November 2002.

[201] "Madame, skolen er muslimsk! – Sharia vinner innpass i Europa," av Helle Merete Brix, www.rights.no, 15 February 2005.

[202] Signand Sign.com, 22 November 2005.

[203] *Frankfurter Allgemeine Zeitung,* faz.net, 16 November 2005.

[204] Helle Merete Brix, see above. The book Brix refers to was written under the pseudonym Emmanuel Brenner and is entitled *Les Territoires perdus de la Republique,* Paris 2004. The same conditions are described in a report that the French Ministry of Education tried to keep secret, "Les signes et manifestations d'appartenance religieuse dans les établissements scolaires" (2004).

[205] *Weekly Standard,* 15 July 2002.

[206] Times Online, 26 January 2004. Regarding my remarks about fetching marriage, there are not, to my knowledge, any official statistics about this topic. Nonetheless it can be established that the fetching of spouses is, as in other European countries, the most important source of immigration. There is no reason to believe that French immigrants fetch spouses from their countries of origin to a lesser degree than immigrants in other European countries. On the contrary, taking the poor integration into consideration, there is reason to believe

that the practice is widespread. In March 2003 I asked the head of the Turkish organization Elele in Paris, Pernaz Hüküm, about the extent of fetching marriage. Hüküm estimated that around 90 percent of young Turks in France are married off in "the interior of Anatolia." Elele works against forced marriage among Turks.

207 *Jyllands-Posten,* 11 April 2005.

208 It was especially Eivind Vesselbo's study of fetching marriage among Turks (described in Chapter 3) and a predicted sevenfold increase in the group of marriageable young non-Western immigrants within twenty years that attracted notice and caused unease. This projected sevenfold increase was viewed in the context of forced marriage and increasing rates of immigration as a result of fetching marriage.

209 "Professoren og prognosen," *Jyllands-Posten,* 21 August 2005.

210 Ibid.

211 *Information,* 28 February 2006. The article takes as its point of departure a seminar about the report "Interesser og holdninger til arbeijde – Fokus på invandrerkvinder og beskæftigelsesindsatsen" (LG Insight, 2005). The report was commissioned by the Danish government and is available online.

212 "Indvandrerkvinder holdes i isolation," *Jyllands-Posten,* 19 February 2005.

213 Ibid.

214 "Interesser og holdninger til arbeijde – Fokus på invandrerkvinder og beskæftigelsesindsatsen" (LG Insight, 2005). The report was commissioned by the Danish government.

215 There is no data to indicate whether or not any of these women may have been pressured by their husbands to present themselves as less resourceful and unqualified for the labour market than they are.

216 "Udlændige på ungdomsuddannelserne – frafald og fagligekundskaper," Tænketanken om udfordringer for integrationsindsatsen i Danmark, 2005.

217 Rockwood Fondens Forskningsenhed, technical note no. 10, by Claus Larsen (2005).

218 Cabinet member Rikke Hvilsøj's comment in the newspaper *Information,* 28 February 2006, after the publication of the report "Interesser og holdninger til arbejde focus på indvandrerkvinder og beskæftigelsesindsatsen," by Lars Larsen in LG Insight (2005).

[219] *Dagbladet Børsen,* 3 May 2005.

[220] *Jyllands-Posten,* 27 May 2005.

[221] *Berlingske Tidende,* 6 April 2005.

[222] Naser Khader has his own website, www.khader.dk.

[223] I am not going into detail about the publication of the Muhammed cartoons, their principal aspects and the many consequences. I will, however, note that the reason for their publication was that author Kåre Bluitgen wrote a children's book ab out Muhammed. He and his publisher thought that the book needed illustrations. But the publisher couldn't find any artist who would take on the job under his or her own name. When an editor at *Jyllands-Posten* heard about this, he invited artists to illustrate Muhammed in order to see if it really was true that a form of self-censorship about Islam had developed in Danish society.

[224] The most famous deception was a picture of a man from a pig festival in France, wearing a pig nose. This picture was taken to the Middle East by Danish imams, who said thast it was one of the images of Muhammed published by *Jyllands-Posten.* Another major lie was that the Danish government was planning to publish a censured and edited edition of the Koran.

[225] *Jyllands-Posten,* 3 February 2006.

[226] "Toneangivende musloimer har kun få med seg," *LO Ugebrevet A4,* no. 11, 20 March 2006.

[227] See, for example, opinion pieces in *Aftenposten,* 24 May and 29 June 2006.

[228] "European Employee Index 2006," from the Danish analytical institute Ennova.

[229] "Udviklingen i udlændines integration i det danske samfund," June 2006, Danish Ministry of Refugee, Immigration and Integration Affairs.

[230] See for example *Ugebrevet A4,* 10 April 2006.

[231] Karen Jespersen and Palph Pittelkow, *De lykkelige danskere. En bog om sammenhængskraft,* Copenhagen 2005.

[232] *Ugebrevet A4,* no. 10, 13 March 2006.

[233] The conflict between cultural rights and individual rights in a democratic perspective is a comprehensive topic. For more discussion of it, see for example David Beetham, *Democracy and Human Rights,* Cambridge 1999, Chapters 5-7.

234 The book *Forsvar for nationalstaten* (2004) by the Danish author Ralf Pittelkow argues that a broad popular society is utterly crucial for maintaining and furthering a peaceful democratic national state such as Denmark or Norway.

235 Ole Jørgen Anfindsen and Jens Thomas Anfindsen have formulated alternative population forecasts and collected extensive materials relating to population change in Norway and Europe at their website HonestThinking.org.

236 The figure is calculated by HRS and based on SSB's population statistics regarding the number of children and young people up to 19 years old with roots in Asian, African, and Balkan countries which already evince a high level of spousal fetching. The estimate is low, since children from countries like China and Chile, only to name a couple, are not included. One may expect that a good many children from countries like China and Chile will also fetch spouses from those countries.

237 The study was performed by the Frisch Centre at the University of Oslo. *Aftenposten,* 2 November 2004.

238 This study was also performed by the Frisch Centre. *Aftenposten,* 4 September 2005.

239 *Aftenposten,* 31 October 2004.

240 "Gjennomstrømning i videregående opplæring," SSB, 2004. The total national dropout rate is 25 percent. There are no figures for the dropout rate among ethnic Norwegian students.

241 *Horisont: Næringspolitisk tidsskrift,* no. 2, 2006.

242 *Oslo-speilet,* no. 3, 4 June 2006.

243 Bredo Berntsen in the book *Gode formål – gale følger?*

244 *Berlingske Tidende,* 6 April 2005.

245 *Memo,* no. 1-2006.

246 In 1998 I had a meeting, in my capacity as a private citizen, with the then leader of the Norwegian Parliament's justice committee, Kristin Krohn Devold. The reason was that I had published the book *Hellig tvang* and I was worried about the abuse of young people as living visas. I had the idea then of increasing the age limit for fetching new spouses to Norway, which I also proposed in *Dagsavisen.* I had gotten the idea from public documents published by the Danish bureaucracy under the social-democratic government.

247 *Politiken,* 24 January 2006.

248 "Ny utlendingslov," Norges offentlige utredninger, NOU 2004:20.

249 Documented by SSB statistics in the report "Innvandring gjennom ekteskap," HRS, May 2005, pp. 69-74.

250 Communicated in conversations with leading Danish politicians.

251 For those who wish to learn more about the new policy, two websites are most useful: that of the department in Denmark that is responsible for the policy, inm.dk, and HRS's site, www.rights.no.

252 "Pardannelse blant etniske minoriteter i Danmark," Socialforskningsinstituttet 2004.

253 There is reason to assume that many of those who apply to study and work and who have been granted residency are people with a partner in Denmark who has lost the required "connection" to Denmark by (for example) residing for some time in the foreign party's homeland. For resourceful couples, then, the loss of the Dane's "connection" to Denmark can be remedied by arranging for the non-Dane to study or work in Denmark.

254 *Politiken,* 24 January 2006.

255 The European Court of Human Rights, 28 May 1985 (Abdulaziz, Cabales and Balkandi).

256 An exemption has been given for the establishment of a Muslim school in Drammen, with a planned start-up in the autumn of 2006. The convert and doctor Trond Ali Lindstad is behind the initiative.

257 In a documentary entitled "I skolens vold," Swedish TV covered conditions in Muslim schools that are highly deserving of criticism (SVT, 8 May 2003).

258 The embassy personnel have told me that some people who are deported from Norway turn up, newly "married," at the embassy with another identity to apply for a visa. At various embassies in Islamabad, in addition to other agencies there that verify documents, it is estimated that 60 to 80 percent of the documents presented at the embassies are false. I myself purchased a valid marriage contract in 1993, stating that on 17 May of that year I married King Harald of Norway in Islamabad.

259 *Guardian,* 10 June 2006.

[260] *VG*, 26 September 1998. Mukhtar has for years been spokesman for Norway's Islamic Council.

[261] "Verdibørsen," NRK P1, 6 May 2006.

[262] "Migrapolis," NRK1, 11 January 2006.

[263] Norwegian-Pakistani Jeanette was married off at age sixteen in Pakistan. For periods of time prior to her marriage, she was put on a strict diet by her family.

[264] Among those who practice "reasonable marriage," the Internet has become a popular means of seeking a spouse. Among people from the subcontinent a common demand is that prospective spouses have a "pale complexion." Nobody ever demands dark skin. The phenomenon can probably be compared directly with the trend in Europe during the Victorian Age, when upper-class women made an effort to avoid sunlight, while workers out in the field grew brown in the sun. Light skin thus signals prosperity; dark skin, poverty. Thus it was that pale skin came to be perceived as beautiful.

[265] In Islam, it is virtually a religious obligation to marry, as recorded in the Koran, sura 24, verse 32. Parents interpret this verse as placing upon them a religious obligation to marry their children off.

[266] Collett was first brought back in from the cold when the Norwegian Association for Women's Rights was founded in 1888. She became its first honourary member.

[267] See, for example, the article "Åpenhet for andre typer ekteskap," *Aftenposten,* 7 April 2006.

[268] *Weekendavisen,* no. 6, 10-17 February 2006.

[269] Online there are a number of photographs of Arab Islamist leaders being visited by the likes of Hitler and of Muslim armies marching in goosestep. See, for example, tellthechildrenthetruth.com/gallery/ and jewishvirtuallibrary.org.

[270] The ties among Mussolini, Hitler, and Islamist leaders in the Arab world were also discussed by Oriana Fallaci in the book *The Force of Reason* (Rizzoli 2006). She quotes Mussolini during a political visit to Libya in 1937, when he greeted a religious leader with the following words: "Fascist Italy wants to secure the Muslim peoples peace, justice, prosperity, and respect for the prophet's laws, and show the world its sympathy for Islam and the Muslims" (p. 99). The neo-Nazi group Vigrid documents on its own website its sympathy for militant Islam: see www.vigrid.net.

[271] *Weekendavisen,* no. 22, 2-8 June 2006.

[272] *Weekendavisen,* no. 6, 10-17 February 2006.

[273] The manifesto was published in *Aftenposten* on 4 March 2006.

[274] *Weekendavisen,* no. 6, 10-17 February 2006.

[275] *Jyllands-Posten,* 23 October 2005.

[276] *Jyllands-Posten,* 30 October 2005.

[277] "Hold religionen indendørs," *Politiken* 20 May 2006.

[278] *Aftenposten,* 5 March 2006.

[279] "Kvinnens stilling i islam," islamic.org.

[280] *Jyllands-Posten,* 23 October 2005.

[281] Helle Merete Brix, "Sløret – islamisternes krigsmachine," rights.no, 1 June 2005. Chadortt Djavann's book is entitled *Que pense Allah de l'Europe? (Hva tenker Allah om Europa?),* Paris 2004.

[282] Opinion piece by Karen Jespersen in *Berlingske Tidende,* 19 February 2005.

[283] www.wikipedia.org.

[284] Communicated in private conversations with intellectuals and politicians.

[285] "The Islamization of Europe?", *Commentary,* December 2004.

[286] Ibid. See also Townhall.com, 17 November 2004.

[287] Pim Fortuyn was the first Dutch politician in modern times to be a victim of a political assassination. The murderer was a left-wing extremist who killed him because of his desire to put the brakes on immigration to the Netherlands. He was killed shortly before a national election in which it looked as if he would be very successful.

[288] *Klassekampen,* 16 November 2005.

[289] *Dag og Tid,* 20 May 2006.

[290] *Dagbladet,* 6 May 2003.

291 See for example the report "Det förnekande hatet: Antisemitism bland araber och muslimer I Sverige" by Mikael Tossavainen (2003). Also see such articles as "Jødehatet lever" (*Aftenposten,* 29 November 2003), "The Murder of Ilan Halimi" (*Front Page*, 7 March 2006), and "Mugged by la Réalité" (*Weekly Standard,* 11 April 2005).

292 The factual details of the triple murder are drawn from the page of *VG*'s website at which the news stories about the murders are collected.

293 *Vårt Land,* 8 March 2010.

294 Statistics Norway, 29 April 2010.

295 *VG,* 19 March 2010.

296 "Hvem er Norges befolkning i fremtiden," HRS N-1 2008.

297 VG.no, June 9, 2010.

298 The report is "Inngifte i Norge. Omfang og medisinske konsekvenser," Folkehelseinstituttet 2007.

299 Those born in Norway fill out the form themselves on which they are asked to check the description which applies to their family relationship to their spouse.

300 Dagensmedisin.no, 8 March 2007.

301 *Tidsskrift for Den norske legeforeningen,* August 13, 2010.

302 Aftenposten.no, August 12, 2010.

303 *Aftenposten,* August 16, 2010.

304 *VG,* August 18, 2010.

305 Ibid.

306 The report is "Kjønnslemlestelse i Norge – En kartlegging," Institutt for Samfunnsforskning, 2008:8.

307 The project called Daphne.

308 Aftonbladet.se, 6 August 2010.

309 SVT.se,.12 August 2010.

310 Hjelm, Ann-Christine, "Är kulturgenererad grov brottslighet myt eller verklighet? brottsoffer och gärningsmän vid grova brottmål i Svea hovrätt 2002," Karlstad 2006.

311 13 March 2010.

312 VG.no, 7 March 2009, and Aftonbladet.se, 7 March 2009.

313 Dagbladet.no, 9 June 2010.

314 I am not ignoring the possibility that racist elements exist in the party's ranks, but so far this has not been shown to be the case.

315 Editorial, dn.se, 6 October 2010.

316 Hd.se, 14 September 2010.

317 This account is based on articles published in Spiegelonline.de on 31 October 2006, in Taipeitimes.com on November 2006, and in Worldpoliticsreview.com on 29 November 2006.

318 The examples so far are drawn from the book *Islams magt. Europas ny virkelighed*, by Karen Jespersen and Ralf Pittelkow (Jyllands-Posten, 2010).

319 The TV clip, in German and English, can be viewed at rights.no 2010, "No-go soner i Berlin."

320 Berlingske.dk, 13 February 2008.

321 Reuters.com, 30 August 2010.

322 Dailymail.co.uk, 30 August 2010.

323 TV2.dk, 16 October 2010.

324 Jav.org, 20 March 2007.

325 Timesonline.co.uk, 11 June 2009.

326 France24.com, 30 April 2009.

327 *Le Monde*, 12 October 2010.

328 Aftenposten.no, 6 September 2010.

329 *The Times,* 23 July 2010.

[330] Independent.co.uk, 8 October 2010.

[331] Thisislondon.co.uk, 20 September 2010.

[332] Metro.co.uk, 16 September 2010.

[333] *Jyllands-Posten*, 10 August 2010. The trial is expected to take place in early 2011.

[334] Sappho.dk, 14 April 2010. When Sappho's editors performed an unscientific study of Google searches, they discovered that during the preceding month the name Kurt Westergaard had been Googled almost twice as many times as the queen's.

[335] Jyllands-Posten.dk, 29 August 2010.

[336] Extrabladet.dk, 17 February 2010

[337] Statistics Denmark yearbook for 2009, quoted in *Islams magt. Europas ny virkelighed*, op.cit.

[338] "Growth, Public Finances and Immigration", Danish National Bank, third quarter report, 2008.

[339] The report was done on assignment for the non-partisan libertarian Danish think tank CEPOS, and is entitled "Immigrants' and Danes' Influence on Public Finances: The Need for a Policy Shift," Cepos.dk.

[340] *Jyllands-Posten*, 14 September 2010.

[341] The 24-year rule, moreover, will no longer be absolute. If the spouse fulfills the other requirements, it can be gotten around.

[342] In 2001, most residency permits were given to applicants from Turkey, followed by Iraq, Thailand, Afghanistan, and Somalia. In 2009, the list was led by Thailand, Turkey, the Philippines, China, and the U.S.

[343] Press release from the Ministry of Justice and Police, 4 December 2009.

[344] Regjeringen.no, 8 May 2009.

[345] Seminar at Litteraturhuset in Oslo, under the auspices of the Nordic Council of Ministers, 7 September 2010.

[346] VG.no, 12 February 2010.

[347] Islam Net has two branches, in Bodø and Tromsø.

348 See its website, islamnet.no, and VG.no, 10 June 2010.

349 Youtube.com: "Every Muslim should be a Terrorist."

350 *Aftenposten*, 18 November 2010.

351 The meeting was held under the auspices of Skeivt Forum in Oslo on 7 November 2007.

352 Nettavisen.no, 8 November 2007.

353 NRK.no, 9 November 2007.

354 *Nomad: From Islam to America: A Personal Journey through the Clash of Civilizations* (2010).

355 This and the following quotations from Hirsi Ali, which were presumably made in English but reported in Norwegian, have been translated back to English from the Norwegian. (Translator's note.)

356 Sharia courts render verdicts in so-called family questions such as divorce, inheritance, family financial conflicts, child support, child custody, and domestic violence. In addition to these official courts, there are several unofficial ones. According to the report "Sharia Law or One Law for All?" by the British think tank Civitas, at least 85 unofficial sharia courts are operating in the British Isles.

Made in the USA
Columbia, SC
09 July 2018